C0-ARP-569

3 3073 10126686 2

DATE DUE

SEP 2 2 2003	

GAYLORD   PRINTED IN U.S.A.

Morris Goodman, Ph. D.
1 Cypress Street
Maplewood, N. J. 07040

INTERACTIONAL PSYCHOTHERAPY

INTERACTIONAL PSYCHOTHERAPY

Benjamin B. Wolman

Editor-in-Chief

*International Encyclopedia
of Psychiatry, Psychology, Psychoanalysis and Neurology*

SETON HALL UNIVERSITY
UNIVERSITY LIBRARIES
400 SOUTH ORANGE AVE.
SO. ORANGE, N.J. 07079-2671

VNR VAN NOSTRAND REINHOLD COMPANY
NEW YORK   CINCINNATI   TORONTO   LONDON   MELBOURNE

RC
480
.W625
1984

Copyright © 1984 by Van Nostrand Reinhold Company Inc.

Library of Congress Catalog Card Number: 83-16952
ISBN: 0-442-20831-6

All rights reserved. No part of this work covered by the copyright hereon may
be reproduced or used in any form or by any means – graphic, electronic, or
mechanical, including photocopying, recording, taping, or information storage
and retrieval systems – without permission of the publisher.

Manufactured in the United States of America

Published by Van Nostrand Reinhold Company Inc.
135 West 50th Street
New York, New York 10020

Van Nostrand Reinhold Company Limited
Molly Millars Lane
Wokingham, Berkshire RG11 2PY, England

Van Nostrand Reinhold
480 Latrobe Street
Melbourne, Victoria 3000, Australia

Macmillan of Canada
Division of Gage Publishing Limited
164 Commander Boulevard
Agincourt, Ontario M1S 3C7, Canada

15 14 13 12 11 10 9 8 7 6 5 4 3 2 1

Library of Congress Cataloging in Publication Data

Wolman, Benjamin B.
    Interactional psychotherapy.

    Bibliography: p.
    Includes indexes.
    1. Psychotherapy.   I. Title.   [DNLM: 1. Psychoanalytic
therapy.   2. Psychotherapy.   3. Transference (Psychology)
WM 420 W865i]
RC480.W625   1984   616.89'14   83-16952
ISBN 0-442-20831-6

A

Preface

My main psychotherapeutic allegiance is to Sigmund Freud, but I am hardly an orthodox Freudian. I view mental disorders not as diseases but as tragedies that involve the total personality.

One may *have* a cold or pneumonia, but one *is* paranoid or a hebephrenic schizophrenic. Psychotherapy need not replicate medical models. A physician does a lot: he administers drugs, performs surgery, and treats sick people. A psychotherapist doesn't do much; a psychotherapist *is* a person one can relate to, have faith in, and depend on, in the process of growing and interacting. *Medicine is doing; psychotherapy is being.*

Mentally disturbed patients are people whose minds have gone astray; they are unable to face life in a realistic and responsible manner. Every patient carries within himself the eternal tragedy of the human race in its Faustian craving for godlike beauty and fulfillment, and in the inevitable frustration and failures of human fate.

Some patients — schizophrenics and schizo-type neurotics such as obsessive-compulsives — resemble fallen angels; they were forced in childhood into premature and unhealthy self-sacrifice. Being human, they were doomed to fail in their angel-like aspirations. Other patients, the sociopaths, have been brought up in an atmosphere of sink or swim, and they swim at the expense of other human beings. Most believe themselves to be innocent, while they are selfish and exploitative. I call this group of disorders "hyperinstrumental," indicating the tendency to use other people. In the middle are manic-depressives and hysterics, who love themselves and hate themselves, love others and hate others. They are love addicts, who love to be loved and hate because no one can love them enough. I call them "dysmutual," for they are unable to develop normal mutual relationships.

Interactional psychotherapy is a modification of classic psychoanalysis. The main modifications are related to an intentional manipulation of transference, in which transference is viewed as an interactional process between the therapist and the patient. I have reduced the number of sessions per week, and I allow much more verbal communication between the patient and the therapist. Although I avoid being directive, I do not avoid it when working with psychotics or when the life situation of patients necessitates it. I encourage patients to make their own decisions, but I do not think they should be allowed to drown just because they are not cured yet. I also ration the amount and the level of interpretation and reconstruction, keeping in mind the relative strength of the patient's ego.

There is no absolute "cure" for mental disorders, and therapists must not be carried away by their ambitions and well-wishing aspirations. In each particular case, one must try to reach the optimum. If one works with a severely regressed psychotic, the restoration of relative mental balance and a reasonable adjustment to daily life may represent the most one can accomplish. There is a limit to how far one can go in each case, and the basic policy should be to keep "one step ahead" of the existing level of severity of the disorder. We are repairmen, and when we repair a house, we must take into consideration the relative strength of its foundations and go as far in our work as is safe for the particular building under repair.

Although the technique one uses is quite important, the *personality of the therapist* is the most important factor in the success or failure of psychotherapy. No human being is perfect, but whoever undertakes to save drowning people must be a good swimmer himself. In the final analysis, psychotherapy is an art based on scientific principles. A good therapist has a keen interest in other people, is willing to help them, and is capable of perceiving correctly their verbal and nonverbal communications.

All living organisms have a beginning and an end of life, and they live their lives without being aware of any meaning. The human species is the only one tragically aware of the fact that nothing can be done about being born and nothing can be done about the inevitability of death. The only thing left in between to human thinking, dreaming, and decision making is what *one can do as long as one is alive.*

The rationale of interactional psychotherapy is derived from the fact that *all* human beings can experience emotional difficulties — not only those people who are called disturbed. Some people are unable to find themselves. They feel confused and perplexed, and they go through life in a state of anxiety and depression.

That's why I propose three levels of psychotherapy. The first phase is *analytic;* its aim is to resolve the emotional problems of the past and heal the wounds, for one cannot accomplish much as long as one is crippled by past errors and miseries. Then comes the second phase — the *search for identity.* The third and last phase is devoted to setting goals in one's life; I call it *becoming: self-realization.*

The aims of interactional psychotherapy are to enable people to have the *courage to be themselves and to have the wisdom to make rational decisions.* To help individuals become aware of who they are and what they can do with their lives is the most relevant therapeutic task.

BENJAMIN B. WOLMAN

Contents

INTERACTIONAL PSYCHOTHERAPY

1
The Patients

I have worked for 40 years with many highly intelligent patients who were quite successful in several aspects of life. I have often admired the business and financial skills of executives who came to my office seeking advice and help. I have had in psychotherapy gifted intellectuals, writers, editors, artists, and performers, whose fame and fortune was quite impressive but who, in some areas of their lives, displayed irrational attitudes and self-defeating behaviors.

Why did these people come to my office? Was it the old dependence on the doctor who was believed to perform miracles? Was it the medical model, and were psychotherapists supposed to "cure" all human ills? Were these people mentally sick?

The term "mentally sick" is a residue from the time of Pinel, who called the inmates of a mental asylum "sick" in order to protect them against inhuman treatment. It was definitely a sign of progress to refer to disturbed people as sick, rather than as devilish, malicious, or obsessed, but today the term "mental sickness" is out of date and out of contact with present-day science. For a person can *have* pneumonia or dyspepsia, but a person *is* neurotic or *is* psychotic. Mental disorder is not a disease of any particular organ; it involves the entire person. When individuals are self-destructive and self-defeating – when their thought is confused, their emotions are uncontrollable, and their actions are not directed to the solution of their problems – they are certainly disturbed.

COGNITIVE FUNCTIONS AND A SENSE OF REALITY

There are several criteria of mental health. The first criterion is related to the cognitive functions. An erroneous perception of oneself and others, an ignorance of danger, and the inability to distinguish wish from reality can seriously jeopardize one's very survival. A realistic perception of what is going on in the outer world and in one's own life increases one's chances for survival and helps in successful adjustment.

Freud (1938) called the ability to see things as they are "reality testing." The neonate, said Freud, is unable to distinguish inner from outer stimuli. Stimuli that come from without are confused with cenesthetic perceptions from within. The "oceanic feeling" pervades, and the images of oneself and of the environment are not clearly separated. Gradually infants learn to "test reality," that is, to distinguish between inner and outer stimuli, between their own feelings and the external world, and between wish and fact.

H. S. Sullivan (1953) suggested another distinction. He believed that the earliest stage in human life is the "prototaxic" mode, that is, a state of diffuse and indistinguishable experiences. In the next stage, the "parataxic," the child perceives the world as a series of experiences related to himself and views himself as the center of the universe. In the third stage, the "syntaxic," the child develops the ability to check his own perceptions against the perceptions of others and to validate them through the consensus of the group. This *consensual validation* is one of the methods by which reality can be tested; the child checks his or her experiences against the experiences of other individuals.

The more one is disturbed, the poorer is one's contact with reality. Everyone makes an occasional perceptual error, but normally, people perceive things as they are and correct occasional errors. In mentally disturbed individuals this ability is impaired or nonexistent.

In most mental disorders, the perception of the outer world is disturbed, but not as a result of some malfunction of the sensory organs as is the case in sight or hearing impairment. Nor is the reduced ability to perceive, compare, and reason a function of mental deficiency as is true for the retarded. In most cases of mental disorder, the mental apparatus is fully or partly preserved, but mentally disturbed individuals are unable to use their mental capacities properly.

People who suffer from mental disorders either have an exaggerated notion of their own importance of else underestimate their own resources. Feelings of superiority and omnipotence on one side, and of inferiority and inadequacy on the other, are frequent mental symptoms. However, the situation can become quite serious when the picture of the outer world is grossly distorted. An individual who consistently misconstrues or misinterprets what he perceives is said to be *delusional.* For example, when a mentally disturbed individual flees a policeman who simply wants to check his driver's license in fear that the policeman will arrest him for a crime he did not commit, or when he ascribes hostile feelings to his loyal and faithful friends, his reality testing is practically nonexistent. Delusions are distorted perceptions; hallucinations are perceptions of nonexistent things, people, or situations. Hallucinations are perceptions without external stimulation, for example, seeing ghosts and hearing voices. Hallucinating individuals are unable to distinguish between inner fears or wishes and the outer world.

THE SECOND CRITERION OF MENTAL HEALTH: EMOTIONAL BALANCE

Human beings react to life situations with joy and sorrow, pleasure and pain. The reactions of mentally healthy individuals correspond to the quality and the quantity of stimuli. Normally, one reacts with pleasure and joy to situations that enhance one's well-being, and feels happy when one's wishes come true. Grief is the normal reaction to failure or loss.

Disturbed individuals may react with sorrow to victory and may enjoy defeat. Their emotional reaction is *inappropriate.* Quite often they act in a self-defeating manner, bring misery upon themselves, and do not find satisfaction in success. They are unable to appreciate what they have and are constantly looking for "greener pastures," but no pasture is ever green enough. Disturbed people tend to perpetuate their misery and refrain from constructive efforts. By avoiding pleasure and seeking pain, they become, as it were, their own enemies.

Normal emotional reactions are *appropriate* and *proportionate* to the situation. Consider a man who has lost money: an emotionally balanced individual reacts in a manner *appropriate* to the fact of loss and *proportionate* to its magnitude and to the ensuing financial hardship. The bigger the loss, the greater is the worry; however, when the loss represents a tiny fraction of one's possessions, the concern should be mild and of short duration.

Well-balanced individuals cope in a rational manner with losses and defeats; they do whatever is possible to regain the loss and to prevent future defeats. Their actions lead to a reduction or an alleviation of past troubles and to the prevention of future ones. In short, normal emotional behavior is *appropriate, proportionate,* and *adjustive.*

Disturbed individuals tend to perpetuate their depressed or aggressive moods. Instead of seeking to remedy past losses and prevent future ones, they tend to indulge in self-pity. Their emotional balance is not easily restored, and their anxiety states are likely to occur again and again. The failure to cope with hardships may lead to increased sensitivity and irritability, and every new frustration creates additional difficulties in restoring emotional balance.

In severely disturbed people, the ability to face frustration and to act in a constructive fashion may be lost altogether. The slightest frustration may throw the individual off balance, cause uncontrollable emotional outbursts of fury and/or panic, and create unbearable tension and depression. The degree of emotional imbalance is an important indicator of the severity of the disorder.

THE THIRD CRITERION: SOCIAL ADJUSTMENT

Interactional psychology, in contradistinction to Freud's theory, emphasizes the role of social relations in mental health and disorder. Human interactions can be friendly or hostile. Friendly means cooperating with others and helping them. Hostile means hurting, harming, and destroying others. The lack of defensive hostility makes one an easy prey; abundant offensive hostility leads to clashes which may be fatal to one who starts them. Some degree of defensive hostility is necessary, provided that it is directed against real threats, and conducted in a reasonably successful way and within socially accepted rules.

Friendly behavior, helping, cooperating, and loving all aim to protect the life of the person at whom they are directed. One tends to help, protect, care for, and support the life of those whom one likes or loves. A group or society in which mutual respect, consideration, cooperation, and friendliness prevail has better chances for survival than a society in which hatred of all by all is the rule. The latter society is likely to find itself in the throes of fratricidal wars and might annihilate itself or be destroyed by enemies who exploit the internal dissension.

There are no ideal societies. Every social group has its share of constructive, life-preserving, and cooperative factors, as well as of destructive and antisocial forces. However, no society can afford a free play of hostile and disruptive forces. If these forces are innate in men, they must be checked; if they are learned patterns of behavior, they must be unlearned, at least to a point at which they do not threaten the survival of mankind. There is great diversity in the prohibitive actions of social groups; some limit their "thou shalt not kill" restraint to members of their own society only. Judeo-Christian civilizations believe in the sanctity of human life, but even the most primitive societies did not tolerate unlimited intragroup belligerence.

Thus, the third criterion of mental health is *social adjustment*. Mentally healthy individuals are capable of living on friendly terms with other members of their group. They may occasionally feel hostile, but their actions are kept under rational control, and when they fight in self-defense, they do it in a manner approved by their cultural group.

Mentally disturbed people are usually socially maladjusted. They are often afraid and suspicious of other people, and ascribe hostile intentions to them. Some of them shy away from people and withdraw into seclusion; others tend to be belligerent and violent. The severity of social maladjustment usually corresponds to the severity of mental disorder, although it is not a simple one-to-one relationship. Uncontrollable hostility is, however, a distinct sign of serious mental disorder.

Social adjustment need not be confused with conformity. Social adjustment is the ability to have peaceful and friendly interaction with other individuals, while conformity implies uncritical acceptance of certain social mores. Were conformity identical with social adjustment, every inventor and discoverer, every creative writer, political reformer and nonconformist, and any pioneer of social, religious, or scientific progress could be branded as socially maladjusted.

Religious, social, and political dissent must not be confused with maladjustment. Quite often, conformists — rather than nonconformists — are the maladjusted individuals. Social adjustment does not imply blind acceptance of prevailing opinions and ideas; on the contrary, it implies the ability to cope with controversies in a realistic manner. Insecure and anxiety-ridden individuals are often afraid to be different and cannot tolerate differences of opinion.

All social relationships can be divided into three types: instrumental (I), mutual (M), and vectorial (V). When people enter a social relationship in order to have their needs satisfied and their expectation is to take rather than to give, an *instrumental* relationship results. The individual regards others as tools or instruments. Human life starts as a parasitic process; the infant must receive all that is necessary for his survival. Thus, the infant versus mother relationship is the prototype of instrumentalism.

Mutual relationships develop gradually. In nursery school or kindergarten, the child is presented with opposition to this instrumentalism. The child learns to share, to take turns, to trade toy for toy, and to accept *mutuality* as a basis for interaction. Mutuality achieves its peak in friendship and marriage. Each partner desires to make the other partner happy and expects the other to feel the same. Successful marriage is based on mutuality; each partner is determined to do his best for the well-being of the other and expects the same from the other party.

As long as a person feels weak, he seeks help, but when a person feels rich and strong, he is inclined to give help. Strong and secure people tend to be generous. Parenthood is the prototype of *vectorialism*. Parents create life, protect it, and care for it, irrespective of their child's looks, health, I.Q., disposition, and success. The more the infant needs their help, the more sympathy he elicits.

Children could not make good parents: they demand that love be given to them; they are instrumental. So are childish adults – they cannot be adequate parents. To be an adequate parent, one must feel strong, friendly, and willing to give, and one must be ready to care without asking anything in return. To give without asking or expecting anything in return is the highest degree of love and the essence of vectorialism.

A normal or well-adjusted individual is balanced in social interaction. He is instrumental in the struggle for survival, mutual in relationships with friends and in marriage, and vectorial in regard to children and to those who need help. He is reasonably selfish (instrumental), reasonably mutual, and reasonably vectorial.

THE FOURTH CRITERION: ACHIEVEMENTS COMMENSURATE WITH ABILITIES AND OPPORTUNITIES

The relationship between *one's potentialities and one's achievements* is an important criterion of mental health. The inability to actualize one's mental and physical potential usually signals some degree of mental disorder. All other factors being equal, the greater the discrepancy between promise and fulfillment, the more severe is the disorder.

In milder cases of mental disorder, one's accomplishments usually fall short of what could reasonably be expected. A bright student ridden by emotional disorder may fail in his studies, and a brilliant adult may miss the opportunities for advancement in life. Some gifted individuals function reasonably well as professionals, scientists, and creative artists, but they are unable to act in a rational manner in their personal lives in interindividual relations. Apparently, many poorly integrated personalities can function adequately in conflict-free areas of business and profession, but they fail in conflict-laden areas of emotional life.

THE FIFTH CRITERION: AWARENESS OF ONESELF AND PERSONALITY INTEGRATION

A realistic perception of the world is the first, and probably the most important criterion of mental health. An individual who does not see things the way they are and who is plagued by delusions and/or hallucinations is severely maladjusted.

The same applies to the way one sees oneself. Individuals who do not perceive themselves correctly may run into tremendous difficulties in life. If they overestimate their abilities, they may do things that bring frustration and defeat. If they underestimate their own abilities, they may be afraid to take the initiative and act in a constructive manner, and they will therefore remain *underachievers*. Awareness of oneself does not imply a blind acceptance of one's faults and shortcomings. *Awareness of oneself is the awareness of the fact that these are the cards one has gotten from heredity and experience, and one should play these cards as best he can.*

A person may realize that if he or she tends to be aggressive, this aggressiveness can be utilized in a rational and productive manner, for instance, in conquering disease and misery, doing research, or engaging in certain creative work, and not necessarily in fighting people. One may neutralize one's energies or sublimate some of them. One need not accept all aspects of his or her own personality, nor does one necessarily have to test all possibilities. One must choose between one's various interests and inclinations, and establish a hierarchy of goals.

Every individual is a bundle of diverse innate impulses and predispositions. As one goes through life, the exposure to other people fosters some of the innate tendencies, puts a damper on others, and conveys, stimulates, and imposes new ideas and new life patterns not necessarily compatible with the innate and already acquired behavioral patterns. A great many people wonder who they are and are unable to come to terms with themselves. I described this "Crisis of Identity and Purpose" in an invitational address at the annual convention of the American Psychological Association in Toronto (Wolman, 1978). I dare to say that all human beings are, as it were, "split personalities" and that everyone's personality is comprised of several diverse — and often conflicting — desires, wishes, feelings, inclinations, and thoughts.

The ability to *integrate* the various aspects of one's personality and establish a hierarchy of goals is a highly relevant aspect of mental health. This applies to the choice of occupation, place to live, marital partner, and most important, one's way of life. Setting a hierarchy of goals and rationally pursuing them are prerequisites for an inner harmony between what one believes one *should do* and what realistically one *could do*.

THE SIXTH CRITERION: SELF-ESTEEM

Self-esteem is the last, but not the least, criterion of mental health. Self-esteem depends on one's own power and on support from others. Quite often it is neither the power one possesses nor the power and loyalty of one's allies, but *how one perceives these factors.* One's self-esteem may or may not correspond to reality and may be a product of a rational or an irrational estimate. A rational self-esteem is based on the ability to see things as they are.

Little children are not capable of precise perception or of sober judgment. They must depend on their parents. When a little boy draws a picture, he cannot evaluate his own work. He depends on his parents' opinion: if they are critical of his work, they undermine his self-confidence and self-esteem; if they praise it, they encourage him and enhance his self-confidence and self-esteem. Parental opinion is the prime source of a child's self-assuredness or of inferiority feelings.

A child who has received a lot of approval at home has a better chance later to win the approval of his peer group and, when necessary, to stand up to peer rejection. A child who comes to nursery school, kindergarten, or grammar school with a homemade feeling of inferiority is likely to be rejected by his peers, and his feeling of inferiority might get worse. Inferiority feelings make a person dependent on what other people think, and the more one seeks approval, the fewer are his chances of obtaining it.

People whose self-confidence was built up in childhood have more courage, and their self-confidence makes them less dependent on others and more dependent on themselves. One's own abilities, efforts, and achievements gradually count more than other people's opinions. Ultimately, self-respecting and self-confident men and women depend more and more on what they think of themselves.

The dependence on one's own judgment is a crucial ingredient of mental health, provided it is based on a realistic estimate of one's own potentialities and environmental opportunities. Every individual faces life with a set of cards, partly innate, partly given by education and training. To know one's potentialities and to play one's cards the best way possible are relevant factors in mental health. The *courage to be oneself* is a highly important element of self-esteem. Courage implies faith in oneself, and it indicates self-confidence and self-reliance. It represents the belief that one has the power to stand up and be counted.

DEFINING MENTAL DISORDER

In the Middle Ages, witch-hunting was the favorite pastime of monks and theologians. The famous Benedictine abbot Trithemius regretted that there were not enough inquisitors to punish all the witches. He wrote:

There is no part in our body that the witches would not injure. Unfortunately, the number of such witches is very great in every province; more than that, there is no locality too small for a witch to find. Yet inquisitors and judges who could avenge these open offenses against God and nature are few and far between. Man and beast die as a result of the evil of these women and no one thinks of the fact that these things are perpetrated by witches. (Zilboorg and Henry, 1941, pp. 146-147)

In 1487, two theologians Sprenger and Kraemer published the book *Malleus Maleficarum* (*The Witches' Hammer*) in which they recommended: "The witch should be stripped of her clothes, her wounds and marks of torture exposed, her head and genitals shaven so that no devil could conceal himself in her hair, and led into court backwards so that her evil eyes might not rest on the judge and bewitch him" (Zilboorg and Henry, 1941, p. 148).

In 1587, the judge Boguet estimated that under King Charles IX, France had 300,000 witches and sorcerers. The witch-hunts continued in Europe well into the eighteenth century, and the last "witch" was executed in Glarus, Switzerland, in June 1782. Even more liberal people, such as the British physician Willis, recommended the following treatment for mental patients: "Nothing is more necessary and more effective for the recovery of these people than forcing them to respect and fear intimidation. By this method, the mind held back by restraint is induced to give up its arrogance and wild ideas . . . . This is why maniacs recover much sooner if they are treated with torture and torments in a hovel instead of with medicaments."

When judged against this background, Pinel's work was indeed revolutionary. On September 11, 1793, Dr. Philippe Pinel was appointed director of the Bicêtre mental asylum. He declared that the inmates were not guilty people who deserved punishment but *sick people* whose miserable state deserved all the consideration that is due suffering humanity. Pinel gave mental patients the status of innocent and helpless victims of unknown diseases. The change from "madmen" to "mentally sick" initiated a revolution in the treatment of mental disorders. One can torture people without knowing anything about them, but one cannot cure diseases without understanding them. Pinel's revolution turned the inmates of mental asylums into "mental patients" and, thus, invited medical treatment. However, in a vast majority of cases, the early medical methods did not work, and the crossroads of the nineteenth and twentieth centuries witnessed a feeling of skepticism concerning the possibility of curing mental diseases.

Freud's discovery of unconscious motivation opened new vistas in dealing with emotionally disturbed people. Freud maintained that the majority of mental disorders did not have an organic origin and, thus, were not related to the nervous system. Although Freud's terminology was rooted in medical phraseology, he strongly objected to the idea that psychoanalysis should ever become a handmaid of psychiatry.

Whether or not one subscribes to Freud's ideas concerning disturbed behavior, one must admit that the shift of emphasis from the medical model to emotional factors has certainly brought about a better understanding of what makes people act in a disturbed manner, thereby permitting a more rational approach to the treatment of their irrationality. However, a great many scientists and practitioners, leaning on Freud's ideas, went beyond Freud and discovered additional factors involved in so-called mental disorders. The sexual aspect of emotional life is certainly a relevant factor in human behavior, but by no means the only one, and possibly not the most important one.

MENTAL DISEASES OR HUMAN TRAGEDIES?

Four decades of practice and research in the clinical field have made me believe that the *drive for survival is of far greater importance in mental health and mental disorder than the sexual drive,* and in my book *Call No Man Normal* (Wolman, 1973), I introduced a comprehensive system of psychopathology.

There are certain cases of mental diseases in the organic sense of the word. For instance, paresis caused by syphilis, Korsakoff disease caused by alcoholism, Down's syndrome (mongolism) caused by an additional chromosome, and so on, are diseases of the nervous or glandular systems. However, the vast majority of mental disorders are *human tragedies* rather than diseases.

Even when the disturbed behavior has organic causes (called genosomatogenic if inherited and ecosomatogenic if resulting from poisoning or any other physical or chemical factors), it is ultimately not a disease but disturbed behavior. Even when the causes are genetic, chemical, or physical, the state of mind of an individual is still always a state of mind of an individual who cannot cope with his problems and is unable to find solutions to his troubles. No human being is "normal," but some human beings are able to search for inner harmony and look for solutions to their problems. Not only are mentally disturbed people unable to find solutions, they may not even be able to look for them.

It is today's fad and fashion to blame parents for whatever happens to their children. In my case studies of hundreds of patients over a period of 40 years, I have arrived at the conclusion that there is practically no evidence for the Freud-Abraham (Abraham, 1953a; Fenichel, 1945) timetable of fixations, and that alleged disturbances related to those fixations don't hold much water. People may have problems at any age, but the age of onset of a disorder is not necessarily related to a particular type of disorder. A great many studies (Ackerman, 1961; Lidz et al., 1955; Wolman, 1966, 1970) have indicated that a *particular type of parent-child relationship* is far more responsible for childrens' mental disorders than is the *time* at which the damage was caused. In other words, it is not the timing of the trauma, but the type of parental relations and the parent-child relationship, that is the main factor in causing mental disorder.

Often, however, it is not a particular parent with a particular emotional problem who causes an emotional disorder in the child. In a great many cases, it is not the parent who should be blamed for the child's disturbed behavior but rather a *totality of sociocultural factors* – the lack of purpose, the decline of moral values, the general trend of disinhibition and deculturation that has affected the family and the upbringing of children.

A great many married couples are unable to relate to one another and transfer their troubles to their children. The intraparental relations of the *sick family* are probably the main cause of the difficulties so many children have in their lives. The sick family is no less a sociological or sociocultural problem than a psychological one. Psychotherapy has limited power; psychotherapists are neither prophets nor social reformers. They cannot reform the family, nor can they undo social systems. Psychotherapists are no more powerful than handymen or repairmen; people come to them with broken souls and disturbed minds, seeking help. Clinical research and experience can, to some extent, help society at large by shedding light on the psychological problems of the present time which certainly differ from those faced by Freud's patients 80 years ago or more in Victorian Vienna. Freud's patients had sexual problems. Today, *insecurity* and a *depressing feeling of helplessness* are the main problems with which psychiatrists and clinical psychologist must deal.

CONTEMPORARY DISINHIBITION AND DECULTURATION

In order to satisfy their basic needs, people have worked and perspired. The development of technology has greatly reduced the number of hours that one must spend at work. With this reduction in the amount of work necessary, the amount of perspiration that is necessary has also been substantially reduced.

Certainly, no society can survive unless it produces food, shelter, clothing, and so on. As technology improves, fewer people are needed to produce the food required by society. In agricultural societies, almost 100 percent of the population tilled the soil. Today, 10 percent of the people can produce enough food for the entire population. With this gradual shift from perspiration to aspiration, human life has become enriched. More people are involved in service, and more people are engaged in noneconomic professions. More people can produce music instead of producing shoes, or paint canvases instead of walls.

The progress of culture, however, also has its dark side. Many people do not actively participate in the process of perspiration, nor do they enter the process of aspiration. These are the opulent people, the parasitic class, the jet set, who possess a good deal of economic power without using it productively. Unfortunately, this class of wealthy and idle people exercises a tremendous influence on the rest of society. Having nothing to gain and so much to lose, they display arrogance in every possible way. Newspapers and other mass media describe their extravagant lives. Magazines are full of pictures of people who marry and divorce, bear children and then reject them, and waste money yawning away their days and spreading anticultural poison. Some people in the past lived this way — kings and courtesans, perverted monks and adventurous princesses — but their lives were private and their impact upon the masses was rather limited. Today, with mass communications, the general admiration of money, and wide-spread conspicuous consumption, these individuals exercise a considerable influence on youth.

In a social climate in which nothing amounts to anything, bored and disappointed individuals often resort to violence. Violence is most often engaged in for practical gain. However, radical groups, who preach impractical revolutionary ideals, refuse to recognize that they do not have a chance of producing any significant social change through violence. The only thing they elicit is counterviolence. Violence breeds violence, and whoever uses violence must be aware of the fact that his violence will be counteracted by someone else's violence. The growing tendency to use force, however, bears witness to the decline of interpersonal cooperation and of the consideration of one individual for another. This decline of cooperation and consideration, which are the fundamental rules of any culture, is ominous.

In times that lack a sense of purpose, the only thing left is to do something for kicks. Thus, our times have brought a widespread wave of violence and terror: Arabs against Israelis, gangs against gangs in America, Catholics against Protestants in Ireland, and so on, and so on. All these acts of terror are patently absurd, because no one has ever won anything in this manner and the terrorist groups cause most harm to themselves. Terror has always produced more terror; thus, from the point of view of society at large, terror has always been an act of suicide. It is significant that most individuals who practice terror, whether in the past or in the present, have been willing to die together with their victims. Terrorists risk their own lives as if their lives have no meaning.

Unfortunately, the wave of anticulture has also influenced the treatment of mental disorders. Freud noticed that many emotional problems of his time were created by restrictive parental authority and a prudish social climate. He rebelled against the exaggerated restrictiveness, and developed a system of psychotherapy in which the therapist helps the patient to remove infantile inhibitions and to evolve more mature and rational adult inhibitions. This occurred 80 years ago. In today's climate of licence and the decline of parental authority, there is little left of the Victorian zeitgeist. Psychiatrists and psychologists who advocate the removal of a too-restrictive system storm an open door, and when they do so, they close useful doors. To be normal does not mean to be disinhibited or "natural." It is perfectly "natural" to press down the gas pedal as far as one likes, but this kind of "natural" behavior can kill a great many people, including the driver of the car himself. The only people who enjoy absolute freedom are the totally disinhibited and deteriorated psychotics in the back wards of mental hospitals. All people who live with other people must practice some degree of inhibition and self-restraint.

Some psychologists and psychiatrists, along with some poorly trained, self-appointed advocates, act as if disinhibition were the panacea for all mental ills. They seem to assume that the only problem which mentally disturbed people have is that they cannot act spontaneously, as if following one's impulses could restore mental health. Very early in his work, Freud realized that acting out leads nowhere. Psychoanalysis does not remove inhibitions; rather, it enables one to overcome infantile inhibitions and develop the rational inhibitions of adulthood. Some "recent techniques" which promote disinhibition, such as touching, acting out, unrestricted sexual behavior, and uncontrollable emotional outbursts, may counteract the exaggerated Victorian neurotic self-restraint, but they also encourage sociopathic behavior.

The fact that some people in the healing professions have fallen prey to the current wave of disinhibition and deculturation is perhaps one of the saddest aspects of our time. A therapy based on total disinhibition and acting out is part and parcel of this process of regression and deculturation. As more people follow the path of "going back to nature" and acting out their impulses, the frequency of violent acts contributes to a suicidal anticulture.

2
The Therapists

Several years ago I taught treatment methods and supervised resident-psychiatrists in the postdoctoral training program of a medical school. Young men and women who had obtained their medical degrees were admitted to a three- or four-year program of post-doctoral training in psychiatry. The training ground was the psychiatric division of a university hospital. Each young resident-doctor treated a few patients, and for every two hours with a patient, he received one hour of supervision with a senior colleague. Like all the other supervisors, I listened to the resident-doctors' reports and offered constructive criticism and guidance.

At a certain point — with the approval of my colleagues of the senior faculty — I decided to observe the residents directly in their daily work on the wards. I took a leave of absence from my other commitments and, as it were, "moved in" with the patients on the locked ward. I spent all my time with them: I ate all meals with them; I sat in the main room, watching TV, playing cards, or chatting; I went with them to occupational therapy; I joined them on walks; and I also spent a few nights on the ward. These few weeks taught me a lot.

At the beginning, the patients wondered whether I was a recently admitted patient, but the nurses told them that I was a research professor. Since I did not interfere in their lives or take any initiative, the patients got used to me and some of them volunteered to talk to me. After a while, they talked more openly to me than to the young doctors I supervised. The informal atmosphere allowed me to learn a lot about the patients and this was a priceless experience in nonparticipant observation.

One day, I sat next to an elderly patient Mrs. Sara Fieldstone. A young doctor, Chris N., came over. He turned to Mrs. Fieldstone and spoke harshly, "Sally, the nurse said you didn't take your medication.

Come on, you better take it! The nurse Adele will give it to you!"
The next day, Dr. Jerry S. came over to Mrs. Fieldstone. He spoke in
a soft and friendly manner: "Good morning, Mrs. Fieldstone, how
are you today? May I sit next to you? Oh, thank you. Did your son
call you? No? Would you like me to call him? The nurse Adele told
me that you had difficulty taking the medicine. Is anything wrong
with the medicine? Let's talk it over. You need the medicine, it is
good for you." He sat down next to her, and after a while, Mrs.
Fieldstone quietly took the medication. Both doctors received the
same medical training from the same school, but their personalities
were quite different.

THE THERAPIST'S MENTAL HEALTH

In the paper "Analysis Terminable and Interminable," Freud (1937)
compared the psychoanalyst to other healing professionals:

> So long as he is capable of practicing at all, a physician suffering
> from lung or heart trouble is not handicapped in diagnosing or
> treating internal disease. The analyst, on the other hand, because
> of the peculiar conditions of his work, is really impeded by his
> own defects in his task of discerning his patient's situation correctly
> and reacting to it in a manner conductive to cure. So there is
> some reason in the demand for a comparatively high degree of
> psychical normality and correct adjustment in the analyst as one
> of his qualifications for his work. And there is another point: he
> must be in a superior position in certain analytic situations and, in
> others, to act as his teacher. Finally, we must not forget that the
> relationship between analyst and patient is based on a love of
> truth, that is, on the acknowledgement of reality, and that it
> precludes any kind of sham or deception.
>
> Here let us pause for a moment to assure the analyst that he has
> our sincere sympathy in the very exacting requirements he is ex-
> pected to fulfill. It almost looks as if analysis were the third of
> those "impossible" professions in which one can be quite sure of
> unsatisfying results. The other two, much older-established, are
> the bringing-up of children and the government of nations. Ob-
> viously we cannot demand that the prospective analyst should be a

perfect human being before he takes up analysis, and that only persons of this rare and exalted perfection should enter the profession. (Freud, 1937, pp. 351-352)

Of course, this would be an exaggerated demand, but a definite level of mental health and maturity must be a prerequisite for anyone entering the healing professions that deal with mentally disturbed people. A physician who suffers from heart trouble can be quite an efficient heart specialist, but a disturbed psychotherapist could hardly help people overcome irrational modes of behavior (Horwitz, 1974). Psychotherapy of all kinds and brands is more being than doing, and a neurotic or alcoholic or depressed individual is unable to cope with emotionally disturbed patients. The requirement of their own psychotherapy for future psychotherapists is more than justified, and most postdoctoral institutes in psychoanalysis and other treatment methods provide a thorough psychoanalysis or some other form of psychotherapy for their candidates, which is expected to prepare them for the highly complex task of psychotherapy. The main question is, however: What makes someone into a successful psychotherapist?

Psychotherapeutic Aptitude

I assume that people who have concluded their undergraduate and graduate studies are endowed with superior intelligence; thus, it is superfluous to point out the necessity of this intellectual element in the psychotherapeutic professions. There is, however, an urgent need to stress the importance of three other factors to the psychotherapeutic professions.

Three factors that determine an individual's success in his or her occupation are *aptitude, knowledge,* and *skill,* or mastery of the technique. The same holds true in regard to psychotherapy. In order to be a successful psychotherapist, one has to have the proper *aptitude* to perform his duties, a thorough *knowledge* of psychopathology, and diagnostic and therapeutic *skill.* Training and experience contribute to knowledge and skill, but they are of little help unless one has the right aptitude. The psychotherapists use their entire personality. This is probably the main reason why, despite differences in theory and technique, all other factors being equal, some psychotherapists are more successful than others. The tool one is using to help people is oneself. The vocational aptitude of a psychotherapist is that of a total personality geared to helping mentally disturbed individuals. This aptitude is the single greatest factor in successful psychotherapy. Having the right kind of personality, the psychotherapist must receive thorough scientific training in his field and acquire therapeutic skill through the personal psychotherapy and close supervision which enable him to learn the art of therapy from his most advanced, skillful, and psychologically gifted senior colleagues.

Empathy

One of the main personality traits of successful psychotherapists is their ability to perceive nonverbal communication. Verbal communication is the main tool used by the therapist and his patients. They verbally report to the therapist their past and present experiences, thoughts, and emotions, and the therapist interprets, explains, and guides. However, a considerable part of mental life is conducted silently, nonverbally, and unconsciously. Psychoanalysts and most other therapists request that patients say whatever crosses their minds, for in free associations the chances for reporting unconscious material are considerably enhanced. The ability to listen patiently and to absorb is of utmost importance in psychotherapy, but one must not view psychotherapy merely as verbal communication, for the patients' unconscious problems might not be communicated verbally. Every patient wishes to open up and tell the therapist everything about himself or herself, but many issues and problems are unconscious and the patient may be totally unaware that his or her behavior hampers the therapeutic process. Past wishes, frustrations, and conflicts are usually repressed, and the patient's unconscious resistance which prevents opening up is a continuation of the process of repression.

Inexperienced therapists tend to accept their patients' verbal utterances at face value. Quite often, a young clinical psychologist or psychiatrist whom I supervise has reported his or her patients' verbal expression of love or hate. Usually, I try to reach out to my younger colleagues and ask for their "gut reactions." Do they, indeed, feel that the patient loves them? Is the response, possibly, merely a resistive reaction as if to say, "Doc, leave me alone, don't pry. I love you, isn't it enough?" *Empathy* — the ability to perceive nonverbal emotional messages — is a universal phenomenon, but people possess various degrees of it, from a bare and insignificant minimum up to a very high level typical of so-called psychics or sensitives.

During my stay at the locked ward in the hospital, I learned a lot about the problem of empathy. One patient told me: "I was in anguish, desperate, suicidal. I did not know what to do with myself, but my doctor did not notice it. He was his usual self, smiling and self-satisfied. He went on with his silly questions as if nothing happened. What could I do? I was chattering my session away, talking gibberish. If he did not sense my mood, how could I communicate with him?" The young doctor was sure he was making fantastic progress with the smiling, chattering, and exceedingly polite patient who was secretly collecting enough pills to put an end to her life.

Besides good intelligence, tactfulness, genuine human interest, sympathy, and so on, *the ability for preverbal and intuitive perception seems to be one of the greatest assets of a psychotherapist.* Patients may be unable to communicate their feelings: often they are unaware of them; sometimes they are dimly aware but unable to put them in words or unwilling to do so. Occasionally, they hide their true feelings or express opposite ones.

To know what is going on in the patient's mind is a sign of therapeutic talent. This is what Theodor Reik called "listening with the third ear." It is the ability to "sense" other people's feelings even if they do not express them verbally or despite their efforts to hide the feelings behind a smoke screen of words. It is *empathy* in the connotation used by Sullivan in relation to infantile, preverbal perception, when an infant is somehow aware of its mother's emotional state.

The ability to empathize is of tremendous help in dream interpretation when the meaning of certain symbols or hints becomes so plain to the analyst that he can obtain a clear picture of the latent dream material, and decide whether and how much to comment. Apparently this aptitude can be increased by didactic psychotherapy, but it is not a mere skill that can be acquired by training and experience. Skill is a result of both aptitude and training; aptitude is the ability to profit by training. Once one has the aptitude; one may learn how to apply it better and better.

Empathy is not a skill but an aptitude. An insufficient ability to empathize should, I believe, disqualify one for the practice of psychotherapy. I came to this conclusion as a result of my own therapeutic practice and my supervisory work ("control") with younger colleagues. I cannot imagine how one can acquire the very important skill of timing interpretations without having sufficient empathetic ability. In working with prepsychotic patients, one could not avoid causing breakdown without a highly developed empathy. Often one is tempted to express an undoubtedly correct comment on the patient's actions or dreams, but the premature comment could lead to a psychotic breakdown. A therapist must "feel" or somehow perceive that this is not the right thing to do, just as the therapist must "feel" that the patient is tense even when the patient is overtly calm.

What actually is the aptitude that I have reluctantly called empathy? It is, undoubtedly, some ability for *preverbal, archaic perception*. It is what poets call *intuition*. It is what Karen Horney described in infants who gain weight when cuddled or what Rene Spitz found in infants who react to what is going on in their environment. It is the ability to be somehow aware of the feelings of other people. This ability can probably be found in animals, infants, great artists, and writers, but it is usually subdued and often nonexistent in normal adults who rely on sensory perception and a logical analysis of its content.

A tentative interpretation of this ability must be related to the archaic ego which perceives reality in a diffuse, illogical, usually pictorial, magic, and primitively symbolic way. This *arche-perception,* as I would like to call it, is exceedingly *sensitive to emotional processes.* The infant may not distinguish mother from bottle or mother's breast from mother's dress, but he will invariably distinguish whether mother is friendly and joyful or hostile and sullen, and *he will in most cases perceive mother's emotional state correctly.* As will be explained, this is a *parapsychological phenomenon.*

Telepathy

Telepathy is an extrasensory awareness of another person's mental state. This parapsychological ability is of utmost importance in psychotherapeutic work. Freud was quite interested in parapsychology and was a member of both the American and the British Societies for Psychical Research. His staunch determinism allowed no loopholes in the study of mental phenomena. Whatever exists, Freud maintained, has a cause and an effect, and must not be dismissed. Parapsychological phenomena were usually bypassed by research workers, and Freud took an empirical approach. He wrote: "First, we have to establish whether these processes really occur, and then, but only then, where there is no doubt that these processes really occur, we can set about their explanation" (Freud, 1932, p. 40). Freud objected to too hasty a condemnation of telepathy; the fact that charlatans busy themselves with occult phenomena does not prove that these phenomena do not exist.

Freud cited several instances of telepathic dreams, intuitive knowledge, and transference of thought. There is no doubt that certain individuals have better access to their unconscious than others and that such people seem to be somehow aware of their unconscious feelings about others, as well as the feelings of other people about them. They may, for instance, display unexplainable foresight that is somehow related to anticipation of risks and dangers.

The psychoanalytic literature describes several instances of telepathy. Servadio (1935) noticed the relationship between telepathy and positive transference. Devereux's collective volume *Psychoanalysis and the Occult* (1953) contains several reports and discussions concerning the use of telepathy in psychoanalytic treatment. Eisenbud (1977) stressed the importance of extrasensory perception and telepathy in therapeutic technique. The therapist's telepathic abilities may be of great help in interpreting the patient's dreams and transference. Ehrenwald (1977) reviewed the entire field of parapsychological phenomena in their relationship to psychotherapeutic techniques.

Telepathy has been of great help in my work with suicidal patients, and on a few occasions has enabled me to save human lives. In 40 years of clinical practice, I have treated several suicidal patients. My decision to work with them or to refuse to work with them has been based on a combination of rational and realistic considerations and telepathy.

The realistic considerations have related to the patient's home environment. The protection of human life has always been my prime responsibility. Quite often, colleagues have referred to me a suicidal patient who has threatened to kill himself or herself or who has already tried to commit suicide. I have never refused to see patients for an initial, usually diagnostic, interview. Then, after one or a few sessions, I have decided whether or not to take on the patient. Whenever suicidal patients are referred to me, I have insisted on seeing their close relatives.

The realistic aspect of my decision is based on family cooperation. Once, a young lady was brought to my office by her relatives who had picked her up from a hospital where her life had been saved after a suicide attempt. I would have refused to treat her unless the members of the family promised to keep a close watch on her 24 hours a day, 7 days a week. I gave them my schedule and all the phone numbers at which they could reach me at any time. However, this was not enough. I also had to be reasonably sure that I myself was psychologically tuned in to an extrasensory awareness of the patient's moods. I felt I was. This was a telepathic feeling, certainly not a realistic or logical judgment. The patient was too depressed to go to work, and for a while, my office was the only place she agreed to go or, rather, to be taken by a relative.

I did not fail in this case, but I cannot claim success in a self-destructive case. Dr. J. was a biologist with a Doctor of Science degree. His knowledge of biochemistry, pharmacology, and physiology was astounding. Originally, he had planned to become a physician, but he was more interested in research than in practice. He spoke with authority on issues within his competence, and psychosomatic medicine was one of his favorite topics. He was a borderline manic-depressive (dysmutual latent psychotic) with a strong self-destructive tendency. His professional career was inconsistent and spotty; after long periods of hard work, he would abandon his projects, run away, and turn to something else. Apparently, he avoided people, shied away from success, and then rationalized his defeats.

Once, he began complaining about nausea and loss of appetite; he proudly declared that he had developed *anorexia nervosa* and was pleased with his new symptoms. I disagreed with his self-diagnostic statements. I believe that physical diseases can strike everyone, and neurotics are not immune to physical illnesses. I have always been opposed to throwing all physical symptoms into the wastebasket of psychosomatics. In all the years of my practice, whenever a patient has complained of a pain or an ailment, I have always demanded a thorough medical examination. Accordingly, I asked Dr. J. to consult his physician. He chided me. "I knew," he said sarcastically, "that you would send me for a physical. That's your old-fashioned philosophy; body comes first." However, at my insistence he did go see his family physician. The next day he reported triumphantly: "My doctor could not find anything wrong with me. It's all in my mind. It's psychosomatic, positive."

As time went on, his complaints became more frequent and he began to lose weight. I worried about him since his symptoms did not look psychosomatic to me. I sent him for a physical checkup, this time to an internist with whom I cooperated closely. The report was optimistic, diagnosing a mild gastrointestinal trouble, and a medicine was prescribed. Although I kept on insisting on a *thorough* checkup, I tried to convince myself that my worries were irrational. The patient, however, adamantly refused to go for further examinations, and I was torn by an inner conflict: my conscious sided with the internist, but my unconscious was full of worries.

A week passed, and Dr. J. reported a strange dream. In his dream, his brother — with whom he had often identified — was hit in the kidneys by a bomb and was dying. At this point, I became absolutely convinced that Dr. J. had cancer of the kidneys or some other serious kidney disease, and I decided to act immediately. I did not communicate my suspicions to Dr. J., but I put an ultimatum to him: either he would immediately go for a GI series or I would refuse to see him any longer. I sent him to a top internist. The examination revealed cancer of the kidneys. He was hospitalized immediately and, unfortunately, never came back.

It was a terrible shock. One gets attached to a patient, and I felt horribly about Dr. J. I should have been more inclined to listen to the voice of my unconscious. Had I been more determined and less influenced by the two physicians, I would have said, "Go to a top specialist, or I will refuse to ever see you again." I did say that the last time he came to my office, immediately after he told me about the dream. I doubt whether early intervention on my part could have helped, but even today I feel sad when I think of poor Dr. J.

Between Mind and Body

The *Handbook of Parapsychology* (Wolman, 1977) describes several theoretical interpretations of parapsychological phenomena. My own hypothesis places parapsychology, as it were, between physical and mental phenomena, quite similar to hypnosis. Hypnotic suggestions can produce "physiological effects such as an alteration in gastric secretions, inhibition of gastric hunger contractions, inhibition or augmentation of allergic responses, reduction of warts, and production of skin changes which resemble warts or dermographism" (Barber, 1973).

There is also a close connection between empathy and parapsychological phenomena. Sullivan (1947) interpreted empathy in organismic terms. *Tension and relief* follow each other, especially since tension and relief are interpreted by Sullivan in purely physiological terms, as a contraction and relaxation of muscles. This physiological process is later modified by social influences. The child soon learns that on certain occasions the immediate relaxation of muscles meets with parental disapproval. Parental disapproval causes a feeling of discomfort. This *empathized discomfort* stems not from the organism but from *interpersonal relationships.* For example, as soon as there is any tension in bladder or bowels, the proper muscles act immediately to bring relief. However, this automatic relaxation may invite parental hostility, which produces in the child a feeling of "empathized discomfort." This feeling will lead the child to learn "to suffer increasing tension in the bladder and rectum and to resist the automatic relaxation of the sphincter muscles concerned in retaining the urine and feces. Failures in this are often accompanied by empathized discomfort, and success is often the occasion of empathized comfort which is added to the satisfaction from relief of tension" (Sullivan, 1947, p. 44).

Apparently, parapsychological phenomena belong to the "transitionalistic" area between mind and body, together with hypnosis, empathy, unconscious, cathexis, and a host of other psychosomatic and somatopsychic phenomena. They are the seed and the tree, the mind and the body. They do not stand alone; modern physics has accepted the dual nature of light, and Firsoff's (1967) theory of the *neutrino* offers an important *sequitur* to Einstein's theory of the transformation of energy into matter. According to Firsoff (quoted from Koestler, 1972),

> The universe as seen by a neutrino eye would wear a very unfamiliar look. Our earth and other plants simply would not be there, or might at best appear as thin patches of mist. The sun and other stars may be dimly visible, in as much as they emit some neutrinos . . . . . A neutrino brain might suspect our existence from certain secondary effects, but would find it very difficult to prove, as we would elude the neutrino instruments at his disposal.
>
> Our universe is no truer than that of the neutrinos – they exist, but they exist in a different kind of space, governed by different laws . . . . In our space no material body can exceed the velocity of light, because at this velocity its mass and so inertia become infinite. The neutrino, however, is subject neither to gravitational nor to electro-magnetic fields, so that it need not be bound by this speed limit and may have its own, different time. It might be able to travel faster than light, which would make it relativistically recede in our time scale.
>
> From our earlier analysis of mental entities, it appears that they have no definite locus in so-called "physical," or better, gravi-electromagnetic space, in which respect they resemble a neutrino, or, for that matter, a fast electron. This already suggests a special kind of mental space governed by different laws, which is further corroborated by the parapsychological experiments made at Duke University and elsewhere . . . . It seems . . . that this kind of perception involves a mental interaction, which is subject to laws of its own, defining a different type of space-time. (pp. 63-64)

Parapsychology may exercise a beneficial influence on the studies of human life, whether they are conducted from the organic, biochemical, and neurophysiological viewpoints or from the psychological angle. Parapsychology challenges the traditional concepts of time, causation, and individualistic isolation so well entrenched in both the organismic and the psychogenic theories. Viewed from the historical perspective, parapsychology introduces new ideas, keeping pace with theoretical physics and the contemporary philosophy of science.

The concept of positive and negative time, introduced by R. P. Feynman in 1961, revolutionized theoretical physics. Strangely enough, hypnotic regression in age has evoked much less interest, although it may serve as empirical proof of moving back and forth in time, which is analogous to moving back and forth in space. Several parapsychological phenomena could be similarly interpreted.

One of the problems in any psychological research, including parapsychology, stems from the notion that every human being is a separate and discrete entity. Psychiatrists and clinical psychologists often try to make prognostic judgments, ignoring the fact that no one lives in a vacuum and that the fate of every individual is greatly influenced by environmental factors. This applies also to parapsychology. Everything that happens in this area is influenced by the subjects involved, the experimenter or the observer, and a host of other factors. Moreover, traditional causal relationships may be applicable to isolated systems and thus preserved in certain psychological situations, but they may not be applicable when human behavior is viewed in the broad context of the universe. Certainly, the transfer of thoughts and images across large spaces could not be interpreted in a narrow one-to-one relationship.

The fact that not all parapsychological experiments yield significant data provides additional proof of the variability of nature. All oaks are not the same size, nor do all human organisms have the same chemistry. Apparently, some individuals are closer to the transitional processes than others. There are far-reaching organic and psychological differences between individuals; for example, the I.Q. correlation between two randomly chosen individuals is zero. Some human organisms vehemently react against penicillin which produces miracles for others. There is, therefore, no reason to assume that all people are equally able to respond to telepathy, hypnotism, or for that matter, to any other stimulus.

Both empathy and telepathy are instances of the *transfer* of psychological elements such as emotional states, perceptions, thoughts, and so on, but such a transfer is facilitated by the particular somatopsychic or psychosomatic nature of the individuals concerned. Future research in parapsychology must, therefore, focus on a most thorough study of "paranormal" individuals, the "sensitives."

Are parapsychological phenomena mind or body? They are either or both. They exemplify the facts of nature, the continuity in change. As such, parapsychology opens new vistas in science, thereby joining psychoanalysis, hypnotism, psychosomatic medicine, and theoretical physics.

Going back to the psychotherapists' psychological makeup, one must appreciate the relevance of the ability to receive nonverbal communication. The tool which psychotherapists use is their total personality, and their unconscious is an important and useful part of this personality. Sullivan's term "empathy" encompasses communication across large distances: thus it borders on, and often transgresses the borders of ESP. The ability to perceive communication which is not expressed in words is a prerequisite for a successful patient-therapist relationship in practically every type of psychotherapy.

Plasticity of the Ego

One must, however, take some precaution against putting too much faith in one's telepathic abilities or being overly reliant on para-psychological messages. The entire field of extrasensory perception represents some arche-perception which is far from precise and is a rather inadequate basis for rational judgment. One must not rely on the dim, often diffuse, telepathic messages typical of some animals and infants (Wolman, 1977a); one must use perceptual data, test reality in a precise manner, and reason with the help of socially agreed-upon verbal symbols. The archaic way of perceiving and thinking must be checked by rational and communicable perception and thought.

However, in dealing with disturbed and regressed individuals, one must have the ability to comprehend the content of their condensed language, pictorial thinking, and preverbal symbols, and "sense" their feelings. Some people possess this ability to a great extent. Borderline latent psychotics demonstrate this facility. Probably like many other psychotherapists, I have often been surprised in group therapy when a latent schizophrenic has easily and almost infallibly interpreted the dreams and other communications of group members. The same thing has happened in individual psychotherapy with schizophrenics or latent schizophrenics, when their ability for "arche-perception" has been amply demonstrated.

However, all this is not meant to encourage training neurotics and psychotics, and making therapists out of them. There are good reasons why they could not be suitable therapists despite their empathetic abilities. The main reason is the *weakness of their ego* and their consequent inability to face the emotional onslaught of their patients. An emotionally disturbed therapist may crack up when faced with outbursts of hate or panic or, at best, respond to his patients' emotions in an irrational way.

Psychotherapy is a *scientifically determined procedure* aimed at the removal, or at least substantial alleviation, of mental disorder. People who practice it must have proper scientific training and must use scientifically elaborated techniques; also, their minds must be capable of *rational implementation* of this acquired skill and knowledge.

The *rational behavior* which excludes psychotics and neurotics from the practice of psychotherapy has to do with the ability to take frustration, to control one's inner conflicts, to perceive reality correctly, to control one's emotions, to think logically, and soon. This involves many personality traits that can be grouped together under the heading of *strong ego*. A strong ego, is the master of the organism, capable of keeping of a satisfactory balance between the pressures stemming from external reality and one's own emotions.

A strong ego is capable of sound judgment and of full use of the mental abilities which themselves represent an important factor in the makeup of a therapist. A mentally healthy individual does not apply in his waking life primitive symbols and pictorial reasoning, and the archaic elements of his ego are carefully analyzed in didactic psychotherapy and then suppressed in a satisfactory manner.

Obviously a strong ego and empathy or telepathy are not one and the same thing. One is tempted to find contradictions between these two elements because, as a matter of fact, infants and psychotics have a weak ego and empathy, which is some sort of arche-perception characteristic of the very early ego.

However, there is no reason for such counterposition. I imagine that anyone with some experience in analytically oriented psychotherapy has noticed the following phenomenon which I call a *split-level process,* that is, one which works simultaneously in two apparently opposite directions that are actually not contradictory but mutually complementary.

Most patients undergo this split-level development in psychotherapy. On one hand, their egos become stronger, and with this, most of their overt behavior becomes more rational. Their egos are better able to take all kinds of pressures and failures, and to withstand the inner pressures stemming from the id and the superego.

This process is closely related to, and dependent on, certain unconscious changes. In order to resolve their inner conflicts and restore their mental balance, patients *have to regress.* Transference (described in detail in Chapter 6) is a regression to infantile dependence, which is of great help in psychotherapeutic work. I shall avoid discussing this problem here, but I would like to mention that I have noticed that most of my patients have simultaneously increased their ability for rational judgment and their ability for empathy. They have undergone the split-level process that has widened the scope of their perception, making them more rational and more empathetic at the same time.

I believe that this personality development is *an increase in the plasticity of the ego.* I would venture to say that the degree of plasticity of the ego is one of the major determinants of successful psychotherapy. For a better explanation of the issue, let us use the Freudian pictorial representation of the mental apparatus as a body floating in water, with a part of it − the ego − above the surface. Let us go further and ascribe to the water the attribute of unconscious, and to the air the attributes of preconscious and conscious. A normal individual could be compared to a boat; a part of the boat is in the water, but the upper part must remain above the surface to be able to function. If too much water enters the body of the boat, the boat will sink. The normal individual keeps unconscious material safely under control, and only a part of it is exposed in a not dangerous way in dreams, slips of tongue, and so on. Neurotics do not function too well and struggle to keep the water (unconscious) out of their mental system. Psychotics are flooded by the waves of unconscious.

The therapist may be compared to a boat that usually moves on the surface of the water but faces no danger when diving in deep waters. The therapist does this at will − goes as deep as necessary and comes back easily to the surface. The therapeutic strategy is always calculated on the surface of water (i.e., in a conscious, rational, and scientific way), but whenever necessary, the therapist dives into the deep waters of the unconscious. The therapist must possess the ability to mobilize and demobilize, to emerge (conscious) and to submerge (unconscious). This is what I call the *plasticity of the ego.*

The plasticity of the ego is related, as it were, to the "wealth" of one's personality. Disturbed individuals use their resources in inner fighting, trying to keep their impulses down. They function with only a part of their mental resources. Average, well-adjusted individuals are in a better position: the ego controls most of their resources, "stores" them in the preconscious ("memory traces"), and has easy access to them. Other people are even more fortunate; they have access to their unconscious mental resources. The great masters of art and literature have penetrated the depths of human nature and expressed in an artistic way feelings which most people are unaware of and unable to discover.

In a way, a psychotherapist is an artist, and psychotherapy involves artistic talent. However, when the happiness − or sometimes the very survival − of a suffering fellowman is at stake, it is the therapist's moral obligation to put the therapeutic activity to the scientific test. Therapeutic talent is a talent like any other, but psychotherapists work not with tunes, words, or paints, but with human beings who desperately need their help. Even great talent does not suffice.

It is good to know about talent. Schools that train psychotherapists should look for talent. Personal psychotherapy should increase one's abilities, but even the greatest talent should be controlled by scientifically elaborated methods that will help the talent to grow, check the treatment strategy, and prove that satisfactory results are being obtained. Aptitude (talent), study, and skill together lead to the best possible results and bring about improvements in psychotherapeutic practice.

Vectorial Attitude

If one wanted to construct an aptitude test or a battery of tests for psychotherapeutic professionals, such a battery should be composed of five tests.

1. The first should be an *intelligence test.* One has to possess a high I.Q. to be able to comprehend the complexity of human nature and to attain mastery in psychopathology and psychotherapeutic techniques.

2. There should be a *test of empathy and perceptiveness.* Personal psychoanalysis or another type of psychotherapy usually increases one's ability to empathize, but most probably this ability is formed very early in one's life. Psychotherapists should be able to join their patients in journeys into the unconscious, should "listen with the third ear'" and must be capable of detaching themselves from the patients' unconscious whenever necessary. When a psychotic patient experiences delusions or hallucinations, the psychotherapist should be able to get a quick and correct insight into these distortions of reality. At the same time, whoever works with psychotics must be aware of the danger of becoming involved in the unconscious processes of the patients (cf. Fromm-Reichman, 1950; Thompson, 1950).

3. Prospective psychotherapists should themselves be in relatively *good mental health;* it is assumed that the didactic analysis they undergo will help them to become even more rational, emotionally balanced, and socially adjusted. These criteria of mental health must be rigorously applied to people who enter the psychotherapeutic professions.

4. Like any other therapeutic process, psychotherapy is a process of interaction. As mentioned in Chapter 1, three types of social interactions can be distinguished depending on the aims of the participants. When the objective of someone entering an interactional relationship is to take, that is, to satisfy his own needs, this is an *instrumental* type of relationship. When the objectives of each participant are to give and to get, it is a *mutual* type of relationship. When one's objective is to give, that is, to satisfy the needs of others, this is a *vectorial* type of relationship. The infant versus mother relationship is the prototype of instrumentalism; sexual intercourse and marriage are the prototypes of mutualism; and parental attitude toward an infant is the prototype of vectorialism. Needless to say, the *therapist's attitude* toward his patients must be *vectorial.* If he lived in a country where therapeutic services were socialized, there would be no patient-paid fee. Patients' fees or hospital salary need not detract from the fact that the analyst is the giver and the helper.

Not everyone is inclined or able to be dedicated to others, but such *vectorial dedication is an indispensable personality trait for all psychotherapists.* The vectorial attitude includes compassion, a friendly and congenial disposition, and devotion to one's therapeutic tasks.

5. Freud did not make his ethical principles explicit; they were obvious and implicit in his behavior inside and outside his office (Jones, 1953). Today, moral standards are rather unclear, and unless therapists take a definite stand, they may lose their raison d'etre as therapists. Consider the case of a sociopathic patient with a criminal record: the therapist must help the patient to discontinue the antisocial behavior and to develop positive and moral attitudes. Therapists do not judge people, but in order to help, they must take a stand and determine the eventual outcome of treatment. I believe, therefore, that *moral convictions, courage, and responsibility are indispensable elements of psychotherapeutic work.* Freud possessed these virtues; following his deeds no less than his words, one must say that personal integrity, self-discipline, moral commitment, and courage are necessary prerequisites for all psychotherapists.

Ethical Requirements

What level of morality should be expected from clinical psychologists, psychiatrists, and psychiatric social workers who assume responsibility for the mental health of other people? The answer is obvious: *Helping others is an act of supreme morality. Men and women who enter the healing professions must act in an impeccably moral manner, and a strict code of ethics must be obeyed by people who take care of mentally disturbed individuals* (Rosenbaum, 1982).

To be ethical implies being truthful. Psychotherapists must not undertake the treatment of cases which they are not capable of offering to adequate help. They must not promise things they cannot deliver. They must terminate treatment when it does not serve the best interest of the patient.

Therapists are not angels or saints and must not represent themselves as such. Psychotherapy is a vectorial process of giving help, but at the same time it is an instrumental process of earning a living. To be moral does not mean to love; one must act in a moral manner to everyone and not only to those one loves.

On some occasions, patients have asked, "Do you love me?" My answer has been unequivocal: "I care for your well-being. It is my moral responsibility to do the best I can, but I am not a magician or an angel. Helping people is my profession: it is the way I earn my living. It is my job to help people, and I will conscientiously discharge my responsibility."

Over years of clinical practice, research, and teaching, I have trained and supervised scores of younger colleagues. Whether it was in the postdoctoral program in psychiatry at the Albert Einstein College of Medicine, the postdoctoral program in psychoanalysis and psychotherapy at Adelphi University, the doctoral program in clinical psychology at Long Island University, or many years of private supervision, the essence of my teaching and guidance has been: *a good psychotherapist gets involved with the patient's case without getting involved with the patient personally. This is our ethical commitment.*

Imagine an individual living on an isolated and uninhabited island: such an individual could not be either ethical or unethical. Morality starts with a relationship to another person; there must be at least two people for moral behavior. Morality implies a manner in which one interacts with another person or persons (Margenau, 1964). Ethical or moral principles (I am using these two terms interchangeably) have been determined a priori by Immanuel Kant, deduced logically by Baruch Spinoza, related to religious principles by Martin Buber and explained in hundreds of different ways by philosophers of all creeds. Apparently, there is no universal agreement concerning what is right and what is wrong.

I believe that the most objective, succinct, and simple definition of morality was given by the ancient Jewish sage Hillel. When a pagan asked him to describe Judaism briefly, Hillel said, "Thou shalt love thy neighbor as thyself. That's all. Everything else is a commentary."

The term "love" might be somewhat ambiguous, and to be safe, Hillel's dictum should be replaced by the following one: "Treat your neighbor the way you want him to treat you." The shift is from the emotionally loaded term "love" to overt behavior, that is, to observable interaction. It is impossible to love everyone, but it is possible to interact with everyone in a fair and just manner. Moral principles are rather vague as long as they are stated in terms of feelings, thoughts, and theories, but they can be clearly stated, objectively observed, experimentally tested, and measured in *overt behavior* (Berkowitz, 1972; Colby et al., 1980; Kohlberg, 1979; Rest, 1979). In other words, *it is counterproductive to define ethics in abstract terms that deal with unobservables, but a scientific analysis of ethics can successfully scrutinize moral behavior. The relevance of moral judgment depends on its application in overt behavior, for what is the good of convictions that are not practiced?*

Daily life and historical evidence provide numerous instances of individuals' making lofty moral judgments while, at the same time, passively condoning, approving, or even actively participating in immoral behavior. Several years ago I supervised psychologists who worked in a prison. I asked them to apply a brief oral questionnaire to burglars, muggers, and killers. The imprisoned sociopaths maintained that they had the right to do what they had done. In my book *Call No Man Normal* (1973), I referred to the sociopaths as "innocent criminals." I was not surprised that most sociopaths and practically all other prison inmates passed the brief moral questionnaire with flying colors. All of them clearly distinguished between minor transgressions and violent assaults, and all of them verbally condemned stealing, cheating, mugging, and other criminal practices. Some of them pointed to the low moral standards of high public officials such as President Nixon and Vice-President Agnew, and the "moral judgment" of the jailed criminals did not substantially disagree with the slogans and catchwords of some public officials.

The famous — or rather infamous — murder of Catherine Genovese is a case in point. Neighbors heard her cries and saw her being murderously assaulted, but no one came to her rescue. Of course, all the neighbors condemned murder, but no one helped and no one acted in accordance with his or her "moral convictions." The behavior of the so-called innocent bystanders has little in common with morality, and a verbal condemnation of murderous activities hardly proves one's high moral convictions (Latane and Darley, 1970). Morality is not a verbal issue; it is a matter of deeds.

I have proposed a theory of moral development that goes through five phases, namely, (1) anomy, (2) phobonomy, (3) heteronomy, (4) socionomy, and (5) autonomy. According to this theory (Wolman, 1982), people are born *anomous*. They know of no restraint, no concern, and no consideration for anyone. The intrauterine life is clearly parasitic: the zygote-embryo-fetus is all out for himself and grabs whatever he can. Mother's body is self-sacrificing: it is ready to give whatever it possesses to feed and to protect the not-yet-born child.

Although the newborn must use his or her own respiratory system, the parasitic-dependent attitude continues even after the umbilical cord has been cut. The infant wants what he wants, and follows his instant stimuli and impulses. He operates on the principle of immediate gratification which Freud called *Lustprinzip.* Infants are *anomous,* that is, amoral and selfish.

Morality means concern for fellowmen, but it starts with restraints imposed from without. Fear of retaliation and punishment is the first, rather small step toward behavior. The earliest restraints and rules are based on fear, and the early and primitive morality should be called *phobonomous.* Fear is not morality, but primitive people and toddlers must be restrained from without. The restraint breaks the ground for more advanced phases of morality.

As the child becomes aware of parental love and care, he begins to appreciate what he gets and tends to reciprocate. Children's "love" is quite selfish, for they love only those who love them. Children need parental love and fear its loss, and their attitude toward their parents is a combination of love and fear. Children willingly and fearfully accept parental rules and prohibitions, gradually incorporating these rules and identifying with parents or parental substitutes. They may blame themselves and develop *guilt feelings* whenever they violate parental rules. Their behavior is *heteronomous,* for they obey norms imposed by others whom they perceive as loving and powerful authority figures. In Freud's personality model, this self-regulatory behavior was ascribed to the *superego.*

Moral development does not reach its full development with the acceptance of parental rules and the formation of the superego. Preadolescents and adolescents develop close interpersonal relations with their peers, and form groups, cliques, and gangs. These new social relations often displace the child-parent attachments, and the rules of peer society frequently become the ultimate source of moral or antimoral group behavior. The willing acceptance of social norms, be they of a certain religious denomination, of a racial or ethnic group, or of a political party, leads to the formation of a new part of one's personality, which I call the *we-ego*, and to the group identification period I call *socionomous*. Most individuals do not go beyond socionomy and the acceptance of the norms prevailing in their particular group, clan, subculture, or society at large; most people follow the rather limited moral rules of their own sociocultural group.

The ultimate moral development goes beyond socionomy and is related to the idea of power. Imagine an Omnipotent Being: an Omnipotent Being does not fear or need anything, and thus cannot hate or hurt anyone. The only thing he can do is to give what he has. He *must* build and create, love and protect. Christ, Prometheus, and Antigone had the *courage to give* without expecting anything in return. They had developed a *vector-ego* which reaches out to help others. Their morality was *autonomous*. Psychotherapists are not divine beings,but they must desire to perfect their moral standards. The higher they go, the better they will be.

Helping people is emotionally rewarding for, as a rule, those who give enjoy more than those who receive. Those who give, feel strong because it is within their power to give. Those who are on the receiving end are glad to receive what they need, but they feel dependent on the goodwill of others who have the power to give.

Small wonder that psychotherapists might err in estimating the usefulness of their work and occasionally, albeit unconsciously, may wish to postpone the termination of psychotherapy. An error in judgment is not a crime, but it may lead to unfair behavior that must be avoided. The termination of psychotherapy might resemble the termination of parental care. The aim of parental care is to help the child become a mature adult, thus making further care superfluous. Even rational parents who know that their child must leave the nest might experience emotional difficulties. Taking care of someone is tantamount to investing one's emotions in that person, and the more one cares, the more one becomes attached to the person one takes care of.

The therapist-patient interaction is a two-way and two-level process. On one level is the *here-and-now* relationship; the patient is aware of the fact that he is going to a doctor whom he pays or who is paid by society and who is supposed to help him to relieve his tensions and resolve his inner conflicts. On the other level, some irrational feelings are directed toward the therapist, who serves as a target for the patient's emotional onslaughts.

Serving as a target for a continuous onslaught of human emotions is a great mental health hazard. It's no wonder that psychiatrists have a high incidence of suicide and that some of Freud's early associates who had been inadequately psychoanalyzed suffered mental breakdowns. Obviously, whoever intends to deal with the emotional problems of other people must put his own house in order and undergo his own analysis. In order to save drowning lives, one must be a good swimmer, well-prepared to do the job of lifesaving.

A good therapist must get involved with his patients without getting involved with their personalities. The psychotherapist must get involved with the patients' causes and be determined to help them. On the other hand, the therapist must not become personally involved with patients or get caught in the murky waters of morbid counter-transference feelings. To be dependable but not involved — this is the task of the therapist. The therapist's attitude toward his patients is a giving attitude; he must enable them to go through *corrective emotional experiences* in order to remedy their past bad experiences and correct their personality deficiencies.

However, to do this, the therapist must be emotionally independent and able to serve the needs of patients and not his own narcissistic needs. If one tries to take a shortcut in defining psychotherapy and asks what its aim is, the answer would be: *the aim of psychotherapy is to make it superfluous.* A good psychotherapist works in such a way that his work becomes unnecessary. He helps patients to grow up, and at the end of his work, they don't need him anymore. Their dependence on him is terminated as they become independent and begin making their own rational decisions.

The termination of psychotherapy often presents considerable emotional difficulties for both the therapist and the patient. A therapist may resist termination initiated by the patient for a good reason such as a job transfer or going away to college. The therapist shows his resistance by labeling the termination "premature" and suggesting that treatment is not "finished." Implicit here are the therapist's anxiety about separation, and his notion that therapy has a definite time limit and that less time means fewer results — as if to say that the efforts and accomplishments of a short time have no merit unless one gets a diploma for the course. By maintaining a neutral attitude and accepting the reality of the external exigencies (let's see what we can do in this period of time), the therapist can avail himself of the opportunity to observe the fact that patients can be exceedingly productive under externally set time limits. The therapist has to learn to cope with the anxiety of letting patients grow up at their own rate, as well as to handle his own anxiety about separation from patients.

Many patients announce their readiness to leave by reviving their original symptoms, long since gone. This revival is a disguise for separation anxiety and is, convertly, a test of the therapist's willingness to let them go. Making explicit the separation anxiety, as well as the fear of leaving, resolves this issue. No therapist should allow a patient to leave treatment without a mutual recounting of the issues covered, description of the goals achieved or missed, and delineation of the varying nature of the relationship, both real and unreal. The discoveries of positives as well as the uncovering of negatives have to be spelled out (Witenberg, 1972, p. 189-190).

An additional *caveat* should be added at this point. One seeks help from a surgeon or a psychotherapist whenever one feels that something is wrong with oneself. When a person goes to a dentist, he assumes that the dentist is competent (i.e., capable of helping) and caring (i.e., willing to help). The dentist and the surgeon are perceived as *strong* and *friendly,* and patients depend on their help. However, outside treatment hours, one does not necessarily look up to them. If the patient is a real estate broker, the dentist or the surgeon may need the patient's help in buying a house. Human relations are not a hierarchic system in which somebody always looks up to someone else; one needs a baker for bread, an accountant for tax, and a dentist for teeth. One looks up to each in his *particular capacity.*

This relationship does not apply to the treatment of mental disorders. The psychotherapist is not supposed ever to ask the assistance of his patients who are dentists or lawyers. The psychotherapist deals with his patients' total personality; thus, patients cannot view the therapist merely as a strong and friendly expert. The psychotherapist has taken the place of the father-confessor, but he is expected to have more power than the priest, rabbi, or minister. Patients depend on the therapist in making the most vital decisions.

The treatment of mental disorders resembles the child-parent relationship. Adult men and women go to someone who is not necessarily wiser, better established, more influential, or more powerful than themselves. People seek psychotherapy because they are unhappy and don't know how to manage their lives. Most of them are unable to adequately cope with their jobs, their families, and the whole complexity of life; some even think about quitting life altogether. Many are in despair; practically all are in quandaries.

Putting one's faith and fate in a therapist makes a person much more dependent than he is in regard to his physician, dentist, or lawyer. In the patient-therapist dependency, the patient necessarily develops an infantile regression, called "transference" by Freud. When one is under stress, one tends to develop regressive moods and to transfer one's emotions onto the supporting person. The therapist becomes a target for the patient's positive and negative emotions, which present a challenge to the therapist's mental health. More about dealing with positive and negative transference as well as countertransference will be found in Chapter 6.

3
The Goals of Psychotherapy

All human behavior is goal directed, but those who act are not always certain of what they are trying to attain. A lack of clarity of goals is totally unacceptable in psychotherapy; people who come to psychiatrists, clinical psychologists, and psychiatric social workers look for help, and the goals of therapy are implicit: the aim of psychotherapy is to make any further psychotherapy superfluous.

The question remains: What can psychotherapy, specifically, do for a particular patient? What kind of help can psychotherapy offer? Is it sort of a medication aimed at assuaging pain? Is it a friendly pat on the back and fatherly reassurance? Is it the removal of symptoms? What can patients expect at the termination of the therapeutic process?

Quite often my patients ask, "When I finish psychotherapy, will I be happy?" My answer is: "Not necessarily. A normal and mature adult cannot always be happy. He or she will react with joy to success and satisfaction, and with sorrow and anguish to frustration, pain, and loss. No human being is immune to loss, frustration, and disappointment, and no human being can always be happy unless he or she is totally insensitive and totally unable to experience normal positive emotional reactions to success and negative emotional reactions to failure."

"So what good is in psychotherapy?" they ask. I answer, "The aim of psychotherapy is to enable people to have the *courage to live* and to face the existential tragedy of humanity, the inevitable fate of death, and the necessary decision to make the best of one's life. The aim of psychotherapy is to help people to have the courage to be themselves and to live in accordance with their convictions. Successful psychotherapy enables people to make the best of every possible situation, and to bring as much happiness and joy to themselves and their dear ones as humanly possible. Whenever events take an adverse course and misfortune or misery hits them, they do not fall apart but cope with dignity and courage with the adversities life brings. *Courage and wisdom* — these are the purposes of interactional psychotherapy."

Some authors have stressed the ability to work and to love. These are the negative aspects of psychotherapy. People who are unable to work, who are unable to relate to other human beings, who have sexual difficulties, must get rid of these and other problems. This is the first step. The psychotherapeutic interaction must be divided into three phases. The first phase is the *analytic;* its task is to overcome whatever emotional obstacles and irrationalities one has developed during one's lifetime. This involves the removal of infantile inhibitions, as well as the resolution of irrational conflicts that cripple one's personality and prevent a person from acting in an adult and mature way. The resolution of past conflicts and the attainment of the first three criteria of mental health discussed in Chapter 1 are the task of the first, analytic, phase of interactional psychoanalysis.

One cannot accomplish much as long as one is crippled by past errors and past emotional conflicts. However, as soon as psychotherapy helps to resolve past conflicts and the patient, liberated from past ills and handicaps, is capable of putting his intelligence and energy to productive use, psychotherapy moves toward two consecutive phases which I call "search for identity" and "becoming: self-realization," respectively.

THE FIRST PHASE: THE ANALYTIC PHASE

In order to be able to find oneself, in order to be able to become a mature adult, one has to go through the analytic phase of psychotherapy in which one acquires a good sense of *reality, emotional balance,* and *social adjustment.* The sense of reality is a necessary prerequisite for any adjustment to life and any chance of finding oneself in life. People who distort reality, who have exaggerated notions of themselves and of the world, or who underestimate themselves or overestimate obstacles can hardly, if ever, live a genuine life.

Emotional balance includes four factors. First, the emotional reaction must be *appropriate* to the situation. We react with sorrow to defeat and with joy to success. Disturbed people react in a paradoxical way, enjoying their defeat and finding success unacceptable. Second, well-balanced emotionality is also *proportionate.* Disturbed individuals overreact or underreact to success and failure. Manic patients, for instance, can be ecstatic about small successes which don't warrant much joy, and in depressed moods, they experience deep sorrow not related to the real situation. The third factor in emotional balance is the ability to *control* and express emotions. Infants and disturbed people are unable to control their emotions; they act under impulse. Mature adults are able to control their emotions and react in a way that will serve their purpose and help them in attaining their goals. The fourth factor in emotional balance is *adjustability.* No matter how deep the sorrow is or how great the joy, life goes on and one cannot live in the past. Neurotics live in the past. Well-adjusted adults never deny the past but instead go ahead in life, being aware of the fact that there is just one road in life which leads to death. This road must be followed with maximum wisdom and maximum courage.

The third achievement in the analytic phase should be *social adjustment.* People who have undergone psychotherapy should be able to develop a meaningful relationship with one or more individuals and to form with others a rational give-and-take relationship which would not hurt them and would prevent them from being hurt by them.

Social adjustment is a necessary prerequisite for good mental health. Mentally disturbed people usually fail in developing rational patterns of social behavior. For instance,the hypervectorial schizophrenic type gets overinvolved with people — overcommitted, overzealous, and overjealous. Some of them form symbiotic relations and are unable to live their own lives. Sociopathic hyperinstrumental types never care for anyone except themselves, and their hypernarcissistic emotions are hypercathected in themselves. They often exploit others and take advantage of whomever they can. The manic-depressive or dysmutual type shifts from one extreme to another, being either overinvolved or underinvolved. Dysmutual depressive patients experience too much love and too much hatred, both for themselves and for others. All these emotional dysbalances must be corrected in the psychoanalytic phase of therapy which should result in a good sense of reality, a reasonable emotional balance, and a flexible ability to relate to people.

THE SECOND PHASE: SEARCH FOR IDENTITY

The three phases in interactional psychotherapy are not closed entities; they may overlap each other. While patients go through the analytic phase and their egos get stronger, they begin to search for sense and meaning in life. The more one advances in the analytic phase, the more one is capable of reconciling one's erotic and erratic impulses, and acquiring a better balance in relation to oneself and to others. One becomes reasonably selfish, that is, capable of understanding that one must take care of one's own needs. At the same time, one is reasonably unselfish, that is, capable of relating to other people and taking care of their needs, according to the degree of emotional involvement with them.

The analytic phase clears up past difficulties and enables the individual to think clearly and to act in a realistic way, but it does not solve the problem of direction in life. What patients are going to do with themselves, what life should mean to them, what the goals in their lives are — these are the problems dealt with in the second phase of interactional psychotherapy, which is called the *search for identity.*

Quite often toward the end of the first phase patients feel an abundance of energy; they feel that so much more could be done with their newly acquired energy which has been liberated from inner conflicts. They crave *self-realization* and *fulfillment,* and *they search for meaning and purpose.*

Perhaps the life of an individual could be compared to a song; he himself is a song, a theme, a melody. Yet he doesn't know which melody or song he is, what he can do with himself, what the meaning of his life is, what is most important to him, how he can utilize his innate and acquired potentialities, how he can make his life in a way that will enable him to feel he has accomplished what he wanted to accomplish in life. I had a patient, a man 60 years old, whose main complaint was that he had wasted 40 years of his life doing things he hated, living a life he despised, and spending all those years pursuing goals which were alien to himself.

The Meaning of Life

The two greatest events of life, birth and death, are beyond our control. We are born before we are ready to live, and we often die when we have just begun to live. Between these two great events, which are determined *without our approval,* there is only *one* decision that we *can* make if we understand its importance and urgency. *It is the decision of how to live.* It is not up to us whether we live or not, but we can — we must — decide *how we are going to live.*

No one lives in a vacuum, and no one has all options available to him. Heredity and environment offer different opportunities and set different limits for each individual. We are given a set of cards, and it is up to us to play the cards we have received, the good ones and the bad ones.

Life is a unique, unrepeatable chance. It is an unsolicited gift — the greatest gift one can ever receive. To be alive is a prerequisite to whatever joy, pleasure, satisfaction, and happiness one can experience. To miss the opportunity of using one's options is both a crime and a punishment. It is a crime not to walk when one has legs; it is a crime not to sing, not to smile, not to give, not to enjoy. Nevertheless, the crime also brings about a most severe punishment — the punishment of futility, of meaningless vegetation and a wasted life.

No one can achieve *more* than he is able to if the following factors are taken into consideration: his *innate potentialities,* such as health, intelligence, and so on; and his *external opportunities,* such as home background, education, peers, economic factors, and the entire fabric of economic, political, and cultural relations of his time. When this totality of factors is considered, no one can be an overachiever. Unfortunately, a great many people realize but a fraction of their potentialities and are underachievers. An underachiever is one who accomplishes much *less* than his capabilities and circumstances permit.

Yet what is it in life that should be achieved? Is it material wealth, which so many people strive for at the expense of physical or mental health, or should both be sought? Is it the political power that people crave over the dead bodies of other men? What is the purpose of life?

Human life is a sheer coincidence: a certain sperm cell meets an egg cell and here you are. There is no purpose in life, nor is there any purpose in death. Some tissues simply fade away, some muscles get tired of working, some hearts stop beating, or some bullets interrupt the process of life. So what is the purpose of living? The truth is simple and obvious: *there is no intrinsic purpose to human life.*

Quite often, my patients ask, "What is the purpose of life? What do I have to live for? Could you explain it to me?" All the while, I know very well that there is no purpose — that life as such is a pure biological fact that involves breathing, taking in food, and metabolism, just like any other organic process which goes its own way without consideration for meaning, values, or other inventions of the human mind.

Human beings seek pleasure and avoid pain. This is an empirical fact. However, this empirical fact is no more enlightening than the facts of perspiration, respiration, and digestion. Suffering is senseless: there is no purpose in suffering; there is no meaning to suffering. Glory and joy and triumph and happiness are also futile, because sooner or later they must come to an end. So what good is living when life doesn't make sense?

A great philosophical movement *existentialism* tried to cope with this problem in various ways. Some existentialist philosophers tried to seek values which transcend human life. Some of them looked for issues that cannot be solved. Perhaps the most brilliant presentation of the existential philosophy can be found in Camus's "The Myth of Sisyphus."

According to Camus, suicide is just as senseless as life. Gleaning the philosophical explanation — what is good about that? Can one escape into religion? Religion is just another illusion that promises something which doesn't exist — life after death. Camus says that the absurd man faces the absurd: he does not want to live with illusions. Camus counterposes Sisyphus. Sisyphus tried to roll the rock up the mountain; as soon as he came close to the top, the rock rolled down and he had to do it again and again, continuing the futility of human life.

What can man do? Man is doomed to live like Sisyphus. Christ is death for hope; Sisyphus if life for death. Which way can human beings go? There are no solutions in Camus, Kafka, Kierkegaard, or any other existentialist. Camus (p. 57) suggests a rebellion against the absurdity of life. He believes that one can restore majesty to life by dying unreconciled in privation of hope and future; death is the liberator from the absurd life.

There is very little consolation or solution to the problems of life with this kind of philosophy. That life is not worth living is obvious.

That suffering is useless is obvious. That there is no profound reason for living is obvious too. So what is the wisdom offered by existentialists? They counterpose their philosophy of despair to a naive interpretation of life as presented by so-called common sense and religion. Perhaps there is a point in this, but to face the futility — to face the absurd with courage — doesn't make much difference. If everything is absurd and futile, where are we going? *Quo vadis, humanitas?*

It is easy to philosophize, to argue back and forth about the futility of life, and pretend that one can accept it with equanimity and pride. However, this kind of approach doesn't offer any solution, nor does it correspond to the true facts. Let us consider a beggar who has nothing else but a small piece of bread: one can ridicule the piece of bread and say that it is no good and it has no future or value. If one eats it, it comes to an end; if one throws it away, one has lost whatever one had. If one holds onto it and hides it, it still doesn't make sense. To defend it is silly; to enjoy it is futile. *Nevertheless, the beggar has nothing else but this piece of bread, and the bread therefore becomes the sense of life.*

Perhaps all humans are a bunch of beggars. We don't have much, but whatever we have can be put under a common name: *life.* Maybe life is not worth living, but the fact remains that *there is nothing else but life.* Life is the only thing that we possess. No matter what we think about — no matter what we plan, invent, desire, hate, love, philosophize about, write books on, or develop religious doctrines around — there is only one thing: *life,* and *life is not an illusion.*

As long as we live, something may happen, something is going to happen, we will *make* something happen. As long as we live "waiting for Godot," we may be waiting for something more than Godot. *Life represents everything that we have, and woe to the beggar who throws away his last piece of bread.*

We, clinical psychologists and psychiatrists, work with people who seek morbid escapes from the perplexing problems of identity and purpose. We see people avoiding responsibility for their lives and seeking solace in drugs and alcohol. We see people escaping into mythical beliefs, pseudoreligions, and obscure fanaticism. We see people who fight their feelings of futility, depression, and helpless anger by acts of violence and antisocial behavior. We see people perplexed and disturbed, at odds with themselves and others, entangled in emotional problems they cannot solve by themselves.

We, clinicians, are not saviors of humanity, but we must be conscientious repairmen. As such, we must not apply remedies that worked 70 or 80 years ago to people who are experiencing quite different problems. Most of our patients come to us with desperate feelings of confusion, futility, and helplessness. We may call our work psychoanalysis, psychotherapy, behavior modification, and so on, but ultimately our work is helping people who need our help.

Perspiration and aspiration are two distinct levels of behavior. Primitive people perspire in their struggle for survival. Many people have enough means to live comfortably and have nothing to fight for. Many young people have parents who support them and can pretend to be poor hippies while their parents pay the bills. When people can obtain sex and companionship without any effort, when the romantic period of trying to win over a man or a woman has almost disappeared, one witnesses a growing wave of disenchantment, depression, and feelings of futility.

THE THIRD PHASE: MEANING AND PURPOSE

In the third phase of interactional psychotherapy, the therapist should help patients to develop worthwhile goals based on *their* interests and abilities. To be a fully developed individual, one cannot remain on an instrumental level; one should be capable of a mutual relationship (marriage, sexual relations, and friendship), but one must also be able to develop the ability and the desire for giving. Getting is limited; giving is unlimited.

Consider two individuals: one stretches out his hand to get something; the other, to give. Who is more happy? The one who gets is fully aware of his inadequacy, of his shortcomings, and of his need to receive from others. He is weak and dependent. The one who gives has the glorious feeling of being able to give, of making other people happy.

Since human life has an inevitable end, the only way one can *become* a full individual is through investing oneself. One may do this on a one-to-one basis; a person may give himself to his children or to his family. One may, however, develop far-reaching goals, giving oneself to social, philosophical, political, or religious ideals.

It sounds paradoxical, but those who give more, have more. Those who hold on to what they have cannot replenish their resources. Consider two individuals of identical physical power. One of them economizes by not using his muscles and saving his energy; the other exercises, works, builds, creates, and constructs. After a period of years, the former's muscles atrophy from lack of activity, but the latter is stronger than ever before.

The third phase of interactional psychotherapy should enable individuals to decide where they are going to direct their energy, and how they are going to utilize their intellectual and emotional resources. In this phase, patients should find the meaning of *their* lives.

No human being can always achieve or always do something that pleases him and others. No human being can always be successful. No human being can reach the sun and the stars every day, but to have goals and to go in the right direction give meaning to one's life. Not to have achieved, but achieving; not arriving at the inn, but walking toward the inn; not resting on one's laurels, but moving toward those laurels and putting one's talents to the most constructive use — this is the main sense of life and the only possible answer to the existential neurosis which cripples human efforts and maims human minds.

All human beings cannot attain the same level of achievement and the same level of fulfillment. That is why every psychotherapist must assess correctly his or her own resources, as well as the resources of the patient, and not to try to accomplish the impossible. Every psychotherapeutic process must come to a conclusion.

WHEN AND HOW TO TERMINATE

When and how should therapy be terminated? In a paper called "Analysis Terminable and Interminable," Freud (1950b) pointed out several important issues related to terminating treatment. Freud asked, "Is there such a thing as a natural end to an analysis or is it really possible to conduct it to such an end?" He wrote:

We must first decide what is meant by the ambiguous term, "the end of an analysis." From the practical standpoint it is easily defined. An analysis is ended when analyst and patient cease to meet for the analytic session. This happens when two conditions have been approximately fulfilled. First, the patient must no longer be suffering from his former symptoms and must have overcome his various anxieties and inhibitions and, secondly, the analyst must have formed the opinion that so much repressed material has been brought into consciousness, so much that was inexplicable elucidated, and so much inner resistance overcome that no repetition of the patient's specific pathological processes is to be feared. If for external reasons one is prevented from reaching this goal, it is more correct to say that an analysis is imperfect than to say it has not been completed.

The second definition of the "end" of an analysis is much more ambitious. According to it we have to answer the question whether the effect upon the patient has been so profound that no further change would take place in him if his analysis were continued. The implication is that by means of analysis it is possible to attain to absolute psychical normality and to be sure that it will be maintained, the supposition being that all the patient's repressions have been lifted and every gap in his memory filled. Let us first consult our experience and see whether such things do in fact happen, and then examine our theory and learn whether there is any *possibility* of their happening. (p. 320)

Further on, Freud stated:

Our object will be not to rub off all the corners of the human character so as to produce "normality" according to schedule, nor yet to demand that the person who has been "thoroughly analyzed" shall never again feel the stirrings of passions in himself or become involved in any internal conflict. The business of analysis is to secure the best possible psychological conditions for the functioning of the ego; when this has been done analysis has accomplished its task. (p. 354)

One must, at this point, make a definite and binding statement. Although there are no generally accepted criteria of "cure," *every therapist has the moral obligation to terminate his or her work as soon whenever he realizes that further work will not bring additional and significant therapeutic gains.*

In supervising younger colleagues, clinical psychologists and psychiatrists, I keep reminding them that *no one can turn an apple into an orange,* and there is no reason for trying to "overhaul" someone's personality. The task of therapy is to make the apple a better apple, that is, to enable the patient to make the best possible use of his or her potentialities. Yet, what are these potentialities?

Termination of any type of healing procedure including psychotherapy is largely a matter of professional ethics. A physician must not keep a patient in a hospital or in outpatient practice beyond the point of being helpful to the patient. Being helpful is to a great extent a matter of judgment — both an objective and a value judgment. A competent physician should know what he or she can do for the patient. A correct assessment of one's own potentialities is one of the main prerequisites for ethical conduct in psychotherapy. Responsible psychotherapists strictly adhere to this principle of not accepting a patient they cannot help and of telling the patient what they can and cannot do for him or her.

Professional ethics hinges on professional competence. An incompetent therapist is unethical for he promises services he cannot deliver. Competence means the power to do things one is supposed to do. Professional ethics means not to promise to do what one cannot do and *to terminate psychotherapy when the therapist cannot do much more for the patient.*

Objective judgment must be backed up by a value judgment. "Thou shalt not do to anyone what you don't wish to be done to you" is the chief ethical principle. In my supervisory work with younger colleagues, I have repeated this same question and asked, "Would you like your doctor or dentist to keep you or your spouse or your child in treatment beyond the point of necessary professional help? Keep this well in mind, and terminate psychotherapy as soon as the *patient* does not need it or as soon as *you* are unable to do more for the patient. In the latter case, refer the patient to a more competent colleague."

Termination of Psychotherapy

The nature of the terminating phase of psychotherapy depends on the nature of treatment, whether it follows in the footsteps of S.

Freud, H. S. Sullivan, J. Wolpe, or any other person. The common denominator of the terminal phase is the awareness on the part of both the therapist and the patient that the task has been more or less accomplished and that further therapeutic interaction would be superfluous.

However, even the most competent psychotherapist cannot avoid some thorny questions: How successful was the therapy? How adequate was the psychotherapeutic process? Finally, can psychotherapy guard a patient against future conflicts and relapses?

Perhaps it is my own shortcoming as a psychotherapist, but I do not believe that psychotherapy of any type can be ever perfectly finished. Suppose the aim of psychotherapy was the removal of certain symptoms (e.g., bed-wetting, insomnia, anorexia, a phobia, and so on). Could one criticize the therapist for not preventing the recurrence of the same or similar symptoms or for their substitution by other symptoms? Is this expected from any other healing profession such as dentistry, surgery, or internal medicine? A dentist can fill a cavity; can he prevent, once and for all, further tooth decay and another cavity? Can a surgeon prevent future bone fractures? Does the cure of a disease prevent future diseases?

I explain to my patients that psychotherapy does not have a clearcut ending, but there is no need to continue it (and pay for it) in a patient-therapist setting beyond its distinct usefulness. Freud called psychoanalysis an after-education, and F. Alexander (1948) called it an emotional reeducation. I explain to my patients that as long as they live, they will have problems and hardships.

The terminal phase of psychotherapy must be directed toward enabling the patient to solve problems and to cope with hardships. The psychotherapeutic process should teach the patient how to face the ups and downs of life. Psychotherapy should foster the *courage* to live and the ability to act in a *rational* way. As explained in previous chapters, my therapeutic technique is a far-reaching modification of Freud's method in which three phases are distinguished, (1) the analytic phase, (2) the search for identity, and (3) becoming: self-realization. The aim of the analytic phase is the resolution of past conflicts that prevent the individual from attaining psychological maturity. The second phase is devoted to increasing one's self-awareness and discovering one's desires, wishes, aptitudes, and options.

In the third phase, the individual should be able to choose his pattern of life, and should have the *courage* to be himself and the *wisdom* to cope realistically with whatever goes on in his life.

Toward the end of treatment, I usually explain to the patient my theory of the "broken-knee syndrome." I say, "Let us imagine that someone broke a knee and underwent surgery. Let us assume that the surgery was successful and the knee is no longer broken, although it may remain quite sensitive for years to come. Of course, the patient should walk around and go about his or her business as usual, but it is not advisable to take unnecessary risks and/or to overexert oneself. It is quite possible that on a rainy day or in the case of exertion or fatigue, the knee will react with pain. The patient will not need new surgery, but it would be advisable to call on the surgeon for a checkup. Of course, should someone hit the cured knee with a sledgehammer, the knee will require new medical care."

Limited Improvement

The task of the therapist is *to be of service* to people who come seeking help. When Freud was asked the best way to terminate psychoanalytic treatment, he said, "To carry it out correctly" (Glover, 1972, p. 152).

Some limitations are related to the nature of a particular type of disorder and to the particular way in which said disorder has affected this particular patient. Moreover, even the most competent therapist cannot attain the same level of improvement with different people. Some patients can make fantastic progress, while with others, one can expect rather limited improvement. A correct diagnosis (see Chapter 4) is one of the main prerequisites for successful treatment, and the therapeutic strategy must be linked to a precise diagnostic evaluation of every single case.

Working with schizophrenic patients and supervising younger colleagues who treat schizophrenics, I have developed a rather cautious and perhaps timid attitude. It is my feeling (I am using the word "feeling" in the absence of objective evidence) that therapists must not press their luck and try to solve all the problems which schizophrenics might have. My attitude is by no means universally accepted, and it might reflect both my theoretical views and my own shortcomings as a person and as a psychotherapist. Ultimately, *psychotherapy is more being than doing,* and every psychotherapist uses his or her own personality no less than the skills he or she has acquired.

I do believe that I have been quite successful in treating schizophrenic patients. In the numerous cases of schizophrenia that I have worked with (described in two books, several chapters, and various journal articles over the last 30 years), I have avoided setting definite goals. Every new patient, in a hospital or in private practice, has presented a challenge to do what I hoped to be able to achieve. On a few occasions, I have refused to treat patients whom I doubted I could help. In most cases, I have been quite careful not to go beyond an improvement that could be reasonably expected. I call this rule "one step up" (Wolman, 1966): it implies cautious support of neurotic defense mechanisms and the acceptance of milder symptoms in order to prevent a total collapse of personality structure. I have been afraid that going beyond that point might cause severe regression. Trying to repair a damaged structure, one must keep in mind how far one can go and how strong the foundations are. When the foundations are not too strong, it might not be safe to be too hasty. On many occasions, I have terminated my work with schizophrenics while accepting limited improvement.

Patients Have the Right to Know

Glover (1972, p. 136 ff.) has noticed that "practitioners who advance in seniority tend to find their case lists loaded with disorders of intractable nature, many of which have gone from pillar to post under the care of a variety of therapists of every description." However, even cases that seem to be exceedingly difficult, or at best capable only of slight improvement, need not be denied treatment. Glover continued: "Organic physicians do not countenance for a moment such highhanded, arbitrary and rather cowardly policies." Thus, "the onus should lie on the diagnostic and prognostic skill of the consultant, who should, of course, forewarn or advise the prospective patient of the possible outcome of his treatment, whether favorable or unfavorable."

Patients have the right to know. Psychotherapists are not supermen; they must avoid megalomania and self-righteous, conceited attitudes.

Every human being has the right to know what kind of service he or she is receiving, or is about to receive, and psychotherapists must abide by this universal rule. Glover (1972, p. 145) recommended that "the obvious course for the analyst to follow in difficult cases is to warn the patient beforehand that, whether after treatment he is better or not, he cannot expect more from this obviously promising form of therapy."

When Therapy Fails

Defeat is indeed a bitter pill — difficult to swallow and even more difficult to admit. It takes a great deal of strength to admit one's weakness. It is impossible to always be successful with all patients, and every therapist can tell many unpleasant and even embarrassing stories of his or her failures. Small wonder that the psychiatric and psychological literature is full of descriptions of successful treatment and rather poor in accounting for frustrating cases and embarrassing defeats (Claghorn, 1976; Eysenck, 1961; Horwitz, 1974; Simon, 1977; Strupp, 1969; Strupp et al., 1977). In a book published in 1972, *Success and Failure in Psychoanalysis and Psychotherapy* (Wolman, 1972), I asked several leading clinicians, among them E. Glover, L. S. Kubie, and others, to write on the subject "When and Why I Failed My Patients."

According to Aaron Stein (1972, pp. 44-45), the general factors leading to failures in all forms of psychotherapy are:

1. Incorrect diagnosis and, therefore, selecting the wrong form of treatment; this stems from errors in estimating the amount of psychopathology. Treatment is begun with patients who present mild symptoms which later are found to mask very severe disorders often inaccessible to exploratory psychotherapy.
2. Untoward external conditions:
   a. Where external conditions are so unfavorable that actual gain through remaining sick seems of greater value than the advantages of good health.
   b. Where the attitude of the family supports neurotic (or psychotic) manifestations in the patient.

     c. Reality factors — education, class, economic status, and the effect of trauma such as illness and loss.

3. Constitutional factors — strength of instincts and of conflicts centering around penis envy in women and passive attitudes in men.
4. Unfavorable modifications of the ego — severe characterological disturbances and so on.
5. Transference and countertransference.

There can be a great many reasons for a particular, well-qualified therapist to fail in a specific case. Nevertheless, it is the therapist's moral obligation to admit failure and, in a most tactful way, explain it to the patient and terminate work that does not serve the patient's well-being.

How to Terminate

There is no one, uniform, good-for-all way to terminate psychotherapy. The therapist must take into account several variables, among them:

1. Was this, in his or her opinion, a successful treatment?
2. If yes, how successful was it?
3. What could be expected in the future?
4. Was treatment a failure?

Other factors, such as the patient's age, occupation, friends and relatives, family obligations, cultural environment, and so on, must also be considered.

    The therapist must carefully weigh his or her words in explaining the termination of treatment. There is, however, one common denominator in all the ways of terminating psychotherapy, namely, regard for the *well-being of the patient.*

4
Diagnostic Procedure

It has been always easier to hurt than to help, to damage than to repair, to destroy than to build. Teams of specially trained people toil for a long time to build an airplane, but one half-wit can destroy it with a hand grenade. A little child can damage complex machinery and set fire to a house built by scores of mechanics, builders, and construction workers.

The same applies to human life and to physical or mental health. One does not need to know much to hurt and to kill, but it requires a great deal of skill and knowledge to help, to cure, and to protect someone's life. One cannot repair a car without knowing what is wrong with it, and certainly one cannot cure mental disorder without a thorough knowledge of the nature of a particular disorder, the degree to which it has affected a particular individual, and the individual's resilience.

A correct diagnostic evaluation is an absolute prerequisite for the treatment of any mental disorder. As long as mentally disturbed individuals were accused of witchcraft and collusion with the devil, their "treatment" was quite simple: they were incarcerated, flogged, and tortured, and if they happened to be accused of witchcraft, they were burned alive. (The last case of judicial murder of a witch took place in Switzerland in 1782.)

Responsible treatment of mental disorders, whatever the method used, must start with a diagnosis of the patient's condition. One cannot plan a therapeutic strategy unless one knows *what to cure*. A thorough knowledge of the patient, of his or her past history and present symptoms, and an understanding of what caused and/or perpetuated the emotional difficulties, are prerequisites for successful psychotherapeutic intervention. There are several steps in the diagnostic procedure. The first step is to decide to what nosological class or category a particular case belongs.

NOSOLOGY

Nosology is the scientific procedure of classifying diseases and disorders. Classification is a systematic arrangement of objects or ideas in categories. Diagnosis means discerning, that is, finding out specific traits or characteristics that enable the clinician to put a particular disease or disorder into a class which contains similar cases.

When a clinician studies a disease or a disorder, and arrives at a conclusion concerning the particular nature of the case, further decisions are greatly facilitated if it is possible to relate a particular case to a class or category of similar cases. An adequate classificatory system enables the clinician to reason, for example, as follows: "Mr. A. cannot go to sleep unless he touches the alarm clock innumerable times. He always brushes his teeth in the same manner, four times up and four times down. He feels miserable when he is unable to have his lunch at 12:15," and so on. These symptoms permit diagnosis of obsessive-compulsive neurosis, provided all other cases with similar symptoms have been put together in the same class. An adequate classificatory system is a necessary prerequisite for a clinical diagnosis and for a treatment strategy.

Imagine a clinician who does not have any classificatory system. Suppose he or she noticed certain symptoms, but was unable to relate them to any nosological categories. What kind of treatment should be applied? In medieval times, headaches were often treated by bloodletting, which could have been fatal for some patients. Some mentally disturbed individuals were treated by exorcism, cold packs, flogging, and so on, irrespective of the nature of their disorder.

Wolman's *Dictionary of Behavioral Science* (1973c, p. 99) defines *diagnosis* as the "identification of diseases, handicaps, and disorders on the basis of observed symptoms; diagnosis is classification on the basis of observed characteristics." A correct assessment of distinct features (symptoms) common to a certain class or group of disorders is the mainstay of clinical diagnosis, and an adequate classificatory system facilitates diagnostic procedures.

Symptomatology

Psychologists and psychiatrists have pointed to four clinically significant criteria for classification of mental disorders, namely, symptomatology, etiology, prognosis, and treatment. Originally, mental disorders were classified on the basis of the patient's overt behavior. Pinel, the first great reformer of treatment methods, divided mentally sick patients into melancholic, manic with delirium, manic without delirium, and dementive (Alexander and Selesnick, 1966). Passive and despondent patients were classified as melancholic; hyperactive and elated patients were divided into delirious and non-delirious; mental defectives formed a separate category.

Soon Pinel's system came under criticism, especially as clinicians noticed that melancholics often become manic and vice versa. This condition was called *cyclic disorder* by Kahlbaum and, after the sixth edition of E. Kraepelin's *Lehrbuch* (1899), has become a standard category of manic-depressive psychosis.

The ninth edition of Kraepelin's *Lehrbuch* (1927) consists of two volumes containing 2425 pages. Kraepelin's systems followed the model of other medical specialties and delved into the etiology, symptomatology, prognosis, and incidence of each disorder. Although Kraepelin offered a detailed description of every clinical entity, his system has linked symptomatology with other aspects of mental disorders, especially prognosis.

Since Kraepelin's time, psychiatrists and psychologists have argued about the value of symptomatology versus other diagnostic criteria. Freud's system stressed etiology. Presently, there is a strong tendency to move away from inferable and not always proven etiological data toward symptomatology (see DSM III, 1980).

Behavior modification methods suggest that diagnostic procedures should be limited to the assessment of observable symptoms. Overt behavior is identified with the disorder, and the emphasis is on visible symptoms and reinforcement contingencies.

A different approach, but one also stressing overt behavior, has been advocated by Albee (1969), Bower (1966), Phillips (1968), Scheff and Scheff (1966), and others. They suggest relating behavior disorders to the patient's level of social competence, adequacy, and capacity for successful adjustment.

In 1974, the American Psychiatric Association appointed a task force on nomenclature and statistics to prepare a third edition of the *Diagnostic and Statistic Manual of Mental Disorders* (DSM). The first edition of this manual (DSM I) appeared in 1952 and the second

(DSM II) in 1968. The third edition (DSM III) was published in 1980, its outline had been presented in 1977 by Pinsker and Spitzer in Wolman's *International Encyclopedia of Psychiatry, Psychology, Psychoanalysis, and Neurology* (Vol. 3, pp. 160-164).

DSM III emphasizes observable data. "When DSM I was published, etiology was emphasized. It is apparent now that much of what was in 1952 thought to be etiology must now be regarded as speculation. The empirical emphasis of DSM III is not intended to detract from psychodynamic psychiatry but emphasize the distinction between observation and inference . . . . Diagnosis should be based upon what is observed and known" (Pinsker and Spitzer, 1977, p. 161).

While there is a good reason for moving away from unproven speculations toward observable facts, one can raise valid objections to the use of symptomatology as the main criterion for classifying mental disorders. For one thing, there is no general agreement concerning the choice of symptoms for classificatory purposes. Edwards (1972) compared American and British psychiatric diagnoses of schizophrenia and discovered far-reaching differences in the choice of symptoms. For example, 68.7 percent of American psychiatrists believe that distortions in perception, and especially hallucinations, are indicative of schizophrenia, while only 25.6 percent of British psychiatrists believe that hallucinations constitute the most significant symptom of this disorder.

Moreover, symptoms are often misleading. High temperature, coughing, nasal discharge, diarrhea, local swelling, weight loss, and so on could signal a variety of mild, moderate, and severe physical illnesses. Depression, impotence, aggressiveness, psychosomatic symptoms, delusions, and hallucinations could be associated with a host of different organic and psychogenic mental disorders. Some symptoms may be related not to a particular mental disorder but to the patient's religious beliefs, cultural background, socioeconomic status, and so on.

Zubin (1967), in an analysis of problems related to the classification of behavior disorders, stressed the question of continuity versus discontinuity in the behavioral patterns of patients. Discontinuous patterns could be coincidental to a particular disorder. Apparently, a classificatory system based solely on overt symptoms leaves too many questions unanswered.

Etiology

Kraepelin (1927) distinguished between endogenous and exogenous mental diseases. He believed, for example, that epilepsy and schizophrenia are caused by internal changes in the brain, while delirium tremens is caused by alcohol, which is an external factor. DSM II (1968) was primarily guided by etiological considerations, albeit not too consistently. For example, the division of disorders into organic and nonorganic is clearly etiological.

Freud's classificatory system was par excellence etiological. Initially, Freud divided all mental disorders into "actual neuroses" caused by organic factors and "psychoneuroses" caused by psychological factors. Freud linked the origin of psychoneuroses to fixation at, or regression to, infantile developmental phases as shown in Table 1 (quoted after Fenichel, 1945, p. 101).

Within the Freudian frame of reference, Glover (1968) suggested a new classification system related to two factors: (1) the Freud-Abraham stage of psychosexual fixation or regression (Table 1) and

Table 1. Freud's and Abraham's Timetable.

STAGES OF LIBIDINAL ORGANIZATION	STAGES IN DEVELOPMENT OF OBJECT LOVE	DOMINANT POINT OF FIXATION
1. Early oral (sucking) stage	Autoeroticism (no object, preambivalent)	Certain types of schizophrenia (stupor)
2. Late oral-sadistic (cannibalistic) stage	Narcissims: total incorporation of the object	Manic-depressive disorders (addiction, morbid impulses)
3. Early anal-sadistic stage	Partial love with incorporation	Paranoia, certain pregenital conversion neuroses
4. Late anal-sadistic stage	Partial love	Compulsion neurosis, other pregenital conversion neuroses
5. Early genital (phallic) stage	Object love, limited by the predominant castration complex	Hysteria
6. Final genital stage	Love (postambivalent)	Normality

(2) the predominance of a particular defense mechanism of introjection and projection. Bour (1966) applied both Freudian and Adlerian systems to diagnosis, and emphasized three sets of characteristics: (1) the changes in aggressive and sexual drives, (2) the psychosexual developmental stage, and (3) the dominant psychodynamic mechanisms typical of a particular disorder.

While etiological factors continue to play a significant role in the diagnosis and classification of mental disorders, one must point to two main difficulties with a classification based on etiology. First, etiological data are often controversial. For instance, some authors maintain that schizophrenia is inherited, while others maintain that it is acquired. The second difficulty is related to the particular nature of causal relations in psychology, for there is no evidence that the same causes always produce the same effects or that a certain effect is always the result of a certain cause.

Consider children's thumb-sucking. Is thumb-sucking always produced by the same cause? Investigators have revealed several possibilities: (1) Some children suck when the holes in the nipple are too small; apparently, they get tired and give up the bottle, but suck their thumbs because they are hungry. (2) When sucking the breast of an affectionate mother, sucking becomes a pleasurable experience; children suck their thumbs any time they are upset, as if seeking the soothing pleasure of sucking. (3) Children who did not suck in childhood or were weaned too early suck their thumbs as if trying to recapture the missed gratification.

Clinical observations are not always conclusive, and often yields a rainbow variety of interpretations. A schizophrenic patient whom I saw in a hospital was defeated in her efforts to set fire to the hospital and reacted with obvious relief. As she explained later, she realized that "she was not as dangerous as she has thought, if one stupid doctor and one moronic attendant could overwhelm her." For a while she screamed, "We are outnumbered," but later she felt happy that finally someone "did not take her nonsense." Apparently, her reaction to frustration was ambivalent and included both protest and relief.

Pavlov's dog suffered a "nervous breakdown" when exposed to conflicting stimuli in an ellipse approaching a circle. Would a man suffer a nervous breakdown if he could not distinguish between his girlfriend and her twin sister? Would he not find a way out?

Therapeutic Considerations

Empirical psychopathological science serves as a basis for the applied sciences which deal with the treatment of mental disorders. These applied sciences can be called *praxeologies,* for they *prescribe actions* directed toward a certain goal. For example, education, which is one of the praxeologies, *sets goals* and *develops means* for the attainment of these goals. Clinical psychology and psychiatry as praxeologies aim at curing behavior disorders and develop physical, chemical, and psychological methods which enable practitioners to attain those therapeutic goals. As mentioned, the empirical science of psychopathology is the very foundation for the praxeological science of treatment. It is a two-way street, for adequate therapy is based on empirical knowledge of mental disorders and the empirical study of mental disorders must not overlook its main application. Therapy which is not based on scientific psychopathology is quackery, and empirical research in psychopathology which is not geared to therapy could be useless because it may deal with irrelevant issues. Apparently, therapeutic goals should serve as the vantage point for any classificatory system. This decision raises several relevant questions concerning the aims, method, and overall philosophy of therapy (Wolman, 1973b).

Other praxeologies have it much easier. Consider education: educational praxeology has a given, built-in, *immanent* goal which is determined by the biological process of growth and maturation. The immanent goal of all educational systems, whether John Dewey's or J. F. Herbart's, American or Soviet, is to help and guide children in the natural process of becoming mature adults. However, since the concepts of maturing and adulthood depend greatly on cultural settings and social philosophies, the educational praxeology must determine *transcendent* goals appropriate for each society and culture.

The fact is that therapeutic techniques based on different schools of thought claim similar results. One can substantially reduce depression by the use of ECT, lithium carbonate, and several other antidepressants, and by highly diversified psychotherapeutic methods such as classic psychoanalysis, existential analysis, nondirective therapy, and so on. Quite often, there is no adequate scientific explanation of why certain methods produce results while other methods fail.

Small wonder that many therapists are given to diagnostic apathy and even to diagnostic nihilism. Many clinicians apply one and the same method to whatever case they deal with. In some cases, their accidental approach may work, but in others, such a hit-or-miss method may prove counterproductive and even harmful.

Some clinicians go still further and reject the very idea of classification. Laing (1967) maintains that diagnostic categories are dehumanizing and self-fulfilling prophecies. For example, schizophrenics behave in a peculiar way because they are treated as schizophrenics. No less extreme ideas have been expressed by Szasz (1961) who maintains that psychiatric classification is merely a strategy of personal constraint.

Unfortunately, all these ideas fail to solve the problem under consideration. Deprived of any classification, psychiatrists and clinical psychologists would have to view every case as a totally new and unique occurrence, a true idiophenomenon that defies any generalization. Unable to generalize and draw general conclusions, would clinicians be able to learn anything and to profit from their experience? There would be no other way but to start from scratch every time they saw a new patient!

Generalization

Disappointment in the existing diagnostic systems has been voiced by several authors (Albee, 1969; Phillips, 1968; Scheff and Scheff, 1966; Szasz, 1961; Wolman, 1978b). The main criticism has been leveled against the term "mental disease." Many authors have stressed the fact that disturbed and disorganized behavior is itself maladjustment, and there is no need to relate it to a medical model. As Philips and Draguns (1971) summarized, at present the importance is accorded to a person's interaction with his environment and adjustment, rather than to a hypothetical disease entity.

There are, however, considerable differences among the advocates of the nonmedical approach. Some authors prefer to deal with overt behavior only, while others also include unconscious elements of human behavior. Furthermore, some authors emphasize flux and change in behavior (Albee, 1969; and many others), while others seek more stable elements (Grinker, 1969; Zubin, 1967).

Zubin (1967) pointed to the chaos existing in this area. One of the main difficulties is related to the specific nature of psychological data and the apparent need for caution in generalization and classification. For instance, such general categories as ascendance-submissiveness, masculine-feminine traits, introvert-extravert, domineering parents or children, "strong" mother and "weak" father, overprotection, overindulgence, and dependence-independence may miss the point entirely. A manic-depressive is both ascendant and submissive, depending on his mood; he is often aggressive toward others and self-defeating to himself. He may be self-sacrificing and overselfish, oversentimental and overbrutal. A schizophrenic may oscillate between overdependence and independence: he may fear a fly and run into a lion's den; he may worry about hurting the feelings of the person he murders. Parents of schizophrenics can be both overprotective and overindulgent.

Physical scientists have an easier job. Their electrons, energy, loads, temperature, sizes, and locomotion seem to behave in a more reasonable way than humans do. Hence, the rules of logic and mathematics are applicable to the study of the physical world. Scientists who study human behavior, however, are in a disadvantageous position. Their objectivity can be questioned; their power to determine the conditions of observation is so great as to raise suspicion; their subjects are irrational. Also, scientific observation or experimentation can easily become a two-way process, in which both observer and observed participate.

The observer's methods and tools are important variables affecting the subject's performance. The observer sets the conditions under which the observation will take place and determines what actually will be performed. The detached position of the psychoanalyst whose armchair was outside the patient's field of vision probably caused further withdrawal in schizophrenic patients and led Freud to believe that schizophrenia was a narcissistic nontransference disorder. Fenichel, Federn, Sullivan, Hill, Fromm-Reichman, Wolman, and others, who took a participant attitude, reversed Freud's notion on transference in schizophrenia.

This does not mean that every case of mental disorder is a unique, unrepeatable phenomenon which renders impossible any generalization and classification. Actually, everything and everybody is an idiophenomenon, but on the basis of a single common trait, sciences can group any number of idiophenomena together and draw generalizations (Wolman, 1981). For instance, no oak tree is identical to any other oak tree; every single tree has something specific and unique about it, if for no other reason than the fact that no two oak trees can grow in exactly the same place. However, all oak trees have at least one common trait which enables us to put them together in one class and draw general conclusions. When a botanist or a gardener "diagnoses" a tree as being an oak, he does not prescribe its future development as an oak or constrain the developmental process, Szasz's and Laing's stern warnings notwithstanding.

Causal-Etiological Considerations

Apparently one must give up the idea of classification based on a single factor, be it symptomatology, etiology, or therapeutic goals and methods. The only possible way out is to base the classificatory system on a combination of several factors. Etiological data seem to be exceedingly valuable, provided that the knowledge of causes can allow the therapist to predict symptoms and can serve as a basis for the selection of an appropriate treatment method.

One could apply here Tolman's (1951) formula of independent, intervening, and dependent variables. If we assume that etiological factors are the independent variable, the clinician, armed with the knowledge of intervening variables, should be able to predict the symptoms (the dependent variable). If he knows the dependent and the intervening variables, he should be able to explain (to "predict" in reverse time order) the cause (the independent variables). For instance, if a patient fears open spaces (agoraphobia), the clinician applies his knowledge of an appropriate conceptual system that could serve as an intervening variable and can explain the causes of agoraphobia. By the same token, when the clinician finds the underlying etiology, he should be able to predict that his patient will fear open spaces. This is the method I use in my psychotherapeutic practice. I have pursued *diagnostic interviews* either starting from etiological data and leading to the anticipatory hypothesis of symptoms or starting from symptoms and hypothetically deducing their causes.

An adequate classificatory system must relate the therapeutic goal to relevant etiological and prognostic factors. This hinges on acceptance of the causal principle in psychology and its application both to past events (i.e., etiology, the study of causes) and to future outcomes anticipated by prognostic studies. The causal principle has been questioned by theoretical physicists and philosophers of science, and Einstein's fourth dimension undermined the concept of temporal sequence that underlies causality. The causal hypothesis in physics smacks of anthropomorphism since it sounds as if, for example, clouds have "produced" the rain or heat has "made" bodies increase in size. Fortunately, neither of these problems exists in psychology. Human life has a clearly time-determined beginning and end, and temporal sequences are self-evident. To deny the fact that human actions produce certain results would smack of *reimorphism.*

CLASSIFICATION OF MENTAL DISORDERS

Mental disorders can be inherited, acquired, or caused by a combination of both. If they are inherited, they are transmitted through the genes. Those mental disorders which are not inherited are acquired through interaction with either the physical or the social environment. Thus, mental disorders can be divided into three categories related to their origins. Those that originate in the organism through heredity or through interaction with the physical environment (injuries, poisons, and so on) are "somatogenic." Inherited disorders are "geno-somatogenic" because they are caused by genes; physically acquired mental disorders are "ecosomatogenic" because they are caused by interaction with the environment (*ecos*). All other disorders stem from faulty interindividual relations, that is they are psychosocial; I call these disorders *sociogenic* or *sociopsychogenic.*

In developing a nosological system, I have attempted to build a bridge between Freud's theoretical system and observable behavior. Interpersonal relations seemed to offer the best choice, for human interaction is not only observable but also an indicator of highly relevant adjustment processes. Freud's personality model requires some modification in regard to social relations. The term "cathexis" is merely a logical construct that enables us to distinguish between various types of object relations. Freud's studies dealt with the cathecting individual and omitted the cathected object. Instead of Freudian love, sexual or aim inhibited, Horney introduced protection and safety; instead of Freud's active cathexis of libido or need to love, she emphasized the need to be loved. Sullivan went even further in his theory of interpersonal relations; he tied personality directly to interpersonal relations. Without using the term "cathexis," he emphasized empathy, describing it as a kind of "emotional contagion or communion" between the child and parental figures. Freud dealt with the individual who cathects his libido in the object; I have suggested inclusion also of the cathected object.

This new concept of "interindividual cathexis" is merely a logical construct and has been introduced because of its methodological flexibility and usefulness. Thus, in instrumental relationships, the individual's aim is to receive libido cathexes from others; in mutual relationships, the individual aims at receiving libido cathexes from, as well as giving them to, others; in vectorial relationships, the individual aims to object-cathect, to give to others. A well-balanced individual is capable of functioning in all three types of relationships. Sociopaths hate whoever refuses to be used and exploited by them; schizophrenics fear their own hostility; and manic-depressives hate those who don't love them and hate themselves for not being loved.

I have translated the Freudian concept of cathexes (Wolman, 1966, 1970, 1973) into observable interactional categories. When an individual relates in a hostile (H) manner to others, his destrudo is object-cathected. If an individual's libido is self-cathected and he expects others to take care of his needs and wishes, his attitude to others is narcissistic-hyperinstrumental because he perceives others as tools to be used. Basically, he is hostile to other people.

If an individual's libido has been excessively hypercathected, especially in parents or parental substitutes, his self-cathexis has been impoverished. Too much libido has been given away in a *hypervectorial* manner. This person cares for others too much, resents his resentment of giving too much without receiving, and tries to control his destrudo out of fear of hurting those he loves.

The third clinical type exhibits dysbalance in his social relations, and in the distribution of libido and destrudo cathexes. He swings from object cathexis to self-cathexis, from love to hate. He loves too much and expects too much in return, and he hates others and himself for the inevitable frustrations. His social, mutual relations are disturbed, and he is therefore called *dysmutual.*

Based on a modified Freudian view of personality and the criteria for mental health, I have suggested three types of "sociogenic" mental disorders. The *hyperinstrumental* type is highly instrumental in any situation and in regard to all people, always asking something for nothing and showing no consideration for his fellowman. This type of disturbed person corresponds to what has usually been called "psychopath" or "sociopath" and has generally been the rejected child. The *hypervectorial* type is always ready to give, to protect, and to sacrifice himself. In childhood, this type was forced into the role of protector of his protectors (i.e., the guardian of inadequate parents). This type covers all that is described under the name "schizophrenia" and related conditions. The third type is the *dysmutual* type characterized by cyclic moods of extreme reactions corresponding to what has been called "manic-depressive." Typically, the childhood of these individuals was characterized by rejection and inattention, except at times of extreme stress (e.g., when sick or injured) when they were showered with excessive amounts of attention and overprotection.

Moreover, there are five levels of disorder moving from neurosis to complete collapse of personality structure (see Table 2). These levels are said to function on a continuum, but not every mentally disturbed individual must go through all or any levels of deterioration: when rocks fall down, some roll one level down and come to a stop; some roll down step by step; some skip a step; some roll down all the way through. The fact that some rocks roll only one step down and some skip steps does not contradict the fact that there are five distinct steps on the slope. These five steps are empirically observable. What has been added here is the *link* between them, the idea of *continuity* in mental processes, counterposed to an unjustified assumption voiced by some workers that a neurotic cannot go psychotic.

The emphasis on etiology offers certain advantages because it helps to distinguish the roots of similar symptoms. Consider depression. Depression as a symptom is a cluster of feelings of angry helplessness and despair. It is a catchall, almost as broad as "high temperature" in physical illness. Actually, it is even more so, because well-adjusted

Table 2. Classification of Sociopsychogenic Mental Disorders.

	NARCISSISTIC HYPERINSTRU- MENTAL TYPE (I)	DEPRESSIVE DYSMUTUAL TYPE (M)	SCHIZOHYPER- VECTORIAL TYPE (V)
Neurotic level	Hyperinstrumental- narcissistic neurosis	Dysmutual neurosis (dissociations, hysterias, and depressions)	Hypervectorial neurosis (obses- sional, phobic, and neurasthenic neuroses)
Character neurotic level	Hyperinstrumental character neurosis (narcissistic character)	Dysmutual char- acter neurosis (depressive and hysteric character)	Hypervectorial char- character neurosis (schizoid and obsessional char- acter)
Latent psychotic level	Latent hyperinstru- mental (sociopathic narcissism border- ing on psychosis)	Latent dysmutual psychosis (borderline depressive psychosis)	Latent vectoriasis praecox (border- line and latent schizophrenia)
Manifest psychotic level	Hyperinstrumental psychosis (psychotic sociopathy and moral insanity)	Dysmutual psy- chosis (mani- fest depressive psychosis)	Vectoriasis praecox (manifest schizophrenia)
Demential level	Collapse of personality structure		

individuals get depressed when they are physically wounded, when they have lost their jobs, or when they have lost someone dear. Such an *exogenous depression* is not a sign of maladjustment as long as it is appropriate, that is, caused by a real harm or loss, proportionate to what happened, reasonably controllable, and leading to adjustive actions.

Endogenous depressions are usually pathological, but they may have a variety of causes and can lead to a host of different behavioral patterns. In a vast majority of cases, the causes of depression deter- mine its course. For instance, in schizophrenia depression is deep and can go on forever except for periods of so-called spontaneous recovery. In manic-depressive disorders, depression reaches a certain low point which may lead to self-termination (there will be more about depression later on). Obviously, psychotherapy with schizophrenics differs from psychotherapy with manic-depressives (Krauss and Krauss, 1977a).

The therapist must find out *why* a patient developed certain symptoms and what for? The combination of a causal and a teleological approach is usually rewarding. Why did a particular patient develop a particular symptom depending on what bothered him and what he wished to avoid or to gain?

Such an approach also facilitates preventive action. While the immediate task of clinicians is to seek remedies for existing ills, their moral obligation to society goes beyond that of a repairman. Armed with the knowledge of causes and results, they must actively participate in developing programs for the prevention of mental disorders.

Parent-Child Interaction

As mentioned in the section classification of Mental Disorders the three clinical types are related to parent-child interaction. As a rule, the earlier the infant is exposed to a noxious interaction, the greater is the damage to his personality. One can distinguish three main parent-child interactional patterns that adversely affect the child's mental health: some parents reject their child, some expect too much from him and overdemand, and some shift from acceptance to rejection and vice versa.

Some parents do not demand love from their children, nor do they offer any love to them. In this kind of environment, the child feels lonely and rejected, and perceives the world as a place where one either exploits others or is exploited by them. Rejected children soon learn to take advantage of other people's weaknesses and assume that everyone else does the same. Viewing the world as a jungle serves as a justification for their own extreme selfishness. They regard their exploitative and hostile behavior as the self-preservation of innocent creatures facing a hostile world.

Clinical observations indicate three prototypical settings which are conducive to fostering such selfish sociopath, (I named them *hyperinstrumental-hypernarcissistic* personalities): institutions, underprivileged homes, and exceedingly wealthy homes. The institutional environment, where anonymous counselors deal with anonymous cases in a cold, uninvolved, matter-of-fact way, distributing so many cups of milk and so many penalties for violation of institutional discipline, is most likely to produce secondary narcissism. Then too, many hyperinstrumentals were underprivileged children, reared in a hostile atmosphere and rejected by parents who resented the burden of taking care of their offspring. Some underprivileged families create an atmosphere in which the entire world seems populated by enemies. In the third category are children of well-to-do families in which parents have characteristically substituted money for affection and nurturance. The child of such a background has no one to love or identify with and is forced to live a hollow, selfish existence.

These narcissistic-hyperinstrumental children usually become sociopaths. Milder cases of hyperinstrumentals are selfish and hostile people who assume that others are hostile. They are sensitive to their own suffering and deprivations, but they have no empathy or sympathy for anyone else. In more severe cases, there is a total lack of moral restraint and compassion for one's fellowman; often, these individuals defy the law while proclaiming and believing in their own innocence. Hyperinstrumentals operate on the principle that weak enemies and neutrals have to be destroyed, and friends are to be used. The destrudo of a hyperinstrumental is highly mobilized and ready to strike at the outer world (object directed). Perceiving himself as an innocent, poor, hungry animal, he views other people as enemies: *either he will devour them or they will devour him.* The narcissistic hyperinstrumental type is actually a coward – brutal and cruel to those who fear him, but obedient and subservient to those he fears. The most severe cases of psychotic sociopaths were referred to by Prichard (1835) as "moral insanity."

At the other extreme are parents who love their children but expect too much love in return. Immature and insecure parents reverse the social roles. They act as if they were the children, and demand the kind of love and affection from the child that would more properly be expected from their own parents. The parents' attitude toward the child is instrumental, and the child is forced into a vectorial attitude toward his parents. The child, in effect, is robbed of his childhood and must prematurely become an adult. The parents, disappointed in one another, expect the child to compensate for all the love and affection they fail to obtain from each other. The child is not allowed to express dissatisfaction, discomfort, or dissent, nor is he permitted to act out childhood tantrums. The child is exposed to immature, overdemanding, and instrumental parents, and is expected to renounce his own desires to please them. The child is forced into an extreme and too early hypervectorial attitude.

This parent-child interaction forces the child to worry about his truly or allegedly weak, sick, or dying parents. The child is forced to become a protector of his protectors (Wolman, 1966, 1970). The child may try, at the devastating cost of impoverishment of his own emotional resources, to overcontrol his impulses. However, as soon as the emotional resources of love (the libido) have been overspent, the emotional energy of hate (the destrudo) takes over. Overspent love turns to hatred for oneself and others. The "fallen angel" soon becomes a hateful devil who is no longer able to control his hostile impulses. He hates himself for hating others, and is afraid of love that becomes overdemanding and threatening. Typically, schizophrenics are individuals who as small children were forced to worry about their parents. Throughout their lives, they have felt compelled to strive for perfection. They appear to treat life as an obligation to be honored, a ritual to be followed, or a mission to be fulfilled. They tend to be domineering and overprotective. The loss of control may result in a full-blown schizophrenic episode, in which they are driven by uncontrollable hatred (Bellak and Loeb, 1969; Hill, 1955; Jackson, 1960; Wolman, 1966).

Depressive states of all kinds and levels have given rise to a good deal of controversy in psychiatric and psychological literature. Obviously not all depressed moods are pathological. One of the main criteria of mental health, which was suggested in Chapter 1, is emotional balance.

Human beings respond with pleasure and pain, joy and sorrow, to situations in which they find themselves. Mentally healthy individuals react to stimuli in proportion to their magnitude (stronger reaction to the stronger stimuli and weaker reaction to the weaker stimuli) so that the best possible adjustment and restoration of emotional balance result. The reaction of the mentally sick or emotionally unbalanced individual may be exaggerated and out of proportion to the stimulus. Even when the loss is negligible and can be easily replaced, the disturbed individual is carried away by his emotions and acts in an irrational manner that certainly will not make matters better. Gradually increasing irritability and growing difficulty in restoring the emotional balance bear witness to an aggravation of the mental disorder. Severe emotional dysbalance is one of the indicators of the severity of the disorder.

There are four clinical syndromes of the depressive psychosis (Krauss and Krauss, 1977a). The dysmutual psychosis is basically a state of depression, but when the patient's ego surrenders to the superego, they merge in a state of blissful *elation* or mania. The second syndrome is *paranoia*. When the failing ego externalizes superego pressure, it perceives the outer world as a rejecting and punishing mother who will eventually be forced to accept her suffering child. This is basically the dynamics of paranoia. The third syndrome is *agitated depression*. This starts whenever the ego is crushed between the cruel superego and savage id. There are no elated moods, no escape mechanisms, no respite from the unbearable depression. Suicidal danger is very high in this syndrome. The last syndrome is *simple deterioration* in which both the ego and the superego are defeated by the id.

The manic syndrome does not bring genuine joy. It is an escape, a desperate reaction to an unbearable feeling of depression. The dynamics of this syndrome represents the surrender of the ego to the superego. When the pressure of the superego becomes unbearable, the ego renounces further resistance and turns away from reality as if refusing to deal with it. In a manic mood, the self-righteous superego determines what is true and false; thus, manic patients may express dogmatic and self-assured opinions about matters they have not heretofore considered. They become omniscient sages and judges who know everything and have the final say on all problems.

Introjection of the image of the rejecting or deceased parent, most often the one of the opposite sex, is typical for the dysmutual disorders. This introjected "love object" functions in a manner analogous to that of the rejecting parent: it is hostile and cruel, but only up to a certain point. The despairing ego tries to reach this point by accepting defeat, by magnifying it, and by making life look more horrible than it is. Then it turns to the superego as if to say, "See how miserable I am! You are right, I deserve to be punished. So beat me, but love me."

Often the dysmutual turns self-hate into self-pity and his mood changes radically. A manic patient becomes everyone's friend: a patient of mine, a married woman in a manic state, invited strange men she met on the street to share her bed; a manic man distributed money to whomever he met. In elation, there is no delay, no reality principle, no planning or caution. Whatever the manic feels like doing, he does immediately. If he is sexually aroused, he may proposition the first girl he meets and become furious if she turns him down. He cannot take the slightest frustration.

The manic-depressive's delusions and hallucinations are related to martyrdom, to being lost and found, to being a Cinderella saved by Prince Charming or by a loving mother. Schizophrenics wish to be God or the Messiah. Since their parents were weak and unreliable individuals, they must fill the void by becoming the omnipotent, omniscient, benevolent, or destructive God-Father, who saves, protects, or punishes. The schizophrenic rescues; the manic-depressive wants to be rescued.

Not all dysmutual psychotics are capable of manic denial. In some cases, there is no escape from the assaults of the superego. The patient may feel happier if he has had the opportunity to outshine others and bask in the glory of his achievements, but since no human being can always be victorious and constantly admired by others, the short-lived moods of good feeling yield to severe depression.

One of the possible psychotic reactions to depression is full-blown paranoia. A way of defending against the self-directed destrudo (i.e., hate of the superego toward the ego) is to project the hate, as if saying, "I do not hate myself, but *they* hate me." In schizophrenia, when the ego is exposed to intolerable accusations from the superego, it develops paranoid projections. In sociopathic disorders, when the patient's aggressiveness evokes hostile reactions, the patient denies that he was ever hostile: he believes himself to be an innocent sheep surrounded by a pack of wolves. In dysmutual disorders, projections become systematized, reproducing the Cinderella story of a persecuted child finally rewarded for her sweetness and goodness. Every paranoid is a martyr, persecuted by a bad mother who is expected to become a good godmother.

When one feels painfully rejected, he may deny the rejection and pretend that he is greatly loved, or he may come to believe that he is the victim of a conspiracy. In either case, the mechanism of projection is employed. In the first case, the individual projects his love for the rejecting love object; in the second, he projects his hatred for the love object whom he hates for turning down his love. Dysmutual patients tend to exaggerate and advertise their feelings. They often take signs of friendliness or even simple kindness as evidence of great love and proceed to fall in love accordingly. Sometimes they are carried away by their own wishful thinking and imagine that other people are madly in love with them. A repeated pattern of this nature can assume the proportions of paranoia.

The Levels of Mental Disorders

There are distinct degrees of severity in mental disorder, but the distinction between neurosis and psychosis is a controversial issue. Pinsker and Spitzer (1977, p. 162) reported that in DSM III, "psychoses" and "neuroses" are not used as principles of classification:

"Psychotic" is used as an adjective to describe certain aspects of severity of illness. "Neurosis" is referred to as a speculative etiologic concept.

The concept of "the psychoses" as a group of conditions seems rooted in the mental hospital, at a time when no one was identified as a mentally ill person unless psychotic. But if the term "psychotic" describes a certain degree of impairment of reality testing, disruption of thinking process, disorganization of behavior, or inability to function, the disorder (or disorders) which causes the psychotic impairment must have been present in mild form before the psychotic level of impairment was reached. Further clinicians do not usually classify their patients as "psychotic" as a precursor to determining whether or not the exact diagnosis is organic brain syndrome, mood disorder or schizophrenia, the historical subdivision of the psychoses (ICDA, 1968).

Some psychiatrists diagnose schizophrenia in patients who have never been psychotic; others insist that psychosis at some time during the course of illness is essential before the diagnosis can be made. Yet even with the more stringent approach, the schizophrenic patient is not psychotic at all times. It is inconsistent to describe a patient as suffering from a psychosis, while acknowledging that he is not psychotic. (Pinsker and Spitzer, 1977, p. 162)

My system assumes a continuum; neurosis and psychosis are levels of disorder and not separate clinical entities:

My assumption is that the normal personality is a balanced personality. Once an imbalance in cathexes starts, the ego, in accordance with Freud's "constancy principle" and its main task of protection of the organism, tries to counteract the maladjustive processes. The struggle of the ego against pressures from within creates profound feelings of anxiety with a great variety of ego-protective symptoms. Although the nature of the symptoms depends on the nature of the threat or damage and is specific in each of the three types of disorder, the common denominator for this level of all three types is anxiety and ego-protective symptoms. As long as the ego is capable of asserting itself using a galaxy of defense mechanisms, it is *neurosis*. It can be a hyperinstrumental neurosis, a dysmutual neurosis, or a hypervectorial neurosis; they are different *types* of neurosis, but they are the same, first level of mental disorder.

When the ego so-to-say comes to terms with the neurotic symptoms and the neurotic symptoms or attitudes become "included in the ego" or "blended into personality" (Fenichel, 1945, p. 463ff.), then neurosis becomes "character neurosis" or "character disorder," or "personality disorder." These three names describe the same category, the same second level of mental disorder.

Sometimes the defenses are inadequate and a neurosis or a character neurosis may turn into a latent (third level) or manifest psychosis (fourth level). A neurosis does not have to become first character neurosis and then a latent psychosis and later on a manifest psychosis. Character neurosis serves as a "protective armor" (Reich, 1945), a rigid set of ego-protective symptoms that prevents further deterioration into psychosis, but sometimes even armor may break. Yet, in some cases, in spite of a severe psychotic deterioration the individual still is not manifestly psychotic. He somehow continues functioning on a slim margin of ego controls; a mild noxious stimulus may throw him into a manifest psychosis. As long as his ego keeps on going and a contact with reality is preserved, it is a *latent* and not a manifest psychosis.

The main difference between neurosis and psychosis lies in the strength of the ego. As long as the ego controls the id and preserves the contact with reality, it is neurosis. Psychosis is a neurosis that failed; it is a defeat of the ego that lost the contact with reality and a victory of the id. (Wolman, 1966, pp. 57-58). The total collapse of personality structure is the fifth level of deterioration.

ASSESSMENT OF THE INDIVIDUAL PATIENT

The awareness of nosological categories and the proper classification of the patient's disorder enable the psychotherapist to arrive at a broadly conceived therapeutic strategy. One does not deal the same way with different entities, and a proper differential diagnosis is the very foundation of successful psychotherapy.

The awareness of the five levels of severity of mental disorder is of great help in delineating precise therapeutic planning. Certainly, one can expect to accomplish most with mild neurotic conditions, less with character neuroses, still less with latent psychoses, even less with manifest psychoses, and very little if anything at all with a total collapse of personality structure.

A *caveat* is needed here, for the above descriptions are general concepts that do not necessarily apply to every single case. For the sake of comparison, let us imagine a house that requires remodeling. Suppose the house is, superficially, in reasonably good shape but was built cheaply and has a weak foundation; an effort to remove a wall in a poorly constructed house may cause a collapse of the entire building. Suppose, however, that the house is a shambles but has solid foundations; in such a case, a far-reaching reconstruction is possible and the ultimate results could be quite rewarding.

Thus, the general diagnostic procedure must be carefully scrutinized and followed by a thorough evaluation of every individual case. The individual case may defy the general rules. I have worked with quite serious cases of manifest schizophrenics who responded well to psychotherapy and, after a bumpy initial road, showed considerable ego strength. Their psychotic breakdown had been recent, and the damage caused to their personality was not severe.

Often, the initial assessment of the patient's strengths and weaknesses must be modified. One cannot be too cautious in assessing the resources of another person, and a rush decision may cause harm to the patient. In supervising younger colleagues, I have often had to temper their therapeutic enthusiasm and craving for quick, spectacular results, and to recommend patience and caution.

Several factors have to be taken into consideration in a diagnostic workup. The first is ego strength. I am using the term "ego" the way Freud used it, namely, as the guardian of reality and sober control apparatus. Another relevant factor is the patient's general outlook, his or her zest for life and determined desire to be cured. These traits must be reinforced during psychotherapy, and on several occasions, I have been fortunate to rekindle the "lust for life" in patients who were at the beginning quite despondent.

In addition to the psychological determinants mentioned, one must take environmental factors into consideration. Human beings do not live in a vacuum, and their life situation affects their mental health. It makes quite a difference whether a patient is single or married, has many friends or is lonely, has good or bad family relations, and so on.

I rarely recommend hospitalization because I do not believe that people with emotional problems, no matter how grave they are, should be deprived of personal freedom. In many instances, hospitalization aggravates the condition, reduces personal initiative, damages self-esteem, and makes an individual more and more depressed. I do, however, recommend hospitalization in two instances: where there is a danger to the patient's life (suicide) or where there is a danger to anyone else's life (homicide). I have worked in private practice with severely disturbed people, provided that I could secure adequate cooperation from those in their close environment. As mentioned in Chapter 2, I have worked with suicidal patients when I was reasonably sure of being able to reach them and when I could be assured of the unswerving cooperation of their close family.

Evidently an individual's good or poor mental health is not an isolated entity. It is produced, sustained, and fostered in *interaction with his or her environment.* With the exception of clearly organic cases, all mental disturbances are caused by interaction in early childhood and are perpetuated, aggravated, or ameliorated by interaction with people during one's life span. The cases described point out the *diagnostic and prognostic importance* of the patient's social environment, which includes one's occupation, job situation, and interaction with superiors and/or subordinates. No less relevant are other social relationships such as one's involvement with religious or other cultural and political institutions, one's peers and neighbors, and one's hobbies or other extracurricular activities.

As soon as psychotherapy starts, a new and highly relevant interactional factor is added. The patient enters a new interactional relationship, this time with the therapist who is determined to help. More about this interaction can be found in Chapter 5.

5
Therapeutic Interaction

The process of treatment, whether surgical, dental, or psychological, involves two parties, namely, the helping professional and the help-seeking public. Patients are people who suffer from, and are aware of, a disease, defect, or malfunction of bodily organs, sensory apparatus, or mental apparatus. They look for somebody qualified and properly licensed to provide the badly needed treatment. This patient-therapist relationship, like any other social relationship, can be presented in two dimensions. The first dimension is *power;* the other is *acceptance. Power* is defined as the ability to satisfy needs. People who can satisfy the needs of themselves and others are strong; those who cannot are weak. The willingness to do so is called *acceptance:* those who help are friendly; those who hurt are hostile.

The concept of power originates in physical strength. Animals and primitive human beings satisfy their fundamental needs, such as food, water, and shelter, by using their physical strength. With the development of higher nervous functions, the human species has been using its mental abilities in order to survive, for survival is the arch-need of all needs.

Most human beings procure their food, water, and shelter not through physical fighting but through work. The use of working skills for producing, providing, exchanging, shipping, and storing goods has become far more important in terms of power than the initial, archaic physical strength.

Power, defined as the ability to satisfy needs, applies also to practitioners in the fields of physical and mental health. People who have certain innate abilities, and have developed these abilities by training and experience, have acquired the power to heal other people's wounds, ills, and shortcomings. They are the competent and skilled helpers, called surgeons, dentists, psychiatrists, psychologists, social workers, guidance counselors, and so on, according to their particular training and skill.

Power can be used to help satisfy needs or to prevent their satisfaction. Thus, the interaction between individuals can be described by the use of quasi-Cartesian coordinates in which the vertical line represents power, from omnipotence at the top to the point of zero power — death — at the bottom. The horizontal line represents a friendly attitude toward the right and a hostile attitude toward the left. People can be friendly or hostile: friendly means willing to satisfy needs; hostile means preventing their satisfaction. Let us call these two dimensions of strong-weak and friendly-hostile *power* and *acceptance,* respectively.

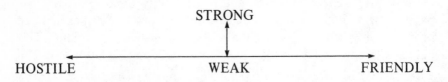

Obviously, when a person has a toothache, he looks for somebody who has the *power* to heal his tooth, that is, a competent, skilled, and experienced dentist; at the same time, he looks for someone who is *friendly,* that is willing to heal him. The dimension of power implies competence; the dimension of acceptance is indicated by integrity, devotion to the profession, and conscientious work with patients.

People interact with one another not on the basis of how things are but of how they *perceive* them. People do not choose a professional man on the basis of what he is: they judge him on his reputation. When the consensus is that a particular psychiatrist, surgeon, dentist, or psychologist is exceptionally gifted and highly competent, it is assumed that he has the power to help. If he has the reputation of being devoted and conscientious, then he is believed to be friendly, that is, willing to help. Strength and friendliness are the traits expected of healing professionals.

The process of psychotherapy is actually a split-level or two-level process. On one hand, it is an interaction between two adults. One of them has an office, obtained an M.D. or Ph.D. degree, passed some examinations, got a licence or certification, and is approved by society for the job he or she is doing. The other can be a lawyer, teacher, accountant, housewife, garbage collector, or diamond collector who feels disturbed and is worried about being disturbed. Usually there is little chance of helping somebody unless he or she feels perplexed by being disturbed and wishes to be helped. On one level, psychotherapy is an interaction of two adults that resembles the interaction which takes place between a lawyer and his client, a dentist and his patient, or an accountant and his customer. The patients believe psychotherapists to be competent in certain areas of life, and they expect to get help. A patient could be a great scholar, a famous surgeon, a multimillion dollar business executive, a brilliant writer, or a famous singer. In the therapeutic situation, the patient looks up to the doctor. Outside the therapeutic situation, the relationship may be reversed, and therapists may look up to their patients. Obviously, the megalomania of psychotherapists is totally unjustified.

THE POWER RELATIONSHIP

One seeks help from a surgeon or a psychotherapist whenever one feels that something is wrong with oneself. When one goes to a dentist, one assumes that the dentist is competent, which means that he is capable of helping, and that he cares, which means that he is willing to help. The helpers are perceived as being *strong* and *friendly*, and the patient depends on their help. However, as mentioned in Chapter 2, outside treatment hours, one does not necessarily look up to them. If the patient is a real estate broker, the dentist may need the patient's help in the purchase of a house. If the patient is a lawyer, his dentist may ask his legal advice. Human relations are not a simple, hierarchic system in which someone always looks up to someone else; we need a baker for our bread, an accountant for our bills, a dentist to fix our teeth. We look up to these people *in their particular capacity,* but they may look up to us whenever *they need* our help. Childhood means dependence on parents or other adults, but adulthood is not independence: it is *interdependence.*

As mentioned in Chapter 2 this interdependence does not apply to the doctor-patient relationship in the treatment of mental disorders. The psychotherapist is not supposed to ever ask the assistance of his patient who is a dentist or a lawyer. The therapist is expected to do more than help in a particular area: he deals with the patient's total personality. Thus, a psychotherapist is not merely a strong and friendly expert. The psychotherapist takes the place of the father-confessor, and he is expected to have more power than the priest, rabbi, or minister. Patients depend on psychotherapists in making the most vital decisions. The role the therapist plays resembles only one person in one's life: *the role of a caring and admired parent.* Small wonder that the treatment of mental disorders resembles the child-parent relationship. Adult men and women go to someone who is not necessarily wiser, better established, more influential, or more powerful than themselves.

Putting one's faith and fate in a therapist makes one much more dependent than one usually is in regard to a physician, dentist, or lawyer. In the patient-therapist dependency, the patient necessarily develops an infantile regression, called "transference" by Freud. When someone is under stress, he tends to develop regressive moods and transfer his emotions onto the person who takes care of him. Freud noticed this first, but transference, which is the transfer of emotions in a state of infantile regression, takes place in all kinds of psychotherapy.

This type of emotional regression creates a patient-doctor relationship unheard of in any other kind of treatment. The dependence on the psychotherapist goes to the gut level. It deals with the deepest layers of one's personality and elicits emotions which might be not related to the here-and-now relationship. I have treated men and women who were wiser, more competent, more influential, and much richer than I. A dentist asked me how to deal with his patient's teeth and jaws; an internist consulted me about how to make a diagnosis; a lawyer sought my advice in complex contracts; and an executive expected me to tell him how to run his corporation. It was rather amazing, although not surprising, that these people asked my advice in areas in which they were far more competent than I and expected me to give them adequate guidance, as if they were little children and I their benevolent and omniscient parent.

Most patients develop affection, admiration, and even love for their psychotherapist. Their love has the infantile element of demanding reciprocation; children expect their parents to love them, to care for them, and to take care of them. Quite often, the patients' love has sexual undertones, and patients, both male and female, develop heterosexual or homosexual crushes on their therapist. Many a patient, despite the fact that he or she pays a fee to his doctor in private practice, or society pays the fees in a clinic or hospital, ascribes to himself or herself a position of total dependence and craves the doctor's affection. Sometimes transference takes a negative turn and the patient uses his therapist as a target for his hostile feelings. Past grievances against parents and other significant adults are redirected against the therapist who may be unfairly blamed for whatever miseries the patient has experienced in life.

The patient versus therapist attitude can be presented on two levels. One level is the here-and-now relationship: patients are aware of the fact that they go to a doctor whom they pay or who is paid by society and is, therefore, expected to relieve their tensions and resolve their inner conflicts. On the other level, a great deal of irrational feeling is directed against the therapist, who serves as a target for the patients' emotional onslaughts. There will be more about transference in Chapter 6.

THERAPEUTIC ATTITUDE

There has been a good deal of controversy concerning therapists' attitudes toward their patients. Freud recommended a neutral and detached attitude of "evenly hovering attention" that facilitates regression and transference. This approach was a logical sequel to Freud's theory of mental disorder. Therapists who assume that mental disorders are produced by *regressive unconscious processes* must follow Freud's reasoning and bring the unconscious to the surface, thereby resolving the buried unconscious conflicts. Freud assumed that most, if not all, unconscious conflicts stemmed from early childhood; thus, therapists must help their patients to regress to early childhood and to reexperience past positive and negative emotional involvements, using the therapists as sort of surrogate parental figures. The patients' reclining position and the analysts' detachment facilitated the patients' regression and transference, and their verbal communication, uninterrupted by the analysts, took the form of free associations which helped to unravel unconscious material.

Gradually, Freud resolved that the analysts' passive attitude required modification, especially in regard to obsessive-compulsive patients who tended to use free associations as a method of resistance. In the paper "The Future Prospects of Psycho-analytic Therapy," Freud wrote:

We are also now coming to the opinion that the analytic technique must undergo certain modifications according to the nature of the disease and the dominating instinctual trends in the patient. Our therapy was, in fact, first designed for conversion-hysteria; in anxiety-hysteria (phobias) we must alter our procedure to some extent. The fact is that these patients cannot bring out the material necessary for resolving the phobia so long as they feel protected by retaining their phobic condition. One cannot, of course, induce them to give up their protective measures and work under the influence of anxiety from the beginning of treatment. One must therefore help them by interpreting their unconscious to them until they can make up their minds to do without the protection of their phobia and expose themselves to a now comparatively moderate degree of anxiety. Only when they have done so does the material necessary for achieving solution of the phobia become accessible. Other modifications of technique which seem to me not yet ready for discussion will be required in the treatment of obsessional neurosis. In this connection very important questions arise, which are not yet elucidated; how far the instincts involved in the conflict in the patient are to be allowed some gratification during the treatment, and what difference it then makes whether these impulses are active (sadistic) or passive (masochistic) in nature.

Freud was even more outspoken in his address "Turning in the Ways in Psychoanalytic Therapy," read in Budapest before the Fifth International Psychoanalytic Congress in 1918 (published in 1919). He wrote:

Lastly, another quite different kind of activity is necessitated by the gradually growing appreciation that the various forms of disease treated by us cannot all be dealt with by the same technique. It would be premature to discuss this in detail, but I can give two examples of the way in which a new kind of activity comes into question. Our technique grew up in the treatment of hysteria and is still directed principally to the cure of this affection. But the phobias have already made it necessary for us to go beyond our former limits. One can hardly ever master a phobia if one waits till the patient lets the analysis influence him to give it up. He will never in that case bring for the analysis the material indispensable for a convincing solution of the phobia. One must proceed differently. Take the example of agoraphobia; there are two classes of it, one slight and the other severe. Patients belonging to the first indeed suffer from anxiety when they go about alone, but they have not yet given up going out alone on that account; the others protect themselves from the anxiety by altogether giving up going about alone. With these last, one succeeds only when one can induce them through the influence of the analysis to behave like the first class, that is, to go about alone and to struggle with their anxiety while they make the attempt. One first achieves, therefore, a considerable moderation of the phobia, and it is only when this has been attained by the physician's recommendation that the association and memories come into the patient's mind enabling the phobia to be solved.

In severe cases of obsessive acts a passive waiting attitude seems even less well adapted: indeed in general these cases incline to favor an asymptomatic process of cure, an interminable protraction of the treatment; in their analysis there is always the danger of a great deal coming to light without its effecting any change in them. I think there is little doubt that here the correct technique can only be to wait until the treatment itself has become a compulsion, and then with this counter-compulsion, forcibly to suppress the compulsion of the disease.

In the treatment of schizophrenics, Freud faced insurmountable difficulties. Schizophrenics reacted to the reclining position and to the analyst's silence with an apparent and far-reaching regression. Freud erroneously believed that schizophrenia was a nontransference neurosis and did not recommend his method for the treatment of schizophrenia.

In the paper "The Effect of the Structure of the Ego on Psychoanalytic Techniques," Eissler (1953) introduced the concept of parameter, which leads to a far-reaching deviation from classic psychoanalytic technique. The parameter method implies direct suggestions or even commands given by the analyst to the patient. Eissler suggested that the basic model for psychoanalytic technique had been developed in relation to hysteria, whereas interpretation, as the essential tool of the analyst, provides the insight that is needed for the achievement of therapeutic goals. Therapeutic factors are not limited to interpretation and insight; other elements are adjuncts to these as specific agencies of analytic technique. In phobias, a point in treatment is reached at which it becomes evident that interpretation does not suffice as a therapeutic tool and that the pathogenic material cannot be attained. A new technical device becomes necessary, such as *advice* or *command* to confront the dreaded situation in real life. This accessory maneuver is termed a *parameter* by Eissler.

In the last few decades, several competent Freudian and non-Freudian therapists have introduced a host of modifications in therapeutic techniques (Jacobs, 1983). At the present time, there are scores of treatment methods, related or unrelated to Freud's classique technique. It is worthwhile to mention that even Freud's faithful disciples, such as Stone (1954), Tarachow (1963), Kernberg (1970), Kohut (1971), Langs (1976) and others, proposed far-reaching and definitely unorthodox innovations in Freud's therapeutic method.

For example, Zetzel (1965) suggested that while retaining an objective and dispassionate role, the analyst must convey to the patient feelings of *sympathy* and *friendliness.* It is not enough to interpret the patient's communication; the psychoanalyst should "respond at all times to affect which indicates the patient's need to feel respected and acknowledged as a real person."

It is my conviction that the therapist's vectorial attitude, described in Chapter 1, is one of the prerequisites for successful treatment. People seek help from someone who is *strong* (i.e., competent) and *friendly* (i.e., willing to help). A passive and detached attitude may foster deep transference and infantile attachment, but it does not contribute to the patient's self-respect and emotional growth.

My fundamental psychological assumption, described in the first two chapters of this book, is that the *fight for survival* is a universal drive and that *the awareness of one's own power, that is, self-confidence, and the power and loyalty of one's allies are the chief needs of every human being.* Accordingly, the therapist must encourage self-confidence in the patient and convey his devotion to the patient's well-being. The task of the therapist is not to please or to pity the patient, but to help him. A friendly and respectful attitude serves this purpose.

THE ABSTINENCE RULE

Since suffering is the main reason for undergoing psychoanalysis or any other form of psychotherapy, Freud imposed the rule of abstinence (or abstention), preventing premature gratification. Patients were requested to postpone major decisions concerning their way of life and to avoid premature solutions of their painful problems.

However, this rule is hardly applicable today, at least in the United States. In Freud's pre–World War I Vienna, people usually lived all their lives on the same street in the same house or apartment, and often several generations occupied the same dwelling. In the United States, people are often on the move: some are recent immigrants who have come from all over the world; others – who may be second, third, or any other generation Americans – move around the country in search of better economic opportunities or for other reasons. No less spectacular is the vertical movement. In Freud's time, children tended to follow in the footsteps of their parents; however, in the contemporary United States, this is the exception rather than the rule. Perhaps Freud was right in advising his patients to avoid radical changes in their lives during psychoanalysis, but today, such advice could be stifling and would often be unrealistic. In a relatively stable environment, patients could refrain from radical changes, but in today's environment, everyone is exposed to change with regard to breadwinning functions, personal life, and sociopolitical situations. A contemporary psychotherapist, Freudian or not, cannot take a neutral attitude when a patient is faced with the loss of a job or with an excellent opportunity for improving his income, when his child becomes a drug pusher, or when his spouse runs away. It might be impossible and, in many instances, antitherapeutic to recommend that patients postpone their decisions until the end of their psychotherapy.

Although, as a rule, therapists should refrain from giving patients advice or directions, on several occasions I have felt that a totally neutral attitude would be tantamount to neglect of my therapeutic obligation and could indeed, be a betrayal of the patient. *The main commitment of a psychotherapist is to help the patient, and no theoretical considerations should blunt or becloud this basic rule.* To let a patient "sink or swim" is a renunciation of the fundamental ethical commitments of the healing professions.

On many occasions, I have felt that I had to take a stand and advise my patients. Once, a young, 23-year-old patient met a woman on an airplane and, after spending an enjoyable weekend with her, decided to marry her. I urged him to learn a little more about her before making his decision. As it turned out, the young lady happened to be a prostitute! On several occasions, I have had to intervene in patients' dangerous neglect of physical health and refer them to competent physicians for a thorough checkup. (The case of Dr. J. has already been described.) The president of a major corporation once outlined a highly speculative plan. I pointed out the apparently self-destructive nature of this plan and suggested consultation with his lawyers and accountants; this fortunately took place and prevented the total collapse of his business. Ultimately, patients have had to make their own decisions, but I believe that it was my moral obligation to offer as much help as I could to prevent irrational, self-defeating, and in many instances, quite dangerous actions.

COUCH OR NO COUCH

At the beginning of his therapeutic career, Freud used hypnosis to force the unconscious to become conscious. After a while, Freud abandoned the hypnotic method and introduced the concentration method: while the patient reclined on a couch, Freud would gently press the patient's head and suggest that he try to recall past experiences which could be related to present emotional difficulties. Later on, Freud realized that the reclining position itself, without any need to press the patient's head and make suggestions, led to free associations. The reclining position protected the patient from being watched by the analyst and encouraged nonrestricted meditation and the free expression of thoughts and feelings. The reclining position facilitated regression to childlike feelings and permitted the repressed unconsciousness to come to the surface.

The patient's reclining position also protected the analyst from being watched by the patient, thereby preventing unnecessary interaction. It thus enabled the analyst to follow Freud's rule of nonparticipation and "evenly hovering attention."

The modifications in classic psychoanalysis introduced by Tarachow (1963) under the name "psychoanalytic therapy" provided for a good deal of flexibility. Apparently, some patients verbalize better in a reclining position, while others are more at ease when facing the therapist. At the present time, most Freudian psychoanalysts do not use the couch with severely disturbed patients, being aware of the fact that the couch may unduly deepen their regression and become antitherapeutic. Non-Freudian, Sullivanian analysts discourage the use of the couch with obsessional patients:

[the] use of the couch tends to increase the depth of the patient's diminished self-esteem and to encourage regression, frequently a risky therapeutic procedure with an obsessional. (Witenberg and Caligor, 1967, p. 431)

The followers of Alfred Adler, who are adherents of individual psychology, strongly oppose the use of the couch. Kurt Adler wrote (1967, p. 325):

The ideal situation is for patient and analyst to sit face-to-face, as equal fellow men. Almost all patients feel it to be a position of inferiority to lie on the couch while the analyst sits in a lordlike fashion above him. Although transference is enhanced, the development of a genuine human relationship is made virtually impossible by such an unequal position.

According to G. Adler (1967, p. 344), Jungian analytical psychology has a flexible approach:

The armchair gives expression to a greater flexibility in the analytical situation and to the "dialectical relationship" between the patient and analyst. . . . [However] the armchair may have its disadvantages in certain situations, for example, when a patient is particularly tense and needs the support of the couch to loosen up, or when transference fantasies are too sharply inhibited by facing the analyst.

Nonpsychoanalytic treatment methods do not use the couch.

The method of interactional psychotherapy that I use leaves ample room for both approaches — the couch and the armchair. I definitely prefer the armchair, with its face-to-face position, since this facilitates interaction. Moreover, being face-to-face enables the therapist to observe the patient's facial expressions and body movements, thus offering nonverbal clues. However, if patients prefer the reclining position, they may use it whenever and for as long as they need it.

HOW MUCH SHOULD PATIENTS KNOW ABOUT THE THERAPIST?

I believe that every psychotherapy is an interactional process between a doctor and a patient, and that the patient has the right to know what is going on in the therapeutic sessions. I have, therefore, always tried to be as open with my patients as *therapeutically advisable.* The decision as to what indeed is therapeutically advisable, is the therapist's, and I recommend a great deal of flexibility.

In many instances, I have outlined my therapeutic plans to patients. Often patients have asked, "Is there any reason why we do not interpret my dream?" or "Why can't we deal with my sexual problem right now?" or "How about my fear of cats?" or "Why do we keep on my job situation?" In most cases, I have felt it advisable to explain that certain problems have priority, while the solution to other problems may follow later. I have often used the following example: "Suppose that a tree blocks our window. Should we cut off the branches which will grow back or should we, rather, pull out the roots?"

Patients are often curious about the therapist's private life. They may look up *Who's Who,* but it is rather counterproductive and wasteful to spend therapeutic time on the therapist's confessions. Nothing is gained by satisfying the patient's curiosity about the therapist's family status or other matters. Divulging personal information may sidetrack the therapeutic process, and on some occasions, I have responded to my patient's inquiries with a jest: "If I talk about myself, then you will charge me!"

There are times when a patient's empathy enables him to read the therapists's thought. When a patient noticed that I was tired, I admitted it. However, when a patient reported a dream that replicated certain events in my personal life, I did not confirm or deny it: I refused to comment.

PROGNOSIS

Quite naturally, psychotherapists are tempted to predict the outcome of their work. Statistical research is full of prognostic studies, but statistical data deal with averages and are not applicable to a single case. Moreover, statistical research can hardly do justice to several complex and changing individual variables. It is my conviction that the very nature of human behavior renders clinical prediction exceedingly difficult if not totally impossible. Human beings do not act in a vacuum, and their behavior represents a *psychosocial field.* Every observer, no matter how objective, influences the observed. In physics, under Einstein's influence, there has been a growing awareness of the fact that any observer-observed situation represents a field. Jeans (1958, p. 143) wrote: "Every observation involves a passage of a complete quantum from the observed object to the observing subject, and a complete quantum constitutes a not negligible coupling between the observer and the observed. We can no longer make a sharp division between the two . . . . Complete objectivity can only be regained by treating observer and observed as parts of a single system."

The difference in the choice of vantage point can lead to far-reaching differences in the results of observation. Compare, for instance, Freud's and Sullivan's ideas concerning schizophrenia. The reclining position of the neurotic patient and the sparse communication from the mostly silent psychoanalyst facilitated transference phenomena. Freud noticed them and made them the cornerstone of his therapeutic method. However, when a psychotic patient was asked to recline with a psychoanalyst sitting behind the couch and watching him, a different reaction took place. Silence was probably perceived as rejection, and the invisible analyst became a threatening figure. The patient withdrew even more into his shell and, if he did communicate, would not dare reveal his true feelings. Such behavior gave the impression of narcissistic withdrawal and lack of transference feelings toward the psychoanalyst.

Sullivan worked in a hospital in which patients moved back and forth, and acted out their feelings. He saw patients in *interpersonal relations* and did not fail to notice the socially induced changes in their behavior. The here-and-now interaction has become the clue to understanding the psychotic patient. Most probably, what has been observed in *participant observation* is not the patient as an isolated entity, but the patient in interaction with the therapist, that is, a *psychosocial field*.

One must, therefore, conclude that the present condition of a mental patient is but one of many determinants of his future behavior. The way he will act in the future can be greatly influenced by his interaction with several other people, among them the therapist, and is, therefore, rather *unpredictable*.

6
Therapeutic Strategy

OVERSTAYED INFANTILE BEHAVIOR

The aim of psychotherapy is to help people to become mature and well-adjusted adults, thus making psychotherapy superfluous. Adults who need psychotherapy are physically mature and, on the milder levels of mental disorder (neurotics, character neurotics, and often even latent psychotics), can function adequately in several areas of adult life. Many of these men and women are quite successful in business and various professions, but in some areas of their life, they act in an infantile manner.

I am tempted to say that mental disorders are a sort of *overstayed infantile behavior.* I once had as a patient the 34-year-old senior editor of a major publishing house. At the initial interview, she told me about her job. After 15 minutes of listening to her, I realized that I was fascinated by her sophisticated description of current American fiction and her encounters with prominent writers. I interrupted her and said, "What you are telling me is most interesting. I really enjoy listening to you, but you did not come here to enlighten me about current fiction. Please tell me about yourself. What made you come to me?"

The change was dramatic: her entire manner of behavior became childlike. Instead of a brilliant editor, I had in front of me a teenage girl who did not make much sense. Her choice of words, her tone, and the content of communication dropped to a childlike level. I could almost physically see the sudden drop. I have had similar experiences with a great many patients. Quite often, they have come to my office, adult men and women, and at the initial interview, they have talked as adults — discussing fees and hours. Sooner or later, however, they have begun to reveal the infantile parts of their personality and to describe behavior which was partly adult and partly infantile. I had in treatment a distinguished college professor, the author of important scientific works, whose behavior at home was sadly irrational, with frequent infantile temper tantrums and sulky withdrawals.

The so-called split personality is probably a misnomer, for no human being is a monolithic structure. Every human personality is a mixed collection of innate drives and acquired wishes built over and over again throughout one's life span. Bodily cells may die and disappear, but psychological cells never die; they sink into the unconscious and stay there forever. Sometimes they are stored without being used, but sometimes they appear on the surface and lead to actions that may surprise or even shock the acting individual. Human growth probably follows certain biologically determined and socioculturally influenced developmental phases, but there are no clear-cut rules concerning any particular individual.

The childish elements in us do not die, but neither do they survive intact. Layer upon layer of deep or less deep unconscious feelings and thoughts pile up on one another or one inside the other. Every human being resembles a house that has been built and rebuilt over the years without a plan or blueprint. No one's life history follows logical rules, and the manifold of successes and failures has nothing to do with rational planning. One can clearly see the chaotic personality development in cases of severe psychotic breakdown (Wolman, 1966). The devastated personality structure does not resemble an orderly regression to an early developmental phase, but rather a house built in spurts and remodeled over the years, which was destroyed by an earthquake; the ruins show the various layers and degrees of destruction.

With the exception of organic cases, almost all mental disorders start in early childhood and are the product of a morbid interaction with parents and/or other significant persons such as siblings, grandparents, other relatives, friends, or enemies. Children are unable to survive unless taken care of. Their own power (defined as the ability to satisfy needs) is insignificant; therefore, support from without (acceptance) is a prerequisite for their survival. A little child is totally dependent on others, and as a rule, the earlier the child is exposed to the harmful interaction, the more serious is the damage.

As children grow, their own power increases and their dependence on others decreases. Ultimately, adult men and women depend on their own resources as well as on cooperation with others. They are no longer dependent; they are interdependent. They need other people, and other people need them. Mature adults develop a reasonable degree of self-esteem, that is, belief in their own power, as well as a reasonable degree of social relations on the instrumental, mutual, and vectorial levels described earlier in this book.

A child's self-esteem is derived from approval by parents and/or other significant adults. Children perceive themselves as weak and passive, and their parents as *strong and friendly,* that is, capable of protecting them and willing to do so. As children grow and develop, their dependence on others gradually declines and their dependence on themselves increases.

Mature adults do not need parental protection. Apparently, something has gone wrong in the lives of people who, being unable to cope with their problems, seek psychological help. In many cases, their "overstayed" childhood attitudes make them create problems for themselves. They seek help, and the need to obtain help puts them, to some extent, in a dependent situation which resembles their past dependence on their parents.

It is not surprising that many people who need help are reluctant to admit it. Moreover, every kind of psychotherapy may look like a temporary regression to childhood dependence in order to surmount the overstayed childhood attitude. Some patients have felt that their dependence was a sort of a crutch. My explanations has usually pointed out the temporary need to use a crutch in order to be able to walk without any support.

Since most psychological difficulties start in childhood, it may be necessary to deal with their origins and unravel their roots, but there is no reason to dig more than necessary. Especially when the tree is not too firm, too much digging can cause more harm than good. On several occasions, I have had to help a younger colleague who – in his therapeutic zeal – interpreted deep mental layers of a shaky personality structure and caused a psychotic breakdown. For each new case, the therapist must decide how much digging out is necessary, but some digging into the past does seem rewarding.

Thus, some degree of regression in which one adult, the patient, relates to another adult, the therapist, in a child versus parent manner is part of the therapeutic process. This regressive attitude produces a highly relevant phenomenon which Freud called "transference."

THE UNCONSCIOUS

It took the courage and wisdom of Sigmund Freud to discover that a great many mental disorders were not diseases in the medical sense nor were they caused by diseased neurons. Freud's topographic personality model, with its distinction of three layers — conscious, preconscious, and unconscious — has opened new vistas in psychopathology. According to Freud, mental disorder is a failure to grow up and become a mature adult. It is a regression to an early level of psychological development. "Regression," Freud wrote in 1900, "plays a no less important part in the theory of the formation of neurotic symptoms than it does in that of dreams" (1900, p. 548). Every human being goes through developmental stages from birth to adulthood; those who have not grown up or who have gone back are mentally disturbed.

Owing to the general tendency to variation in biological processes it must necessarily happen that not all these preparatory phases will be passed through and completely outgrown with the same degree of success; some parts of the function will be permanently arrested. The usual course of development can be disturbed and altered by current impressions from without. (Freud, 1915-1917, p. 297)

Sometimes parts of the libido, or parts of its component impulses, become arrested at an early phase of development. Freud called this arrest *fixation*. The fact that some portions of the libido have become fixated increases the danger that someday the entire libido may regress to those points of fixation. The libido rarely progresses unhampered from one phase to the next. Some fixations are formed, and partial regressions take place. Under trying circumstances, the fixations may become substantial, and a weakened libido is less capable of overcoming external obstacles and proceeding smoothly.

Regression to an early developmental stage of libido is the essence of neurosis.

Before Freud, the treatment of mental disorders closely resembled the healing procedures of physicians or dentists: they "treat" the patient, and the patient is a passive recipient of treatment. Freud revolutionized the doctor-patient relationship. The psychoanalyst took on the role of a reserved listener whose undivided attention was given to the patient's free association.

Free associations facilitate regression in the patient and the uncovering of unconscious processes. The analyst is supposed to restrain himself and avoid giving any stimuli or any reality cues. The stimulus deprivation, the reclining position, and the detached attitude of the analyst produce regression in the patient. In the artificial setting of the analyst's office, repressed unconscious thoughts come to the surface.

Freud did not fight against symptoms but began to unravel the causes of mental disorders. These causes are buried in the unconscious, and must be brought to the surface and resolved. Regression permits access to repressed material and the reexperiencing of past traumas. One cannot fight an invisible enemy; obtaining insight into, and resolution of, unconscious conflicts became a guiding principle of psychoanalytic technique, and it has been incorporated by Freud's disciples and dissidents alike.

As noted, at the beginning Freud tried to force the unconscious to become conscious first by using hypnosis and, later on, by using suggestive pressure to overcome amnesia and resistance. Soon he became aware of the spontaneous help offered by the patient's unconscious. Freud discovered that whatever had been repressed tended to recur again and again. Unhealed wounds called for help, and past traumas forced themselves outward again and again. The principle of *repetition compulsion* was a logical inference from Freud's strict determinism and from the universal law of the preservation of energy, accepted by Freud: undischarged energy calls for a discharge.

The technique of using free association as a gate to the unconscious became the fundamental rule in psychoanalytic treatment. One may deviate from Freud's nosology, reject the Freud-Abraham timetable of etiology, and introduce new stages or concepts concerning personality development; however, no one can deny the fact that mental disorders are the consequence of a cluster of unconscious causes.

TRANSFERENCE

Freud made the regressive phenomenon into a cornerstone of his method. The psychoanalytic situation provides ideal conditions for reliving infantile emotions. The patient comes asking for help, and this puts him in a dependent, child versus parent type of relationship with the psychotherapist, whose willing listening contributes to the patient's feeling of having found a friendly, omniscient parental substitute. Free associations and the reclining position facilitate emotional regression. The patient lets his defenses down and, in a regressive mood, weaves emotional fantasies around the silent analyst who represents, as indicated, a parental figure. Past feelings and conflicts reemerge in the patient's mind, and he relives the family drama as he experienced it in his childhood. The patient transfers his past emotional attachments to the psychoanalyst, and according to Freud, every emotional conflict is "played out in the phenomena of the transference."

What are transferences? They are new editions or facsimiles of the impulses and phantasies which are aroused and made conscious during the progress of the analysis; but they have this peculiarity, which is characteristic for their species, that they replace some earlier person by the person of the physician. To put it another way: a whole series of psychological experiences are revived, not as belonging to the past, but as applying to the person of the physician at the present moment. Some of these transferences have a content which differs from that of their model in no respect whatever except for the substitution. These then – to keep to the same metaphor – are merely new impressions or reprints. Others are more ingeniously constructed; their content has been subjected to a moderating influence to *sublimation,* as I call it – and they may even become conscious by cleverly taking advantage of some real peculiarity in the physician's person or circumstances and attaching themselves to that. These, then, will no longer be new impressions, but revised editions. (Freud, 1915b, p. 116)

Transference is a process of cathexis in a state of regression. If it is a cathexis of libido, it is a "positive" transference; if it is a cathexis of destructive energy, it is a "negative" transference. Transference becomes a neurosis, a neurosis in which the patient relives his past conflicts using the analyst as a target for libidinal cathexes and desstructive assaults. The patient ascribes to the analyst personality traits actually belonging to the patient's parents. Becoming involved with his analyst, the patient becomes less concerned with his own problems. Love and hate for the analyst may reach considerable intensity and, unless treated properly, can impede the progress of psychoanalysis.

The psychoanalyst must neither ignore nor satisfy the transference:

It is, therefore, just as disastrous for the analysis if the patient's craving for love prevails as if it is suppressed. The way the analyst must take is neither of these; it is one for which there is no proto-type in real life. He must guard against ignoring the transference-love, scaring it away or making the patient disgusted with it; and just as resolutely must he withhold any response to it. He must face the transference-love boldly but treat it like something unreal, as a condition which must be gone through during the treatment and traced back to its unconscious origins, so that it shall assist in bringing to light all that is most hidden in the development of the patient's erotic life, and help her to learn to control it . . . . The patient, whose sexual repressions are of course not yet removed but merely pushed into the background, will then feel safe enough to allow all her conditions for loving, all the phantasies of her sexual desires, all the individual details of her way of being in love to come to light, and then will herself open up the way back from them to the infantile roots of her love. (Freud, 1915, p. 185).

Transference may get out of hand if, instead of being merely an emotional experience verbally expressed in the analyst's office, it leads to acting out. Thus, the main task of the analyst is to keep transference as an expression of memories of past experiences, not as a here-and-now experience. Interpretation of transference makes the patient aware of the fact that his infatuation with the analyst is not related to the analyst as a person but is simply a reflection of previous emotional entanglements. The analyst, as the target of the patient's emotions, is merely a substitute for parental figures. Transferred emotions are real emotions, and the interpretation of transferences is an interpretation of the feeling. The interpretation of transferences was believed to lead to far-reaching behavioral changes.

However, Freud realized (1910, 1919) that the passive attitude is not necessarily the choice method with regard to all types of mental disorders. He admitted that in the treatment of phobias and compulsions, direct intervention proved to be necessary. Thus, definite modifications in psychoanalytic technique were introduced, but unfortunately no new interpretation was offered concerning the nature of the interindividual relationships.

Further clinical experiences called for additional amendments in psychoanalytic technique. New problems faced the analyst with the growing attention to character neuroses. Reich (1945) pointed to the transference peculiarities of certain neurotics who seem to accept their neurosis and develop a "protective armor" of character neurosis.

The sociopathic personality and sexual perversions also presented challenges to Freud's technique of handling transference. Modifications in the technique (Fenichel, 1945, Chapter 23) have proved that Freud's method, developed chiefly in the treatment of hysterics, is not a rigid procedure to be followed blindly in all cases.

The treatment of psychotics created new problems. While the manic-depressive psychosis required only partial changes in the psychoanalytic technique, schizophrenics were practically inaccessible to psychoanalysis. Abraham (1911, 1924) suggested modifications only in the initial stage of work with manic-depressive patients; afterwards, the usual psychoanalytic technique was believed to be the choice method because the nature of transference phenomena in manic-depressive psychosis is similar to those in hysteria.

Hysteria and related disorders have been the bedrock of Freud's concept of transference. However, the fact that transference is a *sine qua non* for psychoanalytic treatment has sometimes created insurmountable problems. The overgrowth of transference neurosis has been a major factor in analysis' becoming interminable (Freud,

1937). It is no wonder that the demand to keep transference under reasonable control led to modifications introduced by Alexander and French (1946) and to the idea of "corrective emotional experience."

Corrective Emotional Experience

Alexander and French believed that treatment is a profound emotional experience and that what occurs during its course is more than transference. Though the patient relives in transference the emotional involvements of his childhood, the mere reliving cannot be healing. Past emotions must be reexperienced in a setting that enables their correction. Thus "corrective emotional experience" must be offered to the patient.

This experience must be geared to the patient's needs: a rigid everyday schedule may not be appropriate for some patients. Alexander maintained that in many cases, less frequent interviews were just as productive as the classic procedure with daily sessions.

At propitious moments the analyst may manipulate the frequency of analytic interviews or recommend a temporary interruption of treatment. In some cases, as for example, with acting-out patients, it may be necessary to increase the frequency of the interviews in order to develop a more intense transference relationship. This encourages a tendency toward identification with the analyst, who then has an opportunity to exert a restraining influence on the patient's impulses. Frequently, however, especially with those patients who use analysis as a substitute for life experiences, it is better to reduce the frequency of the interviews or to set a tentative termination date for the analysis. Owing to these experimental manipulations, dependency on the analytic situation becomes a focal issue. The patient may discover that he can manage quite well without the analyst, and soon a more permanent separation may be recommended. Preparatory interruptions were found to be an excellent means of gauging the proper time for terminating the treatment. Alexander, French, and some of their colleagues at the Chicago Psychoanalytic Institute learned that the emotional reaction to previous interruptions is a more important clue than such criteria as recollection of infantile memories or the depth of intellectual insight. In cases when, during interruptions or reductions in frequency, feelings of yearning for the analyst become more intense upon returning to the analysis or upon increasing the frequency of the interviews, the patient may be able now to verbalize those feelings and thus gain greater insight into the nature of his dependent strivings. It is insight based on emotional experience, especially with regard to the transference, that is the aim of these strategems. (Selesnick, 1967)

Corrective emotional experience implies flexibility in the analyst's attitude toward the patient. A patient whose parents were discouraging, hypercritical, and derogatory needs a corrective emotional experience with an encouraging, noncritical, and respecting analyst. The analyst must somehow convey to the patient a friendly, encouraging, and respectful attitude, offering not only insight but also *support* to the patient's emerging ego. He must enable the patient to relive the past in a new and corrective setting so that there is no reason to seek secondary gain and escape into neurosis.

The Widening Scope

Alexander's ideas inspired new developments in psychoanalytic technique; some of them will be briefly described. In 1954, Stone published a seminal paper "The Widening Scope of Indications for Psychoanalysis." According to Stone, psychosomatic and psychotic elements in a patient's personality reduce the prospects of success in classical psychoanalysis, and addictions and perversions require far-reaching modifications in treatment methods. In all cases, the therapist must take into consideration, in addition to transference, the realistic, here-and-now patient-doctor relationship (Downey, 1983).

In the same year, 1954, Rangell defined psychoanalysis as "a method of therapy *whereby* conditions are brought about favorable for the development of transference neurosis in which the past is restored in the present in *order that . . . .* there occurs a resolution of that neurosis (transference and infantile) *to the end* of bringing about structural changes in the mental apparatus of the patient to make the latter capable of optimum adaptation to life."

In 1963, S. Tarachow published *An Introduction to Psychotherapy* which advocated a close-knit system of psychoanalytically oriented psychotherapy. According to Tarachow, the therapist must not attempt to uncover and analyze all unconscious infantile conflicts, and must prevent excessive regressive manifestations of transference. Tarachow recommended direct support of the patient's ego and superego, frank discussion of the patient's problems of daily life, and active participation in the patient's life decisions.

Over the years, several modifications have been suggested by psychoanalytically oriented therapists. Langs (1976) introduced the concept of *bipersonal field* which includes the physical conditions of the analyst's office, the overt behavior of the patient and the analyst, and their interaction, as well as other modifications in the analytic technique. Zetzel (1965) introduced far-reaching deviation from the passive approach of "evenly hovering attention." She recommended that the analyst *verbally* respond to the anxiety and lack of self-esteem of the patient. The works of Kernberg (1976), Blanck and Blanck (1974), and Kohut (1971) and numerous articles in Wolman's *International Encyclopedia of Psychiatry, Psychology, Psychoanalysis, and Neurology* (1977b) and in the *Progress Volume of the Encyclopedia* (Wolman, 1983) bear witness to the awareness of mental health theoreticians and practitioners of the necessity of keeping up with sociopsychological changes and adjusting their treatment methods according to the needs of their patients.

Interactional Treatment of Transference

Transference phenomena are not limited to a doctor's office. Transference is a common state of *reliving past emotional experiences.* People often repeat past errors and act as if the present situation were a replica of a past situation. A man may fall in love with a girl to whom he ascribes the physical and mental traits he ascribed in childhood to his mother. A man may transfer his oedipal hate from his father to his superiors in the army or on a job. Preference for colors, fashions, odors, music, people, and places is frequently a product of transference.

Whether one experiences likes or dislikes on a transference or nontransference basis, the likes and dislikes affect one's here-and-now behavior. Here-and-now behavior includes transference and non-transference phenomena. Transference is but a fraction of the totality of human interaction. Human interaction is a multilevel process: some elements of human attitudes are rational; some are not. Some attitudes are dictated by present needs and circumstances, while others are residues of the past. When a patient expects instinctual gratification in psychotherapeutic situations, it is mainly because he has transferred his infantile wishes onto the therapist.

I believe that all kinds of human relations, called "object relations" by Freud, represent cathexis or an investment of one's emotions in the other person. However, while Freud was concerned with the person who cathects, I have developed an additional concept which takes into consideration the person who is at the receiving end of cathexis. Thus, instead of using the term "cathexis" as described in classic paychoanalysis, I deal with the concept of "interindividual cathexis" which represents the emotional load directed by one person toward another and received by the other person. When a mother loves her child, the mother is cathecting her sublimated or neutralized libido in the child, and the child is on the receiving end. The way the child feels about this, and how he perceives the mother's love, are highly important factors in his emotional balance and personality development.

Psychotherapeutic interaction is also a process of interindividual cathexis. Patients cathect their emotions in the therapist, but the therapist cannot be unaware of the fact that the patients are investing some of their emotions, positive or negative, in him. However, since the nature of this cathexis differs for different clinical types, the psychotherapist must not deal with all the cathected processes involved in transference in the same way. Alexander and French (1946) maintained that transference *should be* regulated, but I would say that *it is always wittingly or unwittingly, regulated by the analyst.*

Every psychoanalytic treatment is, as Fenichel (1945, p. 447) put it, "based on the analyst's influence on the patient." I suggest that this influence be made explicit and that therapists become *aware* of the nature of their influence, for no matter what their point of view is, they always regulate transference. They regulate it by imposing the "basic rule," by suggesting or not suggesting the reclining position, by asking or not asking how the patient is, by smiling or not smiling, and so on.

Several years ago I observed interindividual processes on a closed ward in a mental hospital. Although my policy was one of strict nonparticipant observation, my very presence on the ward influenced the behavior of the patients. In the one-to-one relationship, everything affects the patient and influences the transference irrespective of the therapist's intentions.

Marmor criticized the classic approach. He wrote: "The original theoretical dictum that an analyst must be a shadowy, neutral, impersonal, and a value-free figure is coming to be recognized not only as a practical impossibility, but even as being in some instances at least of questionable therapeutic value?" (Marmor, 1960). My contention is that since no therapist can be "shadowy, neutral," etc., *he should be aware of what he is and what he is doing.* Instead of influencing by default, I prefer influencing in a rational and planned manner. Instead of a purely intuitive approach, I suggest a carefully chosen therapeutic strategy related to the three clinical types and to the five levels of deterioration.

Freud's difficulty with schizophrenics compared to Federn's success with them is a case in point. The insistence on a reclining position facilitated topographic regression; this regression was promoted even more by the "basic rule" of free association; and finally, the analyst's remoteness and silence contributed to the schizophrenic tension and withdrawal. No wonder Freud believed that schizophrenia is a nontransference disorder (Freud, 1915-1917). Federn, however, who admitted schizophrenics to his home, witnessed the most profound transference (1952).

My contention is that, wittingly or unwittingly, psychotherapists manipulate transference. Even the most passive psychoanalysts and nondirective Rogerian therapists exercise a profound influence on their patients, and even nonparticipant-observation affects the behavior of the individuals observed. The very presence of another person cannot be unnoticed, especially when the observing person is expected to offer psychological help and to relieve anxiety, tension, and pain. The impact of the observer on the observed is an accepted fact in contemporary physics, and it is certainly an unmistakable and unavoidable fact in psychological interaction.

My conclusion is self-evident: instead of denying the obvious and implicit facts, wouldn't it be more rational to accept them and put them to therapeutic use? Why not control the phenomena of transference? Why not consciously manipulate them instead of letting them follow an unpredictable and not always useful path? Why allow them to go deeper than necessary for successful therapeutic interaction and, thereby, lead to unnecessary regression and infantile dependence on the therapist which postpones and, in some instances, prevents the successful conclusion of psychotherapy?

Transference is part of here-and-now behavior. The patient relates partly on the basis of past experiences, partly to the real situation. His demands for instinctual gratification are mainly transference: they represent a reactivation of his past infantile wishes. However, an adult patient is not an infant. He is an adult who pays for therapeutic services, and his demands — rational or irrational — are part of the here and now.

In the process of treatment, the therapist is never truly passive. His very presence, his age, sex, looks, manner of speech, and certainly his sparse comments are interactional phenomena. They are powerful factors in shaping the patient's feelings, thoughts, and actions, partially in transference and certainly in the realistic part of the patient's attitudes.

Thus, whatever goes on in therapy is a process of interaction. It is always an *exchange of cathexes,* perceived correctly or misinterpreted by the patient and sometimes also by the doctor. The silent analyst may be perceived by his patients as a taciturn or unfriendly individual, who is, pretends to be, or tries to give the impression of being an omnipotent figure. If the analyst really tries to impress, it is his countertransference blunder. Nevertheless, whatever he tries to do and whatever he says or does, there is always interaction.

Working with a great many hypervectorial (schizo-type) patients, I have noticed how easily they become overcathected and overinvolved in the transference. Some of them worry about the analyst the way they used to worry about their parents. They notice the slightest change in the analyst's voice; they notice whether he looks pale or suntanned; they worry about his future; they would like to take care of him. On the other hand, hyperinstrumental narcissistic psychopaths don't worry about the analyst at all; they worry only about themselves. Being narcissistic, they display strong paranoid tendencies and are almost unable to develop positive transference. They often display a demanding and exploitative attitude toward the therapist. They expect him to take care of them and are very surprised or disappointed that he charges them for his work. Most often, they develop negative transference and blame the doctor for their misfortunes or lack of achievement. The dysmutual depressive type, whether on the neurotic level of hysterics or the psychotic level of manic-depressives, displays ambivalent transference phenomena. The moods of these individuals swing from one extreme to another, and they love and hate their analyst. When they think the analyst loves them, they are elated, cheerful, and full of love. When they don't believe so (and they usually don't), they develop a gloomy, aggressive, hostile attitude toward themselves and the analyst. Quite often, manic-depressive patients threaten to commit suicide, hoping that this would elicit the doctor's compassionate love.

Apparently, the *treatment of transference* must be adjusted to the particular type of patient and manipulated to produce the best results. There are no foolproof methods of dealing with transference. One of the main aspects of interactional psychoanalytic psychotherapy is individualization, that is, dealing with each case as if it presented a totally new situation never witnessed before. Of course, the therapist must deal with transference within the framework of the clinical types described in Chapter 4 and must also take into consideration the life history of a particular patient. In addition, one should remember that transference does not represent the totality of interactional relations in psychotherapy.

What is happening in psychotherapy is a series of libido and destrudo cathexes in which both the patient and the therapist participate. Therapists cannot escape the fact that they may like or dislike their patients, but they must *control* their countertransference feelings for otherwise they are guilty of a violation of professional ethics. Therapists must be aware of the fact that they do not react in the same way to all people, and the awareness of one's shortcomings makes one a better therapist. The psychotherapist must bear in mind that if transference is allowed to go astray, one risks the treatment's being interminable. The psychoanalytic or any other psychotherapeutic process that encourages transference must not permit the transference to become the overwhelming element of treatment; transference must be regulated, modified, increased, or decreased, according to the therapeutic goals of a particular interactional process, the personality of the patient, and the personality of the therapist.

On several occasions, in supervising or teaching younger colleagues, psychiatrists and psychologists, when I have demonstrated how I deal with certain cases, I have warned them that they should not emulate me because they are not me and their patients are not my patients. Certainly one can learn from other people by following ideas and general patterns, but in all kinds of therapy, two individuals interact — the patient and the therapist. The fact that they are two distinct individuals and not just statistical cases must never be forgotten during the process of treatment.

No human being can avoid being somewhat influenced by what is going on in relationship to other people. Some patients display flattering love for the therapist; some patients show resentment and even hatred. One of the main duties of the psychotherapist is always to be aware of what is going on and never to be carried away by his emotions. A psychotherapist who assumes that he is a godlike creature and, driven by megalomania, thinks that in response to a patient's flattery or seductiveness, he should bestow upon that patient the grace of his personality, is violating the fundamental rule of any psychotherapy. A responsible psychotherapist gets involved with the *case* of a patient for this is his moral obligation to society and to the person who seeks his help; however, under no circumstances must the psychotherapist become involved with the *person* of the patient.

I have heard, on occasion, from some of my colleagues that sexual involvement is good for their patients. Perhaps it is good for the therapist, provided the patient is a good sexual partner, but I don't see any reason to assume that sleeping with the therapist has more "therapeutic" value for the patient than sleeping with anyone else. No one has ever proved that sexual intercourse as such is a healing device in mental disorder.

Treatment of Dysmutuals

Transference, as a repetition of past cathexes, greatly depends on past interindividual experiences. I have been trying to make this issue more explicit and to explain it in terms of the concept of three clinical types. The hyperinstrumental type represents self-hypercathexis and object hypocathexis of libido; the hypervectorial type is based on self-hypocathexis and object hypercathexis of libido; the dysmutual swings from one extreme to the other.

Freud's description of transference, given in 1920 in *Beyond the Pleasure Principle*, fits the dysmutual type of neurosis (conversion hysteria, etc.).

Loss of love and failure leave behind them a permanent injury to self-assurance in the form of a narcissistic scar, which . . . contributes more than anything to the "sense of inferiority." The tie of affection, which binds the child as a rule to the parent of the opposite sex, succumbs to disappointment . . . .

Patients repeat all of these invented situations and painful emotions in the transference and revive them with the greatest ingenuity. They seek to bring about the interruption of the treatment while it is still incomplete; they contrive once more to feel themselves scorned . . . . None of these things can have produced pleasure in the past . . . . But no lesson has been learned from the old experience of these activities having led instead only to unpleasure. (Freud, 1920, pp. 22-23)

This repetition compulsion is undoubtedly a universal phenomenon, but not all neurotics repeat the same behavioral patterns. This description of rejected love is typical of dysmutuals.

It seems that noninvolvement is the best way to handle this type of transference. The dysmutual neurotic quickly develops positive transference. He or she falls in love with the allegedly omnipotent and benevolent parental figure. The therapist's attentive attitude is perceived as keen interest by the patient who, in turn, responds with glowing love to the meager signs of approval. The therapist does not criticize the patient no matter what the patient says. The true parents, especially the mother of the hysteric, were highly critical of the patient. Only when the patient was very ill or in great danger did the parents show any affection. The dysmutual dreams of the "lost paradise," when he or she was one with the mother, and tries to recapture it by self-defeat. As long as dysmutuals believe they are loved, they reenact in transference the oral love for themselves, the analyst, and everyone else.

Dysmutuals easily swing from positive to negative transference. As long as they imagine that the analyst loves them, they experience a blissful euphoria. Most symptoms disappear, and the analytic hours become, as one of my patients put it, "the happiest hours in one's life."

However, this imaginary love does not suffice for long. Pretty soon, dysmutuals begin to demand more attention, more love, and more tangential proof of love for them. A male hysteric who developed a homosexual crush in transference demanded an increased number of sessions and the right to call me several times a day. A young woman complained: "You are nice to all your patients. But I am not just a patient. I love you. Why can't you make me happy?" A male patient said, "I know that you are a homosexual. Why can't we?" A learned female patient assured me that "active" psychoanalysts slept with their patients.

The dysmutuals' love turns easily into hate: object hate of the analyst and self-hate. The libido recedes and the destrudo takes over. Dysmutual patients either hate the analyst (interindividual cathexis of destrudo) or hate themselves (intraindividual cathexis of destrudo), or both. "I know you hate me, you detest me, you cannot stand me," said a 28-year-old female hysteric. "You are right. I hate myself too. I know I do not deserve to be loved," she said with a charming smile.

Woe to the therapist who lets himself be drawn into the treadmill of the emotional ups and downs of a dysmutual patient! The detached, objective, matter-of-fact treatment of transference, combined with an incisive interpretation of resistance and transference used as a resistance, is the choice method of treatment.

Treatment of Hypervectorials

The peculiar difficulty in working with hypervectorial neurotics lies in their excessive resistance. One of the motives for resistance is a strong need for punishment, associated with masochistic wishes. This unconscious need for punishment corresponds to a piece of aggressiveness which has been internalized and taken over by the superego.

Freud (1933) wrote:

> We are in doubt whether we ought to suppose that all aggressiveness that has turned back from the external world is bound by the superego, and so used against the ego, or whether a part of it carries on its silent sinister activity as a free destructive instinct in the ego and the id. Probably there is a division of this kind but we

know nothing further about it. When first the superego is set up, there is no doubt that the function is endowed with that part of the child's aggressiveness against its parents for which it can find no discharge outward on account of its love fixation and external difficulties; and for this reason, the severity of the superego need not correspond to the severity of its upbringing. (p. 150)

Further on, Freud (1933) wrote:

People in whom this unconscious guilt feeling is dominant distinguish themselves under analytic treatment by exhibiting . . . a negative therapeutic reaction. In the normal course of events, if one gives a patient the solution of a symptom, at least the temporary disappearance of the symptom should result, with these patients, on the contrary, the effect is momentary intensification of the symptom and the suffering that accompanies it. It often needs only a word of praise of their behavior during the cure, the utterance of a few words of hope as to the progress of analysis, to bring about an unmistakable aggravation of their condition . . . . Their behavior will appear as an expression of an unconscious sense of guilt, which favors illness with its attendant suffering and handicaps. (pp. 150-151)

A passive attitude and nonparticipant listening to free association on the part of the therapist, certainly do not constitute the choice method of dealing with hypervectorial neurotics. Such an attitude produces too much anxiety and may, therefore, foster serious topographic regression. Silent and passive listening may be perceived by hypervectorial neurotics (obsessive, phobic, and neurasthenic) as a rejection. They do not protest against rejection; they tend to accept it as well-deserved punishment. One cannot cure a masochist by rejecting him. Freud recommended *active interpretation and direct influence.* As soon as transference is established, the analyst must induce the phobic patient to modify his phobic overt behavior prior to the resolution of the underlying unconscious motives.

Negative transference can turn into resistance. The hypervectorial neurotic is *afraid* to give up his defenses, especially the compulsions and phobias. Compulsions and phobias serve as a protection against the patient's own hostile feelings toward his parents, reenacted in transference. "I am afraid I may hurt you," said a 28-year-old patient. "I feel like doing something very bad. I better control myself before I do something I will regret."

Hostility requires a thorough interpretation; otherwise, the patient may repress it and turn it inward. The patient's fear of his own hostility might result in prolonged periods of arid silence that resemble the stuporous attitude of catatonics who fear to say and do the wrong thing. The expression of hostility must be encouraged, but the need for interpretation and working through of hostility is not limited to hypervectorials.

In the process of treating hypervectorials, a passive, detached attitude on the part of the therapist will unduly prolong the treatment and, perhaps, make it interminable. The therapist must be vectorial, that is, genuinely friendly, but must not transgress the professional role or violate the ethical and professional rules of frustrating the patient's instinctual demands. He must never fall into the trap of countertransference and become a copy of the incestuous, seductive or seducible parent. A moderate, aim-inhibited interest in the patient's well-being is necessary. Such an attitude of friendliness and respect for the patient will help to increase the patient's self-esteem and improve the intraindividual balance of libido cathexes (cf. Wolman, 1966, p. 197).

The dictatorial, overdemanding, irrational superego of hypervectorials must be reshaped. Its irrationality must be exposed, and the ensuing severe guilt feelings must be interpreted and worked through. The armor of resistances has to be taken apart before any significant progress can be made.

The best method for handling the exaggerated accusations of the superego is to support the ego. Hypervectorial patients tend to ascribe to the therapist the role that their parents played and their superego continues to play, and the therapist may soon discover that these patients ascribe dictatorial and punitive tendencies to him. A continuous checking and rechecking to test reality is necessary to support the ego and counteract the patients' deep-rooted tendencies toward rationalization, projection, and displacement.

It is necessary to *prevent* too deep a transference in all hypervectorials, especially in the more severe cases. The more outspoken the therapist is, the smaller are the chances for a deep transference. When a hysteric showers the therapist with personal questions, either the therapist does not respond or he analyzes the patient's curiosity. However, when a frightened obsessive neurotic or latent schizophrenic poses the same questions, frank and honest answers seem to be advisable. The patient's questions "Are you married? Do you have children?" and so on, should be answered in a matter-of-fact fashion. There is no reason to surrender to countertransference and confide in the patient, but a clear-cut answer can keep a patient close to reality and reduce the danger of too vehement a transference.

Treatment of Hyperinstrumentals

Suffering is the main motive for seeking professional help. Small wonder that hyperinstrumentals (sociopaths) rarely seek help. They have little reason to, for they rarely suffer severe inner conflicts; as a rule, they make others suffer. Being highly self-cathected, these individuals may occasionally suffer from hypochondriacal fears, anxiety states caused by erupting id impulses, or inferiority feelings stemming from defeat or frustration. They may also seek secondary gain by assuming a sick role or wearing the mask of innocent victims of misfortune. When they come for help, they seek immediate results and are prone to break off the therapy as soon as they feel better.

In some Veterans Administration hospitals, hyperinstrumentals have become hard-core cases who resist any therapy. They prefer staying in the hospital and continuing a parasitic life. One of my sociopathic patients used to hospitalize himself frequently with a variety of imaginary physical illnesses. Whenever he faced difficulties in business or in marital life, he escaped into illness. He came to me for treatment to "get something out of it" and to "get the right guidance." Of course, he bragged to whomever he knew that he had serious mental problems and was undergoing psychoanalysis.

The sociopaths on all five levels are not inclined to invest their libido in anyone and their transference, if any, stays shallow. Whereas I recommend prevention of too deep a transference in hypervectorials, the crucial task with hyperinstrumentals is to foster as deep a transference as possible and mollify their negative transference. Needless to say, hyperinstrumentals hate whoever frustrates their wishes for immediate gratification.

Manipulation of transference in these cases is not an easy task. Hyperinstrumentals learned in childhood to defend themselves against rejecting, absentee, or overindulgent parents. In any case, the pre-hyperinstrumental has never had the opportunity to identify with either of his parents. Although hyperinstrumentals are usually aggressive, they perceive themselves as defenseless, innocent children. This attitude colors their oral-aggressive transference in psychotherapy.

One patient spent hour after hour directing the most malicious accusations at me. Whatever wrong had been done to her by her parents (truly or in her imagination) was ascribed to me. She expected retaliation on my part, which of course never came. Her amazement at the lack of hostility was, as Alexander would put it, "a therapeutic corrective experience."

Another patient described his fantastically ingenious deceits and frauds. "Everybody does it, don't they?" he asked. His father and mother had been exceedingly permissive, but the outer world was less permissive; he was caught and punished. He believed that the world was hostile to him and developed paranoid fears.

Whoever treats sociopaths cannot stay neutral. Normality includes social adjustment, and a reasonable balance of inter- and intraindividual cathexes: it includes a balanced love for oneself and others, as well as a balanced criticism of oneself and others. A rational superego is an indispensable part of a healthy personality. Thus, the therapist faces a complex task. Silent permissiveness may be misinterpreted as siding with the id. An expression of disapproval by the therapist is not good either, for this may lead to the inclusion of the therapist in the paranoid picture of world conspiracy against the poor, innocent patient. The therapist must take a stand and help in developing the patient's superego, but he must wait till the transference is sufficiently strong. Interpretation must wait until the patient is ready to accept it, and even then, firmness must be combined with caution. An exceedingly passive intervention, or one which is too early and too active, may lead to a breaking off of treatment.

THE FREQUENCY OF THERAPEUTIC SESSIONS

Freud saw his patients six times a week, but in the United States, even orthodox Freudian psychoanalysts see patients no more than five times a week. This reduction in the number of sessions has nothing to do with psychological issues; it was simply determined by the five-day week in American factories, offices, and schools. Moreover, even the five-session-per-week schedule has been challenged for practical and psychological reasons. First, very few people can afford to pay for five sessions a week; second, very few people need them. Several psychoanalysts, most notably F. Alexander, (1948) have introduced the idea of a flexible number of sessions. Too frequent sessions deepen the patient's transference and thus unduly postpone the conclusion of psychotherapy.

I believe that in many instances frequent sessions might be contraindicated. The aim of all psychotherapeutic procedures — Freudian, behavioristic, or any other — is to bring therapy to a successful conclusion within a reasonable time and with as little cost as possible. It has been my experience that two sessions a week are adequate in the vast majority of cases. However, when patients are dangerously suicidal or severely psychotic, I have seen them initially as much as seven times a week; then, as they improve, the frequency of therapeutic sessions is gradually reduced. In some instances, I have felt that even once a week was sufficient to produce adequate results.

RESISTANCE

Quite often, I have had the impression that patients' nonverbal communications have delivered the following message: "My dear Doctor Wolman, what the hell do you want from me? I attend our sessions regularly and promptly pay my monthly bills. I even talk to you and tell you many interesting stories that have little to do with why I am here. I don't feel like talking about what really bothers me. It is painful. Please, leave me alone. It is nice to come to a friendly guy who is willing to listen to me and I would like to come here forever, but don't ask me to talk about unpleasant things, okay?"

Apparently, the existence of pus inside a human body is less frightening than surgery that will let the pus come out, and the fear of pain is often stronger than the fear of disease. Many people who are aware of their emotional problems refuse to seek help. To seek help implies the admission of one's own weakness, and many people prefer the illusion of power and refuse to accept the fact that they need help.

It is easy to accept the fact that one cannot be one's own farmer, builder, or shoemaker and that one needs their cooperation to get food, lodging, and shoes. It is not too difficult to accept the fact that one cannot fill one's tooth cavities or cure one's diseased eyes or lungs. Most people have no qualms in admitting their apparent physical weakness and their occasional need for dental or medical care, since in these cases they can still retain the belief in their own powers while admitting a temporary and partial weakness.

This reasoning is hardly applicable to seeking psychiatric or psychological help. Psychotherapy implies an admission of one's overall inability to run one's own life. Small wonder that many people deny the need for help and that when, convinced by friends or relatives, they finally agree to see a psychiatrist, psychologist, or psychiatric social worker, they unconsciously resist the help that is offered to them. It is certainly easier to sit in a dental chair and let the dentist do the job or to lie on the physician's examination table and let him do his work. The psychotherapist asks: "Please tell me everything that comes into your mind, pleasant or unpleasant, relevant or irrelevant. Tell me everything that crosses your mind, and do not withhold anything at all."

Nothing seems easier than compliance with this simple request — yet patients find it difficult and resist it. Freud compared resistance to a "demon" who refuses to come to light because to do so might mean his end. Patients act as if they were afraid of letting their thoughts flow freely, and in most cases, they obstruct the process of treatment. Apparently, resistance is a fight against being cured, based on the fear of becoming a mature adult. People do not easily relinquish their infantile hang-ups.

There are altogether five types of resistance (Freud, 1915, 1919; Glover, 1955; Spotnitz, 1967):

1. Repression resistance
2. Transference resistance — repressed materials being reenacted instead of being recollected
3. Resistance aiming at secondary, or epinosic, gain
4. Id resistance — dictated by repetition compulsion
5. Superego resistance that originates in the need to be punished

Repression Resistance

Resistance is a process of intraindividual cathexis. The same inhibitory forces of ego or superego that acted as anticathexes and repressants are reactivated as resistances in the psychoanalytic process. *Present resistance is a continuation of past repressions.*

Resistance can take almost any form and shape: failure to verbalize in free association, periods of prolonged silence, breaking appointments or coming late to them, acting out impulses, blocking memories, and antagonistic reaction to treatment are the most frequent signs of resistance. Patients resist by producing hosts of long, foggy, and involved dreams that belabor the same theme; by discussing their problems with outsiders; by producing nonsensical associations; by being irritable and hostile to the analyst; and so on.

In repression resistance, the patient may forget most recent events. He may be unable to free associate, or the associations may go in every possible direction, thereby preventing a continuous flow. The patient may even accept the therapist's interpretations and apply them to everyone except himself.

Unresolved resistance can bring about a stalemate in analysis. Obsessive-compulsive patients will continue to overelaborate insignificant details, while other types may ruminate interminably. Each clinical type — indeed each individual — displays a variety of resistive patterns related to the level of fixation, the type of disorder, and the patient's life history.

Transference Resistance

Transference is both the greatest help and the greatest obstacle in all kinds of psychotherapy. In negative transference, the patient views the therapist as an unfair, unloving, rejecting parental figure, and accuses him of all past parental injustices and rejections. The patient becomes irritable and hostile, looking for errors and unfairness in the psychotherapist.

Positive transference, however, can also erect stumbling blocks on the road to cure. The enamored patient requests special attention. At the peak of positive transference, the patient is interested not in the treatment of his or her neurosis but rather in obtaining love from the therapist. Transference-love may be mild and easily controllable, but it can also be vehemently acted out. Quite often it is sexual love. The therapist must transform the acting out of past feelings into a recollection of them. In some cases, the patient may substantially deteriorate, as if to prove how much he still needs help. Some patients refuse to improve so as to be able to continue their visits to the beloved parental figure.

Epinosic Resistance

Mental disorder is most often an *escape* from the hardships of adult life into an imaginary haven of protected childhood. *Neurosis is a regression to the role of a child and, thus, offers some morbid gains.* These gains can be either primary (i.e., effecting an alleviation of inner tensions and anxiety) or secondary (i.e., achieving social approval and sympathy).

Resistance may be epinosic and aim at the perpetuation of secondary gain. The patient may wish to stay neurotic and win all the sympathy and consideration that can possibly be wrung from the sick role. The patient may not like his headaches, nausea, depression, and other unpleasant symptoms, but the bittersweet taste of being pitied is not readily renounced. Epinosic resistance occurs frequently at the beginning of treatment and in the final stage, when the patient is expected to grow up and to abandon infantile modes of emotional life.

Id Resistance

The id blindly follows the constancy principle, and what has happened once tends to be recapitulated. Repetition compulsion is one form of resistance and a very stubborn one. The stronger the resistance, the greater is the inclination to repeat rather than to recollect. Id resistances cannot easily be lifted because they hinge on the basic rules of unconscious behavior, namely, the constancy and pleasure principles. A prolonged process of working through is needed.

Superego Resistance

Guilt-torn patients resist cure because, unconsciously, they wish to suffer. These patients feel that they do not deserve a better lot and passively surrender to what they believe is well-deserved punishment. This pessismistic outlook about the self and the feeling of one's own worthlessness form serious stumbling blocks to treatment.

Quite often, patients introject the true or imaginary superego of the analyst and identify with it. Glover (1955, p. 65), in *The Technique of Psychoanalysis,* maintains that this is one of the most common causes of stalemate in analysis. The patient assumes that the analyst condemns him, and a silent resignation to what he believes is a justified rejection destroys the patient's motivation for being cured and presents a formidable obstacle to psychoanalytic treatment.

Dealing with Resistance

As a rule, patients are unaware of the fact that they are resisting. They came to be cured, and they cannot believe that by their behavior they intend to sabotage their treatment and recovery. In transference resistance, the patient's love or hate has been misaddressed. Neither the therapist's charm nor the lack of it has anything to do with the patient's feelings: these would have been the same with another doctor.

Thus, the interpretation of resistances must come first, even before the interpretation of transference and the neurotic conflict itself. Unless resistance is overcome, interpretations will fall on deaf ears.

It must be stated clearly that no cure can be obtained without the resolution of resistance. The handling of resistance requires skill, precision, tact, proper timing, and individualization. All resistances cannot be resolved in the same way. For example, resistances coming from the id cannot be handled directly. The only way of handling them is through a prolonged "working through," which will be discussed later on. Repression, superego, and epinosic resistances can be resolved by lifting the lid of repression. This can be accomplished at the peak of resistance, when the patient's resistive behavior can easily be brought to his attention and recognized for what it is.

Freud was aware of the necessity of adjusting the technique to the type of disorder. In his critique of a "wild" analysis he wrote: "My impression was that the lady in question was suffering from anxiety-hysteria, and the whole value of such nosographical distinctions, one which quite justifies them, lies in the fact that they indicate a different etiology and different therapy" (1910e).

Psychoanalytic technique developed mainly in the treatment of conversion hysterics. Hysterics, as a rule, oscillate between positive and negative transference attitudes toward the analyst. Both attitudes, encouraged by the passive-receptive attitude of the analyst, allow the patient to reexperience his neurotic conflict in the analytic situation. The resolution of resistances, the reconstruction of the past, and the interpretation of the unconscious conflict relived in transference constitute the appropriate method of treatment.

In some cases, resistance leads to acting out and demands the immediate gratification of emotional needs. Sometimes acting out takes place outside the sessions, and some patients act under momentary impulses. At this point, a radical change in the life situation of a person is rather inadvisable, and crucial decisions should be avoided while the whole motivational system is undergoing far-reaching changes. Rush decisions may be simply an acting out of infantile impulses and, as such, may represent resistance. The therapist's task in this case is not to sit idly and watch, but to offer insight and, whenever necessary, even guidance.

INTERPRETATION AND INSIGHT

Freud's early technique was a logical sequence of his topographic theory. The unconscious represented sexual drives pushing toward gratification. The conscious censorship represented the forces of self-preservation. The conflict between sexual drives and self-preservation, or the repression of sexual desires, constituted the cause of neurosis. The task of psychoanalysis was to depress the repressed material and to offer a rational solution to the conflict. Thus, reconstruction and interpretation of the past were supposed to offer a resolution of infantile conflicts and a better integration of personality.

The success of interpretation depends on *timing.* Too early an interpretation may evoke the patient's resistance; in some instances, it may be so alarming as to make him discontinue treatment altogether. In other instances, it may bring relief too soon and reduce the patient's motivation for being cured. In still other cases, an early interpretation can arouse the patient's curiosity but have no effect on his emotional life.

The question of *what* to interpret was never answered by Freud in a final manner. Bernstein (1965, p. 1179) pointed to nine distinct areas of psychoanalytic interpretation; these involved the patient's (1) dreams, (2) free associations, (3) symptoms and symptomatic behavior, (4) behavior during the analytic sessions, (5) behavior outside the analytic sessions, (6) past experiences, (7) attitude toward the psychoanalyst, (8) past and present relations with other people, and (9) overall style of life and personality makeup.

Psychoanalytic interpretation plays a dual role. In regard to *topography,* interpretation transforms unconscious into conscious and helps it become integrated into the preconscious-conscious system. The second task of interpretation is *economic,* that is, pertaining to the balance of cathexes. Repressed material is, topographically speaking, unconscious, but at the same time it carries an emotional load of libido or destructive energy. Interpretation by means of verbal symbols may modify the direction of cathexes and neutralize impulses. The ego operates with symbols, and it is capable of binding and neutralizing great amounts of hitherto blind, id-seated energy. To talk about impulses and to understand them are great steps toward their neutralization and control.

However, the idea that cure could be obtained through making the unconscious conscious suffered several setbacks. Even when the patient became convinced that his symptom was rooted in a certain past experience, and even when the interpretation of dreams and other unconscious material brought about correct reconstruction of the past, cure was not forthcoming. Some patients showed considerable intellectual grasp and comprehension of the psychoanalytic theory, but this did not make them well. Certainly insight into one's own mental state is of more help in treating mental health problems than is the understanding of one's teeth or gums in dental treatment, but ultimately something else is needed to produce both mental and dental cures.

As Freud moved away from an intellectualistic bias, digging out the unconscious and making it conscious remained an integral part of his technique; its value, however, became dependent on emotional factors linked to the structural theory and to human interaction. In the paper "The Handling of Dream Interpretation in Psychoanalysis" (1911), Freud tried to cool the enthusiasm of his disciples for dream interpretation. Sometimes patients bring to analytic sessions more dreams than could ever be interpreted. Some patients may even use their dreams as a resistance. Dreams are merely a part of the unconscious life, and there is no magic cure in their interpretation. The interpretation of dreams should follow the same rules as the interpretation of any other material brought by the patient, but interpretation as such cannot single-handedly effect a cure.

Only for a while did psychoanalysis suffer from a sort of intellectual bias, and only at the beginning did Freud fail to distinguish the patient's awareness of past experiences, regained in the process of free association, from the analyst's comprehension and interpretation of the repressed material. Freud had to work through his entire psychological theory before he arrived at the conclusion that neither insight nor abreaction was crucial in psychoanalytic treatment. Ultimately, dealing with transference and resistance became the cornerstone of the psychoanalytic method.

Even before the introduction of the structural theory in 1923, transference and resistance had become the backbone of psychoanalytic technique. Interpretation and insight retained their usefulness, but only in conjunction with the treatment of transference and resistance.

The interpretations given by Freud and orthodox Freudians remained scarce, and occasionally periods of silence occurred. The interactional technique does not allow silence; the therapist should encourage the expression of thoughts and emotions, comment whenever necessary, and never abandon the patient to a feeling of loneliness and lack of concern.

I believe that silence on the part of the therapist is itself a sort of interaction, often perceived by patients as indifference or even hostility. Psychotherapy must always be encouraging and supportive, and the active participation of the therapist in the therapeutic dialogue should serve this purpose.

Interpretation of Dreams

In a great many instances, dreams convey unconscious wishes and fears, and the interpretation of dreams can therefore be of considerable help in psychotherapy. One patient of mine, the 29-year-old Mr. Z., had a serious sexual problem. Whenever a woman turned down his advances, he had a good and lasting erection, but when a woman was receptive, his erection disappeared instantly.

He told me the following dream. He was much younger in his dream, probably a child. He was in a harbor watching a ship leaving for a cruise. A king was departing, and the general feeling was that the king would never come back. The queen stood on the shore crying, for she knew the king would be gone forever. Suddenly, the dreamer felt that it was up to him to console the abandoned queen, and this thought was very disturbing.

The meaning of the dream was quite obvious. The patient's father was personified by the departing king, and the queen represented his mother. The dream conveyed the oedipal wish to get rid of the father and possess the mother, and the disturbing fear of incest. The interpretation of this dream proved helpful in overcoming Mr. Z.'s sexual problem. The dream was followed by several other dreams in which the girls he dated looked like (or somehow resembled) his mother and the fear of incest caused a rapid loss of erection. It took a while before the patient was able to function normally in sex, but the interpretation of his dreams was of great help.

Another patient Ms. W., a 30 year old, reported considerable difficulties in her dating behavior. She was quite attractive and lovely, and was very popular with men. She was, however, in a state of acute anxiety whenever a man tried to embrace her and kiss her on the mouth. She was in a state of severe panic when her dancing partner held her close and she could feel his erect penis.

Ms. W. denied ever having any sexual relations whatsoever. She said she was a virgin and maintained that she would have her first intercourse with a future husband, provided that therapy could help her to overcome her anxiety. She assured me that she had never seen a penis and planned to go to the public library to look up an anatomical atlas.

Her story was rather strange. She admitted to me that in childhood she had often seen her father in underwear, but she had somehow managed never to see his sexual organs. She also took care of her baby brother who was eight years her junior. She dressed and un-dressed him, and even took him to the bathroom and gave him a bath, but she could not remember ever looking below his belly.

One day she told me the following dream: she was a little girl and she was stretched out naked on a bed or a sofa. Suddenly, a Christmas tree grew over her body; all the lights on the tree went on, and her underbelly got wet. The message of this dream was quite obvious: the tree represented erection; then someone ejaculated and wet her underbelly. I decided to delay the interpretation of the dream. Ms. W. described more dreams, and her dreams became more vivid and more transparent. In one dream, she was sucking a big fat pencil. In another, she was playing with her hands with a heavy stick attached to two wheels.

One day, she told me that she had developed some itching in the pubic area and was going to see a doctor. When she came to my office the next time, I could hardly recognize her. She was no longer exuberant, lively, and talkative. Her eyes were red from crying, and her face was wrinkled. She looked like someone severely ill or gravely injured.

She wept for a while, then said, "You knew it all the time, didn't you? You never believed me, am I right, Dr. Wolman? I asked the doctor, 'Am I a virgin?' Guess what he said? 'Who are you kidding? You are not a virgin for God knows how long – 15, 20 years?' "

Apparently, she had been raped in childhood, and this had gone on for years. In dreams that followed, she recalled someone giving her candies and threatening to kill her if she told her mother about them. Finally, she dreamt about a sailor. In free association, the sailor was a salesman – a traveling salesman, her own grandfather.

She recalled that as an 11- to 12-year-old child, she had often stayed with her grandparents. Her grandmother held a regular day-time job and was never home. Her grandfather was a traveling salesman who was often at home, and who forced on her a variety of sexual experiences.

Dreams of Borderline Cases

A cautious interpretation of dreams is often useful in unraveling unconscious and disturbing problems. There are, however, many cases in which there is no need to dig deep into one's unconscious. In fact, when there is a weak personality structure, especially on the latent psychotic or even more manifest psychotic level, extreme caution is recommended.

In some cases, the interpretation of dreams might be inadvisable or even dangerous. When unconscious, morbid wishes are piercing weak defenses, interpretation could bring about a total collapse of personality structure and turn a latent schizophrenic into a manifest one. Interactional psychotherapy implies gradual improvement by substituting lesser symptoms for more dangerous ones. In some cases, helping a manifest schizophrenic to become a hypervectorial neurotic may be all that can be accomplished. My policy has been *one step up,* for in many instances, supporting neurotic defenses may prevent further deterioration and psychotic breakdown.

The main aim of interactional psychotherapy is to strengthen the patient's weak ego. In neurosis, the ego is struggling against undue pressures from within; the *ego-protective,* neurotic symptoms bear witness to this struggle. In psychosis, the ego has lost the battle, and psychotic, *ego-deficiency* symptoms develop, such as loss of reality testing (delusions and hallucinations), loss of control over unconscious impulses, deterioration of motor coordination, and so on.

Therapy aims at strengthening and reestablishing the defeated ego. The therapist must never become part of the irrational transactions of the psychotic mind, be they delusions, hallucinations, or anything else. He must never offer support to erroneous perceptions of reality. The therapist must not dig into the unconscious if this might undermine weak defenses and cause a harmful deterioration.

I did not interpret the following dream at all because I was afraid that an interpretation could lay bare an unconscious wish the patient feared might come true. An interpretation would have thrown this latent schizophrenic into a state of panic and possibly precipitated a psychotic breakdown.

The 40-year-old patient, the mother of two, dreamed that she was in a car with her sister-in-law, the mother of three, and that the car burst into flames. She did not worry about herself being burned, but about her two children who were playing safely on the lawn. The dreams of schizophrenics are usually lucid and apply classic symbols. Fire meant sex, in this case homosexual, and the patient worried about what would happen to her children if she gave in to her homosexual impulses.

A 30-year-old patient, who blamed himself for his father's poor health, told of having a dream in which his father is very, very ill, and no one wants to help. He badly needs an operation on his chest or he will die. The patient feels desperate; he is a little boy and does not know what to do, but everybody seems to expect him to perform the operation. So he does it, restrains various veins, and saves his father. However, he knows that he has done a poor and unsanitary job and that his father may still die.

Dreams of Schizophrenics

The dreams of schizophrenics may not require interpretation, for their content is obvious and sometimes devoid of symbols. Many patients have reported dreams of being beaten, raped, kidnapped, lost, rejected, left alone, and brutally assaulted. The fear of death is the prevailing theme of these dreams.

Schizophrenics often dream of neglecting their duties, forgetting to do things, missing appointments, failing to prepare homework for school, breaking things, and being blamed and accused for all kinds of transgressions and misbehavior. These dreams often represent their own aggressive impulses and fear of them. One patient had a dream in which she was supposed to watch lions in cages, but the lions broke loose and attacked people. The patient woke up screaming for help. Another patient saw reptiles and tried to fight them off in his dreams.

Dreams about wild animals, which usually represent their own sexual and aggressive impulses, frequently occur in latent and manifest schizophrenics. One patient reported the following dream about her hated stepmother: "My stepmother and father fought. Father killed her. I cut my stepmother into pieces, and we ate her. I woke up in horror, and I was upset all day. I must be a very mean person. I hate my stepmother, but it was terrible to eat her."

A 30-year-old patient dreamed about an infant's being burned alive. She woke up and felt that she was the child destroyed by flames. Another patient dreamed that people poisoned him. Another dreamed that someone came to strangle him. Still another reported a dream in which she was hiding behind several doors and a gorilla (her father) broke through and raped her.

Apparently, interpretation of the dreams of latent and manifest schizophrenics is contraindicated and, in some cases, actually harmful. For one thing, latent and manifest schizophrenics have an uncanny insight into their own dreams, and interpretation is unnecessary. My schizophrenic patients usually offer a correct interpretation of dreams themselves, thereby making any further comments superfluous.

I am very cautious in interpreting the dreams of schizophrenic patients, but I eagerly listen to them. The interpretation of dreams might be contraindicated in cases of latent schizophrenia and certainly in manifest ones, but the content of dreams is very valuable in diagnosis. The dreams of schizophrenics are usually transparent and point to what is going on in the patients' minds, and their content may offer the therapist valuable hints as to how to proceed in psychotherapy.

A schizophrenic's dream is usually a call for help. Its message reads: "Doctor, see what is going on with me. I am running away from real life because it is too frightening. But the world of unreality that I am escaping into is even more frightening. Please, help!" This call for help must not be ignored. The dream may point to a highly significant aspect of the disorder. It may also indicate an emergency, such as an intent to commit suicide.

In several instances, after listening to patients' dreams, I have adjusted my therapeutic strategy. Sometimes a dream has indicated that the patient was ready for a remission; in other cases, the dream has called for a slowdown in therapeutic intervention. In practically all cases, patients' dreams have forced me to rethink my therapeutic plans.

BEHAVIORAL COROLLARIES

Imagine a patient with a broken leg who has undergone surgery. Following the successful surgery, the patient uses crutches for a while, but after a certain time, the surgeon advises the patient to give up the crutches and begin to walk, slowly and cautiously, but without crutches.

The surgeon has done his job, but he cannot walk for the patient. The patient must practice walking; otherwise he or she will never regain normal walking ability. Successful surgery does not make one walk; the patient must exercise and walk in order to overcome inertia and fear.

Similarly, in psychotherapy, insight without implementation might become a futile intellectual exercise. I have frequently applied such reasoning in psychotherapy. I once had a patient Ms. S., a 35-year-old, highly intelligent woman. Ms. S. was afraid to use the subway. Needless to say, subways in New York City are neither the most comfortable nor the safest means of transportation, and certainly no one would advise a woman to take the subway at night. Ms. S. lived in Manhattan, but she worked in a distant part of Queens. She had to go to work early in the morning at rush hour and come back home late in the afternoon, again at rush hour. She had a car, but the traffic at these hours was exceedingly heavy and the trip took at least an hour and a half each way. Travel by subway was less than one-half hour, but Ms. S. could not bring herself to travel this way.

The fear of subways was not related to personal safety, for no one would attack her in crowded subway stations or in the more than crowded subway trains. Obviously, the fear of subways was not caused by real danger but was related to other, most probably unconscious, factors. Ms. S. wished to overcome the fear of subways which forced her to spend almost four hours every working day in bumper-to-bumper traffic, but she was unable to do so.

It took us a while to unravel the hidden motivation. Ms. S. was an obsessive-compulsive neurotic (that is, hypervectorial neurotic) whose compulsive behavior was directed toward controlling her intense anxiety and guilt feelings. She was a typical "over-demanded child" (see Chapter 2) who strove for mastery and perfection in all avenues of her life. She was meticulously dressed; her house was immaculately clean; and she was quite domineering, almost busy, in regard to other people.

In her striving for perfection and mastery, Ms. S. liked to drive for she felt that she controlled the steering wheel, the accelerator, and the brakes. Driving made her feel independent and superior, high above the pedestrian crowd. Subways frightened her; she felt she was becoming one of the crowd, a mediocrity, an insignificant passenger on the train. The minute the subway door closed she felt trapped, unable to stop the train and get out.

It took a great many sessions to cope with the need to excel, to be above everyone, and to exercise a total, albeit imaginary, control over her behavior. However, the resolution of her irrational striving for superiority (there will be more about superiority-inferiority in the following chapter) could not be completed without adequate reality testing in terms of actual behavior. Ms. S. had to apply in overt behavior her freshly acquired, realistic attitude. To use the surgical comparison, her leg was cured, and now was time to throw away her crutches and walk.

Despite her freshly gained awareness of the irrational need to always be in control, Ms. S. was still somewhat afraid to use the subways. She already knew that her fear was irrational and that driving back and forth from work every day cost her time and money. Now she needed behavioral experience to overcome the residues of her fear.

I asked her to go to a nearby subway station and call me on the phone. Of course, I praised and reassured her. I asked her to enter the subway, ride one stop only, and call me again from that station. She did it. We repeated the rides and telephone calls a few times, each time increasing the distances. Further encouragement became superfluous, and Ms. S. was able to take the subway whenever she needed.

I had more difficulty with Mr. A., a business executive whose new job required travel but who refused to fly. He simply could not force himself to go on an airplane; he would drive long distances, wasting time and money, missing appointments, and risking his prestigious and well-paid job. This was a serious problem which added one more burden to the man's shaky and depressive personality. The main complaint that brought him to my office was his lack of self-confidence which affected his sexual behavior and caused frequent loss of erection. It didn't take much time to discover the connection between his low self-esteem and self-confidence, and his sexual problem, but it took more time to discover that his fear of a plane crash was a symbolic representation of a loss of erection which he called the "collapse of the penis." The next step was behavioral: the patient was asked to take a shuttle flight from New York to Boston and back, and to call me from both New York and Boston airports for reassurance. We repeated the behavioral experience a few times until the patient was able to overcome his fears, and both his flight and his sexual abilities reached satisfactory levels.

In these two cases, as well as in all others, the patients' *motivation* was the crucial issue. Nothing could have been done without the patients' strong desire to solve their problems. As in all cases of psychotherapy, the patients' determination to get help and to solve their problems is the prerequisite for therapeutic success.

DIRECT GUIDANCE

As a rule, therapists must not tell patients what to do. Direct guidance implies the assumption by the therapist of the parental role and perpetuation of the patients' childlike dependence. The aim of psychotherapy is to help patients to assume full responsibility for their deeds and thus become mature adults. Guiding patients could hinder their growth and harm the psychotherapeutic process.

There are, however, times when direct guidance is absolutely necessary. It is certainly advisable to learn to swim before jumping into the ocean, but the lifeguard does not teach a drowning individual how to swim, he saves that person's life. A psychotherapist's task is to help patients to learn to swim in the stormy waves of life, but his first and foremost moral commitment is to protect their lives. A therapist who rigidly adheres to whatever theoretical rules he believes in even when he faces acutely suicidal patients is not only a stubborn fool but also an immoral individual who violates the ethical principles of his profession and of all civilized humanity.

On several occasions, I have been guilty of violating therapeutic rules, but in 40 years of clinical practice, no human being I have worked with has committed suicide. I have worked with several patients who harbored suicidal thoughts, some of whom were referred to me after one or more suicidal attempts.

On several occasions, I have had to persuade patients to seek medical help. The hyperinstrumentals (sociopaths) tend to overdo in seeking medical help; most of them are hypochondriacs, overconcerned with their health, who tend to visit their physicians frequently. The hyper-vectorials (obsessive-compulsives, phobics, and latent or manifest schizophrenics) tend to neglect their physical health. The dysmutuals (hysterics and manic-depressives) are highly inconsistent; they overdo and underdo seeking medical care in accordance with their swinging moods.

Over 40 years of practice, I have come across practically every disease possible and, I believe, have never neglected to refer an ailing patient to a competent physician. On many occasions, patients have argued that their ailment was psychosomatic. In all instances, my answer has been categorical: "I do not exclude the possibility that your symptoms are psychosomatic and therefore could be cured, or at least considerably alleviated, by psychotherapy. But neither you nor I am competent to make such a judgment. You must go for a thorough medical examination that will determine the nature of your problems. One must always give priority to a medical examination that analyzes the physicochemical aspects of the human organism before one can tackle the psychological aspects. I will not deal with your problem unless I receive a green light from an appropriate medical expert."

Usually patients take my advice. On several occasions, I have had to find the name of a highly competent specialist, make an appoint-ment for the patient, and ask the physician to send me a detailed diagnostic report. In some instances, I have developed a joint treat-ment program with the medical expert. When there has been nothing wrong with my patients' physical health, I have continued a usually successful psychotherapy of their psychosomatic symptoms: I have treated a nonexistent pregnancy, a psychosomatic skin rash, a phony heart trouble, and so on. However, when a patient has refused to go for a thorough medical examination, I have had no choice but to discontinue my work with that patient.

COUNTERTRANSFERENCE

Psychotherapists, like all other human beings, go through the wear and tear of life: they may fall in love and be disappointed; they may be physically ill or suffer car accidents; they may lose somebody dear to their hearts; and they may react like all other human beings. However, one expects that even in their personal lives, therapists should be at least as mentally healthy as the patients they have cured, which means that they act like rational human beings. They should be able to maintain rational and self-controlled reactions, irrespective of the upheavals they have experienced. A therapist who carries his personal troubles to his office does an injustice to his patients; thus, one of the main criteria for a good therapist is a strong ego, which implies an objective, calm, realistic attitude. Severely disturbed people drown in their unconscious. A good psychotherapist is like a good diver; he should be able to join his patients in their unconscious journey, but he should always come back. He must be able to empathize, that is, be capable of receiving nonverbal messages from his patients.

It is certainly not easy to maintain equanimity in the face of emotional onslaughts. Expressions of love are flattering; expressions of hatred hurt and offend. The professional obligation of the therapist toward his patient is not to react to the patient's emotions but to interpret them.

Freud warned the analyst:

> The analytic psychotherapist thus has a threefold battle to wage — in his own mind against the forces which would draw him down below the level of analysis; outside analysis against the opponents who dispute the importance he attaches to the sexual instinctual forces and hinder him from making use of them in his scientific method; and in the analysis against his patients, who at first behave like his critics but later on disclose the over-estimation of sexual life which has them in thrall, and who try to take him captive in the net of their socially ungovernable passions. (1915, pp. 171-173)

In order to help others, the psychotherapist must be able to control his own impulses. Holding countertransference in check and preventing any personal involvement with the patient are ethical and professional prerequisites for clinical practice.

Most people are sensitive to criticism, and enjoy praise and admiration. It is not easy to be exposed to the nagging criticism of a patient in the throes of negative transference. Many young therapists who are not sure of their competence take criticism poorly and often accuse themselves of failure. The fear of being hated looms as large in countertransference phenomena as the need to be loved. As mentioned in Chapter 2, the therapist's unbalanced personality may interfere with his work, making him sensitive to the patient's positive and negative transferences, and disrupting the required objective, professional attitude. Thus, successful completion of personal psychotherapy is a necessary prerequisite for analyzing other people.

Several years ago I supervised a younger colleague who had completed his postdoctoral education and started private practice two years before. I was seeing him once a week. This young colleague, Dr. C. developed a bad case of pneumonia and had to be hospitalized. A few weeks after he left the hospital, he came for the usual supervisory session and told me the following story:

> As you know, I was gravely ill. I could have died. Last week I decided to gradually start my practice, and I have seen only three patients. One of them was the young guy Joe. I felt he needed me desperately, and I called him first. I still felt shaky, but I believed that I owed it to him. And guess what he told me at the first session? He had a dream, and he saw me dead in his dream! Imagine, my first thought was to help him, and he wished me to drop dead!

At this point Dr. C.'s voice sounded as if he were crying. He was quite upset by Joe's obvious lack of gratitude and what he believed to be hostile attitude.

Dr. C.'s reaction seemed to me to be a case of countertransference. I calmed him down by saying, "You should be very pleased. Joe wishes his father to drop dead and in the dream you play a paternal role. This was a useful expression of negative transference, which invited a thorough interpretation and working through. You should learn not to confuse your fear of death with the patient's emotions."

7

The Analytic Phase

The principles of therapeutic strategy discussed in Chapter 6 apply mainly to the first phase of interactional therapy. This phase is called *analytic* for two reasons. First, it is mostly concerned with problems treated by classic psychoanalysis and its offshoots, while the second and the third phases go beyond the hitherto known treatment methods. Second, this phase *analyzes* the etiology and symptomatology of mental disorders, and its aim is to remove the stumbling blocks that prevent the attainment of psychological maturity. If a neurotic could be defined as a person who lives in the past, the main task of the analytic phase should be to help him or her to *overcome the past.*

The interactional approach to mental disorders requires both causal and teleogical investigation, for whatever human beings do has past *causes* that are followed by *effects,* and whatever human beings do is done for a *purpose* (whether or not they are of that purpose). Neurotic and psychotic symptoms have their causes, most of which have been described in Chapter 4. However, the symptoms also serve a certain purpose in the patient's life, of which the patient is usually unaware. The therapist should help patients to understand their behavior in terms of what they are doing, the reason for their doing it (*why*), and the purpose for which it is done (*what for*). This brings us again to the problem of interpretation and insight.

Some patients, especially highly educated ones who read psychological or psychiatric literature, tend to use interpretations as resistance. They like to intellectualize and try to engage the psychotherapist in theoretical discussions related to true or imaginary causes of their difficulties. Unfortunately, the understanding of causes does not necessarily remove their effects. A hyperinstrumental sociopath remains a sociopath even when he realizes that he was a rejected child; a hypervectorial schizophrenic does not improve as soon as he understands that his parents were overdemanding; a dysmutual depressive is not cured simply by the awareness of parental inconsistencies.

The question *what for* is, therefore, more relevant than the question *why*. The therapist must be aware of what *caused* (why) a particular set of symptoms (see Chapter 4), but it is more important that the patient become aware of the *purpose* (what for) of this particular behavior. The following case descriptions will illustrate my point of view.

A young woman Kathy M. was referred to me by a physician who unsuccessfully tried to cure her frequent spells of throwing up. When she entered my office, she politely remarked that she might throw up and perhaps I should remove my carpet. I felt that removing the carpet could invite her to throw up. I reassured her that the small carpet was old and that I did not mind replacing it with a new one. My words apparently had a soothing effect on her, and Kathy sat down in the armchair facing me and told her story.

I am 28 years old. My sister Helen, who is three years younger, married last year. She is a beautiful girl and very popular with men. She is my parents' favorite. They always set her as an example. I was a sickly child; maybe that's why they didn't like me. I knew I always gave them a hard time. Parents prefer happy and healthy children like my sister Helen, don't they?

Doctor, I always had an eating problem. My mother is a very impatient person. When my sister married and left home, my mother started nagging me. She called me an old maid! You know, my mother is old fashioned. Now my parents have introduced me to a son of their friends. George is a nice guy, but he is 40, a widower, and they force me to marry him. I am scared of marriage. My mother is such a competent person. You should see our house! How can I be like her? I am not ready for marriage! Doctor, believe me, I can't stomach this! I can't! I wish I could; I force myself to be nice to George, but when he touches me I feel like throwing up!

Kathy belched but did not vomit. She cried. She looked at me with the look of a beaten child who calls for help. I worked with her to overcome her feeling of inadequacy. I saw her twice a week for a while. She never threw up in my office.

Dysmutual depressive patients act in a self-defeating manner. They make themselves miserable in the unconscious hope that their misery will be rewarded. Psychosomatic disorders (in Kathy's case, gastro—intestinal disturbance) are their means of escape from difficulties they believe they cannot manage into much worse troubles. It took a while before Kathy realized the purpose of her throwing up. She was, unconsciously, regressing to her childhood gastrointestinal problems which had not affected her for 20 years. Her fear of failure in marriage made her escape into a psychosomatic disorder aimed at evoking her mother's compassion.

A few years ago, a 35-year-old man Mr. Otto N. was referred to me by his mother. The man somehow managed to fail in every possible way. The question was what he really intended to accomplish by his skillful avoidance of accomplishments. His father was a rather un-successful college professor, a conceited and despotic individual, who looked down on his wife and could not tolerate the achievements of his gifted son. As long as the little boy brought home straight A's from elementary school, the father did not pay much attention to him and, occasionally, boasted to friends and relatives about his son's good marks. However, as the boy grew older, the father became more and more envious of him. Whenever 11-year-old Otto opened his mouth at the dining table, his annoyed father ridiculed and/or harshly rebuffed him. Soon Otto could not say anything without inviting his father's criticism and ridicule.

Otto learned to keep silent and not to share with his parents the wonderful things he learned in junior high school about science and society. He noticed his father's disapproval of his high marks in school. "What do they know, your stupid teachers," the father used to say, "if they give good marks to you?"

Since getting good marks invited his father's anger, getting bad marks became a way of escape. Otto's grades dropped sharply. His school attendance became spotty; his attention in class and his home-work were reduced almost to zero. His father seemed to be happy. He called Otto "dummy," but he did it in a cheerful, almost affec-tionate manner. Otto learned that failing in school and pretending to be stupid were his only means of avoiding his father's wrath. He soon saw that his mother followed the same policy: she was an intelligent and quite outspoken woman, but at the dinner table, either she was silent or she asked silly questions that enabled her husband to put her down and to receive such apparent pleasure from his self-aggrandizement.

Otto was an exceedingly bright, perceptive, and understanding man, but he did not dare to go to college — so he held a menial job. He came to my office, at his mother's insistence, two years after his father's death. His self-defeating attitude was an overstayed continuation of the past experience of avoiding his father's wrath.

THERAPEUTIC ALLIANCE

It is always easier to slide down than to climb up, and for many people it is both tempting and frightening to become mature adults who must make their own decisions and be responsible for their consequences. It is easier to go back, and be a child, dependent on parental care and protection. Regression comes easy; progression requires effort. Many people crave mother's love and wish to go back to the bittersweet helplessness of infancy. Some people act in a constructive manner most of the time and suddenly undercut their own efforts as if wishing to win their mother's love by failing. When they go for psychotherapy, they often offer strong resistance to being cured. Obviously, the handling of resistance is of prime importance in psychotherapy.

In many cases, the patients' complacency makes therapy more difficult. People unaware of their problem are not motivated to cooperate with the therapist, while people painfully aware of their difficulties are more cooperative and, therefore, improve faster. The patients' desire to change, to grow up, and to assume responsibility greatly contributes to successful psychotherapy. The patients' *motivation* is a highly relevant factor for it is exceedingly difficult and sometimes futile to treat patients who really do not wish to be helped. My policy in private practice is to refuse to work with patients who were forced by relatives to come to my office. Usually, at the first session, I make it explicit to the patient that both of us are entering an alliance. My commitment is to put all my knowledge, skill, experience, and efforts into my work with patients, but they are also committing themselves to full cooperation with me. Psychotherapy, unlike other healing processes, requires the active cooperation of both therapist and patient.

CUTTING THE UMBILICAL CORD

One of the main aspects of psychotherapy is to help patients overcome past problems and prepare to face present and future tasks. Emotionally disturbed people tend to regress to infantile modes of behavior that are totally inappropriate for their present situation. Their behavior resembles that of the man born in Alaska who migrated in his childhood to Texas. On a cloudy day in Texas, he puts on a fur coat despite the heat because in his childhood he was expected to wear a fur coat on cloudy days. Apparently, all mental disorders, with the exception of those caused by organic genetic or organic environmental factors, constitute an arresting or regression in personality development. They represent a failure to grow up and become an adult.

"Regression," Freud wrote in 1900, "plays a no less important part in the theory of the formation of neurotic symptoms than it does in that of dreams" (1962a, p. 548). Every human being goes through developmental stages from birth to adulthood; those who have not grown up or who have gone back are mentally disturbed.

> Owing to the general tendency to variation in biological processes it must necessarily happen that not all these preparatory phases will be passed through and completely outgrown with the same degree of success; some parts of the function will be permanently arrested. The usual course of development can be disturbed and altered by current impression from without. (Freud, 1915-1917, p. 297)

The past does not die; it is merely buried in the unconscious. It may come up in a haphazard, deformed, fragmented, and disguised manner in dreams. Chunks of the past could be revealed in free associations; huge chunks can be unraveled in hypnosis; some elements of infantile impulses, wishes, and emotions may suddenly surface in crisis situations. It is not always necessary to dig out forgotten traumas. As mentioned in Chapter 6, digging into the unconscious of a weak personality structure can cause the total collapse of a weak personality structure and lead to a psychotic episode. The therapist must carefully weigh (1) how much digging in the patient's past is necessary and (2) how deep one can safely dig without jeopardizing the patient's personality structure. Certainly, one must not use a bulldozer to remove a pimple.

The child in an adult person never dies, but it must not be in charge of the adult's life. Once in a while, on vacations, at a lively party, and so on, one may allow oneself to act in a childish manner. Ernst Kris pointed to such a relaxing "regression in the service of the ego." The regressing person acts as if one part of his personality has willfully regressed to a childlike, carefree behavior, but the other part actually holds the reigns and is in full control, capable of stopping the regression and restoring adult behavior. In alcoholics and drug addicts, such control is suspended and often totally lost, and the regression to a carefree, euphoric mood leads to irresponsible and self-destructive behavior.

The task of psychotherapy is to help patients to progress toward adulthood and to counteract infantile regression. Transference is a regressive phenomenon that facilitates corrective experience and the resolution of past emotional problems, but it must not be allowed to go haywire. Manipulating transference and preventing it from going too far or too deep, as explained in Chapter 6, greatly contribute to the success of psychotherapy. Inadequate transference does not provide an adequate climate for the recall and recollection of the past and the healing of past wounds, but too deep a transference may make the therapeutic process interminable. Transference should be viewed as a partial and temporary step backward that prepares the patient to take several steps forward toward mature behavior. Deep transference might substitute one umbilical cord for another.

SELF-DISCIPLINE OR SELF-DEFEAT

Newborn infants have no inhibitions. Their reactions are immediate, impulsive, spontaneous, and disorganized. They may respond with a mass reaction of the entire organism to a local stimulus. They are unable to exercise control over their impulses: they vacate their bladders and move their bowels instantly. They cry if they are in pain, scream in anger, and fall asleep when tired. Their mental apparatus, called *id* by Freud, operates on the principle of immediate reaction and total disinhibition, which Freud referred to as *Lustprinzip* (erroneously translated as pleasure principle). Actually Freud's *Lustprinzip* means lust principle, or the principle of urgent reaction and instant gratification.

In many instances (especially those observed by Freud many decades ago), parents imposed harmful taboos, restrictions, and inhibitions on their children. Quite naturally, some infantile inhibitions should be removed in psychotherapy, and patients should develop their own adult and rational inhibitions. Mature adults do not follow momentary impulses but exercise rational control over their behavior. They control their bladders and bowels; they do not cry or scream when upset; they weight their words and deeds; and they try to anticipate the consequences of their behavior. Their egos exercise control over their ids, and they apply the mature reality principle instead of the infantile pleasure principle.

The inability to control one's emotions and the impulsive acting out of one's wishes, whims, and desires are clear indicators of a weak ego; the weaker the ego, the more severe is the mental disorder. Neurotics may not be able to control their impulses in certain areas, and their lack of self-discipline leads to self-defeating behavior. Character neurotics tend to rationalize and justify their neurotic behavior, and latent psychotics may not be able to control it. Manifest psychotics are usually unaware of their self-defeating actions, and at the lowest level of psychological deterioration, one does not have any inhibitions whatsoever. Disinhibition does not lead to mental health but to psychosis, and those therapists who advocate disinhibition play havoc with their patients' mental health.

The first, analytic phase of interactional psychotherapy aims at the removal of infantile neurotic inhibitions and helps to develop the self-imposed inhibitions of adulthood that enable one to act in a rational manner. The second and third psychotherapeutic phases aim at perfecting the self-control that leads to a mastery over one's own life, thereby helping the patient to develop the courage to be himself and to make rational decisions. Overcoming anxiety states prepares the ground for self-confidence and the courage to live one's life the way one wants.

ANXIETY

Although the words "fear" and "anxiety" are often used interchangeably, it is useful to make a clear distinction between them. The physical reactions to fear and anxiety are similar and involve the autonomic nervous system, specifically its sympathetic part, which affects the activity of the gastrointestinal system, increases the secretion of adrenaline, speeds up the heart rate, and so on. However, *fear is an emotional reaction to a specific real or unreal danger,* such as vicious dogs or goblins, whereas *anxiety denotes a general feeling of impending doom.*

Fear is a *momentary* reaction to danger. It is based on a low estimate of one's own power compared to the power of the threatening factor. *Fear disappears with a change in the balance of power.* In the presence of an adult who is perceived by the child as offering protection, a child's fear will be allayed or obliterated. The disappearance of the threatening person, animal, or object puts an end to one's fear.

Anxiety, on the other hand, is a *general* and *lasting* emotional state that reflects one's feelings of weakness, ineptitude, and helplessness. Anxiety is tantamount to the loss of self-esteem, and it can paralyze one's life. If one anticipates impending doom, one may withdraw from people and from one's own usual activities, and become tense, irritable,and unproductive. Anxiety may even affect one's intellectual functions. The state of anxiety may make a person forget things he knows, stutter or stammer, and be unable to communicate his thoughts as if his mind had gone blank.

Anxiety results from an overall feeling of weakness and inability to cope with dangers. A frightened person feels he cannot stand up to a *particular* danger. An anxiety-ridden individual continually underestimates his ability to cope with life in general or at least with a great many situations. The presence of an ally and a familiarity with the situation do not resolve this feeling of uneasiness. Anxiety does not come from without; it comes from within, from the unconscious.

This distinction is especially significant in child psychology. A child who fears dogs may otherwise be a happy child, active and outgoing. His problem is a limited one, and whoever tries to help him can depend on the child's resources. Moreover, the sheer process of growth and development will increase the child's powers and faith in himself, and increased self-confidence may help him overcome his fears. An anxious child does not have an external problem; the problem is himself and his total personality. He feels insecure and most probably will carry the anxiety into adult years. An anxiety-ridden individual often acts like an anxious child.

Anxiety states are indicative of overall feelings of helplessness and worthlessness. Fear is a temporary reaction to danger. Anxiety is a prolonged state of tension and apprehension. Anxious people, who expect impending doom, become irritable and afraid to take the initiative.

Anxiety states are common to all types and levels of mental disorder, and dealing with them is very important in the analytic phase of interactional psychotherapy. The therapist must unravel their causes and arrive at a diagnostic evaluation. Anxiety states are indicative of feelings of one's own inadequacy and inferiority, and the resolution of these feelings should bring about a significant diminution in, and the eventual disappearance of, these nagging and paralyzing anxiety states.

Anxiety is the feeling that things will never go right and that no matter how hard one may try, defeat is inevitable. Anxious people predict defeat. They are, therefore, discouraged from productive effort for they assume that the future will bring more disappointment and more frustration.

One method of coping with anxiety is *testing reality*. Statements about the past and the present are either true or false, but statements about the future neither true nor false — they are sheer guesses. When a patient describes some future doomsday, I force him to examine his statements: "How do you know what will or will not happen?" It is rational to plan one's future and to act in a prudent manner, but both pessimists and optimists say things they cannot possibly know. Some of them see the future in bright sunlight because yesterday was sunny. Others expect a stormy life because there was a flood a year ago. Neither makes sense, and facing things as they are is one of the main prerequisites for mental health.

A patient of mine Dr. H., who applied for a teaching position in sociology at the City University of New York, expressed profound anxiety: "I made a mistake. I feel panicky. I don't know what to do," he said. "Who needs it? What for? I applied for a teaching position in City University — I worry they may reject me and I worry should they accept me. I am sure I'll make a fool of myself. The students will find out my ignorance and I will be exposed. Either way, I feel hostile. I better withdraw my application." Dr. H. had received his Ph.D. with distinction. He was a gifted young man, highly qualified in his field. His former professors wrote glowing letters of recommendation, and he had a good chance to be appointed to the faculty of the City University.

"Let's check all this against reality," I said. "We can't predict the future, but we can explore the possibilities. Should they turn you down, still there will be no reason for despair. There are more than 50 schools of higher learning in the metropolitan area. Were you the dean, you too would have probably chosen the best qualified candidate. If you are the best one, they will hire you; they may, however, hire someone who is a better qualified candidate. Should they turn you down, it is not rejection; one cannot lose what one has not got, and you will apply to other schools. In case they hire you, you will have several months ahead of you to prepare yourself. No one can predict the future, but one can do one's best to prepare oneself for what could be reasonably expected. There are no assurances for either success or failure, but a realistic appraisal of a situation improves the chances for success."

COGNITIVE FUNCTIONS

As explained in Chapter 1, a realistic appraisal of oneself and one's environment is the first, and most important, ingredient of mental health. Mentally disturbed individuals tend to over- or underestimate their own resources, to misjudge or totally distort the picture of the outer world, and therefore, to make decisions and embark on actions that are doomed to fail.

The denial of reality removes the motivation for change. As I mentioned earlier, when — in an initial interview — the patient tries to assure me that he has no problems but a relative or friend suggested he come to my office, I know that this will be a difficult case. The awareness of one's weakness is a sign of strength and augurs good therapeutic results, while the denial of one's weakness is a stumbling block that requires a good deal of therapeutic skill and effort to overcome.

No less important is the awareness of one's strengths. As will be explained in the next section, many patients are tortured by feelings of inferiority, and some of them cover up these inferiority feelings by making themselves believe they are superior. Testing reality and helping patients become aware of their potentialities are important tasks in psychotherapy.

INFERIORITY AND SUPERIORITY FEELINGS

Joy and sorrow are normal reactions to success and failure. As explained in Chapter 1, human emotions are normally appropriate to real situations: one feels great when his wishes come true and miserable when frustrated. Moreover, a great success elicits great job, and a minor failure evokes moderate sorrow. Every human being experiences these feelings in reaction to his or her victories and defeats, and fluctuations of mood are daily occurrences.

No one can always succeed and always be a winner, and anyone may lose several skirmishes but not lose the war of life. However, many people believe themselves to be losers, irrespective of their realistic situation, and suffer mild or severe feelings of inferiority. A feeling of inferiority is the source of anxiety and of depressive states. It is a feeling of weakness and inadequacy in regard to the tasks one believes one must face, and it affects practically all aspects of human behavior.

The hyperinstrumental (sociopaths) tend to perceive themselves as innocent victims of a selfish and hostile world. They feel entitled to use and exploit, to lie and cheat in what they believe to be self-defense. Many of them go further and act in an overtly hostile manner, and some of them resort to extortion and violence.

Hyperinstrumentals have no guilt feelings. They believe they are always right. One of my women patients physically assaulted her old mother, and the only thing she could say was: "You know, my mother thinks I am stupid and she can push me around. So I taught her a lesson. Now she knows who is the boss." Taking advantage of other people and using physical abuse give sociopaths a feeling of superiority. This proves to them that they are not helpless creatures, and they tend to boast about their victories.

Maturity is synonymous with responsibility. Responsibility means the willingness to do the things one wants and to accept the possible consequences. Most sociopaths do what they can as long as they believe they can "get away with murder." They usually believe they can do this, and they are often unaware that whatever one does will have certain consequences. They somehow assume that they can outsmart everyone and thus compensate for their basic feelings of inferiority. Psychotherapy with the hyperinstrumental (sociopathic) type is not an easy task. These individuals rarely seek psychotherapy, unless their deeds have brought them a good deal of disappointment or they have developed psychosomatic symptoms.

I once had in treatment a young businessman who was cheating his customers and partners, and who justified his actions by saying, "If they are so dumb as to allow me to cheat, they deserve it. It is tough luck!" I asked him whether he checked my monthly bills. "No," he said with a smile, "I trust you." "Well," I said, "I will tell my secretary to inflate the bills. If you don't check them, you deserve to be cheated. Tough!" "Doctor Wolman," he exclaimed, "I would lose all respect I have for you!" "Okay, and what do you think of my respect for you?" I asked.

When an adequately friendly relationship has been established, the patient's inferiority feeling and the need for antisocial compensation are gradually reduced, and the doctor's approval and respect help improve the patient's self-respect.

Hypervectorial obsessionals and schizophrenics are children of overdemanding parents who expected perfection. No matter how hard these children tried, they could not meet the exaggerated expectations of their parents. Small wonder that as adults they continue to wish to attain perfection and, in their dreams, see themselves as omnipotent heroes, demigods, prophets, or executioners. When they deteriorate and become manifest schizophrenics, especially of the paranoid type, they tend to act in a self-righteous manner which demonstrates their carved-for superiority and omnipotence.

Hypervectorial neurotics, character neurotics, and some latent psychotics set unattainable goals that give them the illusion of superiority. They view themselves as being above the rest of humanity because they, and only they, reach out to the stars. While they feel superior in their strivings, they feel inferior in their achievements, which inevitably fall short of their aspirations. Thus their strivings constitute a self-defeating device, for whatever they do, it is never good enough, and whatever victories they may have, they are always below the dreamed-of and unattainable great victories. The therapist should explain their superiority-inferiority game to them and help them understand it in the perspective of their parents' overexpecting attitudes.

The first rule in working with latent and manifest schizophrenics is that the therapist must offer *unconditional support* to them (Wolman, 1966). Unreserved support that is a positive emotional cathexis helps to improve the patients' intraindividual cathexis and increases their self-acceptance and their self-esteem. "There must be something good about me," a patient said, "if you think highly of me."

The second rule involves *ego therapy*. In neurosis, the ego is struggling against undue pressures from within; the ego-protective, neurotic symptoms bear witness to the struggle. In psychosis, the ego has lost the battle, and psychotic, ego-deficiency symptoms develop, such as loss of reality testing, delusions and hallucinations, loss of control over unconscious impulses, deterioration of motor coordination, and so on.

Ego therapy means the strengthening and reestablishment of the defeated ego. Thus, the therapist must never become part of the irrational transactions of the psychotic mind, be they delusions, hallucinations, or anything else. He must never offer support to erroneous perceptions of reality. The therapist must not interpret unconscious motivational processes if this interpretation could weaken the patient's ego.

Physical appearance and bodily cleanliness are important factors in one's self-image. Uncombed hair, untidy clothing, an unshaved face, and dirty hands foster the patient's feeling that he is what he deserves to be. Scratching one's own face or banging one's own head against the wall is a clear indication of an inadequate self-cathexis and a lack of self-esteem. The vectorial attitude of the therapist increases the self-love of the patient and reduces self-depreciation, for love and respect from without enhance love and respect from within. Gradually, improvement in a realistic self-appraisal will reduce inferiority feelings as well as the need to escape into dreams of superiority.

An inability to make decisions and the restraint of motor freedom are typical of the hypervectorial schizo-type disorders. One should not encourage a young painter to follow her need for free expression which would inevitably lead to a panic state. Nor would it be wise to enhance self-restraint that could produce unbearable tension. Thus, the best method is to foster self-esteem: with increasing self-confidence, the painter becomes less afraid to express her feelings on canvass, and begins to believe in herself despite her past experiences.

"One step up" is the third rule. It implies the support of less dangerous symptoms against more dangerous ones, while one keeps in mind that the ultimate goal is to strengthen the patient's ego. Schizophrenia is regression for survival. The psychotherapeutic interaction must make it unnecessary. It calls the patient back to life to growth, to joy, to normal self-protection, and to self-esteem.

Dysmutual hysterics, depressive neurotics, character neurotics, and latent psychotics frequently play the superiority-inferiority seesaw game. They are basically depressed. They feel unloved, undeserving of love, and angry at themselves for being unable to win everlasting and all-embracing love. They tend to put themselves down, belittle their own achievements, punish themselves for uncommitted sins, and resent the world for not loving them. However, their endogenous depression is a discontinuous process, and once in a while, an elated mood takes over, stimulated by a friendly encounter or without any outside stimulation. In their elated moods, these individuals believe in their superiority and bestow their love on themselves and on whoever is in touch with them.

The therapist's task is to reduce the dependence of these patients on approval from without. When a patient says, "I wish you would love me," I counteract the need to be loved by a cold, realistic remark: "What would you gain by my love? What would my loving you change in your life? Suppose you saw not me but another therapist — should he love you too? Why do you want only my love? How many people should love you? And think about it — what for?"

Sometimes gainfully employed dysmutual patients complain that their boss does not show affection. Apparently, their transference takes place wherever they are, and their unsatiable need to be loved produces profound feelings of inferiority with occasional outbursts of elation and superiority. The main therapeutic task is to shift from a need for interindividual cathexes to intraindividual cathexes and to increase the patients' love for themselves. As long as dysmutual patients depend on receiving unlimited quantities of love and affection from without, they may regress to their childhood behavior in which parental love was forth coming only when they were sick, injured, or in any other state of misery. Their masochistic tendency to win love by self-defeat presents considerable danger to their well-being and sometimes to their very survival.

There are three main ways of coping with these deep-seated feelings of inferiority and the occasional, flamboyant feelings of elation and omnipotence. The first method is reality testing. When a patient told me that he had "lost everything" in the stock market, I asked him whether he had enough money to pay his rent. Of course, he had not lost "everything" and was still a very wealthy man with a substantial, regular income. I have had similar experiences with many hysterics, and straight and blunt reality testing has always been therapeutically helpful. The second method applied to depressive moods is to point out the futility of self-defeating behavior, aimed at gaining compassion and love, in my office or anywhere else. The emphasis has been on fostering self-respect and self-cathexis. The third method involves counteracting the passive withdrawal that has inevitably fostered feelings of inferiority and helplessness. Encouragement of the pursuit of goals and of productive efforts contributes to a patient's self-esteem and reduces his dependence on love and approval from without.

REASSURANCE AND SUPPORT

Apparently one of the main tasks of psychotherapy is to support the patient's ego and its functions. The ego which has been battered and/or damaged by inner conflicts needs outside support that must be offered by the therapist. In hyperinstrumental sociopaths, the ego is, as it were, inflated by an abundant self-hypercathexis, and they are overconcerned with themselves. In hypervectorial neurotics (obsessionals) and psychotics (latent and manifest schizophrenics), the ego is impoverished by excessive object hypercathexes and inadequate self-cathexis; hypervectorials are overinvolved with others and underconcerned with themselves. Dysmutual depressives (hysterics and manic-depressives) go from one extreme to another. In addition, the therapist must consider which of the five levels of damage may have been caused to the ego's normal functioning: these are usually considered to be the neurotic, character neurotic, latent psychotic, manifest psychotic, and total collapse of personality structure (see Chapter 4).

Interactional psychotherapy *aims at strengthening the ego,* and the therapeutic strategy must be adjusted to the three types and five levels of mental disorder. At this point it is necessary to reintroduce the concept of *interindividual cathexis.* A lot of nonverbal communication goes on in psychotherapy, and the *therapist's attitude* is often more important than his words. Patients usually perceive the therapist's attitude, and vectorial, unconditional giving by the therapist is a most important source of interindividual cathexis which helps to restore the patients' intraindividual balance of cathexes. The therapist's friendly and reassuring attitude cathects (charges, invests) loads of neutralized libido. It makes patients feel accepted, and conveys the therapist's sincere concern for the patients' well-being and his determination to help them. It resembles the vectorial attitude of parents who care for their children irrespective of the children's good or bad behavior. However, unlike parents, the therapist must adjust his attitude to the type and level of disorder, and to the personality makeup of each individual patient.

Hyperinstrumental sociopaths tend to be suspicious of everyone including the therapist. On several occasions, sociopathic patients have accused me of being a selfish SOB who sides with their enemies, tries to take advantage of them, and at best, does not care. There were negative transference elements in these accusations based on their past experience, but there was also a good deal of here-and-now testing of the therapist's attitude and intentions. It is easy for a therapist to get hurt, insulted, or angry, but such reactions are clearly antitherapeutic. The task of the therapist is to help, even when those who need help act in an irrational manner. The therapist's patient and friendly attitude has a calming and disarming effect on sociopaths who expect to provoke an angry and rejecting reaction that would confirm their view of the world as a place full of enemies and, thus, justify their own enmity.

Hypervectorials on the neurotic, character neurotic, and latent psychotic levels doubt whether anyone is capable of helping them. They believe that it is *their* obligation to take care of others. Some obsessive-compulsive and schizoid character neurotics and latent schizophrenics have expressed concern for my health and well-being, as if it were their obligation to help me. Apparently, they did not care enough for themselves, and their self-hypocathexis and object hypercathexis were reenacted in overconcern for the therapist who was supposed to help them. The therapist's friendly and encouraging attitude supplies (if one may use this term) the badly needed inter-individual cathexes. The impoverished ego requires the replenishment of emotional resources, and unswerving support, respect, and reassurance constitute the main task of the psychotherapist with all hypervectorial patients.

Offering reassurance and support to dysmutual neurotics (hysterics) and psychotics (manic-depressives) entails certain risks since, no matter how friendly the therapist is, these individuals expect and often demand more than is appropriate for therapeutic interaction. Their childhood experiences of being usually rejected, but accepted when their misery was sufficient to elicit parental love and compassion, are often reenacted in the therapeutic situation. They usually exaggerate in describing their sufferings and quite often report nonexistent miseries. Some of my patients have started therapy sessions with a short "hi" and immediately embarked on a tirade about their "excruciating pain," "unbelievable suffering," and "bottomless misery." Others have boasted, as it were, of their true or imaginary misfortunes. A few hysterics have maintained that I had never encountered as difficult a case as theirs and have vociferously declared their "disease" to be incurable.

Woe to the therapist who allows himself or herself to be caught in the web of these unsatiable demands for love and affection. It is, therefore, necessary to state clearly the therapist's position when male or female patients ask the trapping question: "You don't love me, do you?" My answer has always been unequivocal. I say, "I care for you and your well-being. It is practically impossible to do what we are doing without liking one another, but I am not in love with you. My responsibility to you is to help you and not to please you."

It is also difficult to handle depressive self-hating moods. Depression can be *exogenous* if it is caused by real misfortunes such as serious disease, the loss of someone beloved, financial catastrophe, and so on. Such depression, if related to the patient's own neglect or error, presents quite a challenge in psychotherapy and requires a head-on, realistic appraisal of the situation and a rational search for remedies. *Endogenous depression* is not related to any true setback or defeat. Sometimes a patient says, "I know I have no reason to be so upset. Everything is fine — my personal life, my job, and every-thing else. I have no reason to complain, but I feel miserable. Every-thing bothers me and I don't know why."

There are no shortcuts in dealing with severe depressive moods. Simple reassurance does not work, and showing compassion makes the situation worse because if the doctor is so concerned, it must be pretty bad. The therapist's calm and steadfast attitude alone is reassuring because it shows that there is no reason for alarm. It also enables the therapist to apply the three methods described earlier for dealing with depression.

WORKING THROUGH

Once a man in his fifties called my secretary and said that his was an emergency case. It was hardly an emergency. The man was a business executive. In the morning, he had a meeting with his sales staff and they brought bad news. Suddenly he noticed that everyone was staring at him. He was shocked: he realized that he was sucking his thumb. He said, "Dr. Wolman, I read Freud. I know it's oral, or whatever they call it, but I'm still doing it. Fifty-two or fifty-three years ago my mother told me, 'Don't suck your thumb, you're a big boy.' It didn't help. My mother smeared my thumb with God knows what, but it didn't help. Twenty-five years later my fiancée told me she would not marry me if I did not stop this. So I stopped for awhile, but I do it again whenever I am upset. I know all the reasons for my thumb-sucking: my mother was a disciplinarian and did not allow for a sufficient amount of oral gratification; I was orally frus-trated and orally fixated and now orally regressed. So what? I know everything and I do it anyway. Today I was so embarrassed that I decided either you see me right away or I kill myself."

Obviously, insight is a relevant factor in treatment but certainly not a cure. Even if the patient obtains all the insight necessary and relives all his experiences in transference, the next step must be working through. Working through in psychoanalysis includes two fundamental tasks: the resolution of transference and the strengthening of the ego.

The resolution of transference is a prerequisite for the discontinuation of psychotherapy. As long as a patient is in the throes of transference, he will refuse to go away. If the therapist tries to dismiss a patient prematurely, the patient may develop a "miniature neurosis." Suppose the therapist worked with a patient for whatever period of time and decided that this was enough: if the patient was still involved emotionally with the therapist, the dismissal would only aggravate the symptoms. Transference is cathexis of libido and/or destrudo in a state of regression. If the patient still has so much emotion involved in the doctor and the doctor tells him to "go home," the patient feels rejected. Being rejected, he may go back to the only way he knows of forcing attention — by becoming more neurotic. He needs the therapist and forces him to offer therapeutic services. He is just like a child who cuts his finger to get mother's attention. The patient may go back to all the old symptoms. In my younger years, when I thought I was through with a patient, I would say, "Well, we are finishing next session." The patient would come to the next session with all the symptoms he had had two or three years before, at the beginning of therapy. Then what could one do with him? Sometimes, a patient has accused me: "You failed me; you never helped me. You see I have all the same symptoms: I bite my nails, I get depressed, I get migraine headaches — all the things I had before!" If the therapist does not know what to do, he feels horrible. Yet what is one going to do — start again from the beginning?

In order to avoid miniature neuroses and what Freud called "analysis interminable," one must not end treatment as long as the patient is still in the throes of transference. How does one resolve transference? The therapist should gradually interpret the transference phenomena: "You do this or that for this or that reason: you want to please me; you want to displease me. You try to fight with me as you did with your parents, but I am not your father or mother. Do you want to evoke my love and sympathy? What for? What do you need me for?"

The therapeutic process is a two-way street. On the one hand, we as therapists offer the interpretation. On the other hand, as unconscious conflicts are resolved, the patient has less and less need to depend on us. There is an additional dimension that must be considered at this point: the *dimension of power*. The patient versus therapist relationship must be viewed in the dimension of power. Transference, in addition to being cathexis in a state of regression, is also a *power relationship*. Someone whom we call "patient" looks up to someone whom we call "therapist." The patient assumes that the therapist has the power to help him. This is one of the most important reasons why therapists are not allowed to get involved with their patients. The patient should not be allowed to develop unrealistic ideas concerning the doctor and believe the doctor is God's gift to earth. Transference must be manipulated and must not be allowed to go wild. Transference must be kept within therapeutic bounds and used as much as necessary for curing a patient. In no case should the transference be allowed to become *the* neurosis of the patient, as sometimes happens in classical analysis. Transference, being always kept under control, must be resolved at a certain point. It is being resolved when the patient becomes more and more capable of using his or her own judgment, and less and less dependent on the therapist. The resolution of transference is, on the one hand, a conscious process on the part of therapists who offer sufficient insight and dispel the myth that they are parents, omniscient and omnipotent human beings. On the other hand, while the patient resolves his inner conflicts and becomes stronger, he has less and less need to put the therapist on a pedestal. The patient may notice that the therapist's hair is gray, that his shoes are not shined, that he sometimes look tired, and so on. In my case, I enjoy it very much when patients begin to notice that I speak with a foreign accent. It usually takes them a while to say this. As they discover more about the therapist, the patient-doctor relationship shifts from transference to a realistic relationship between two people. The patient who is a lawyer or a dentist knows much more about law or dentistry than we therapists can ever know in our lifetimes. He still believes that we can be of some help in his emotional problems, but the unlimited infantile admiration disappears.

The resolution of transference also hinges upon the strengthening of the ego, for the patient believes he is not capable of functioning independent of therapy. Let us briefly review the main functions of the ego. One of its main functions is reality testing, that is, finding out what is true or untrue, real or unreal. Frustration is a prerequisite of reality testing. When an infant lifts his hand, he becomes aware that it is *his* hand, for he can lift it. However, when he tries to lift the door or the table, he cannot do it so he learn to distinguish between me and "not-me," as Sullivan put it. The child learns to distinguish between his own wishes and the outside world. In the beginning, the child has an oceanic feeling − everything is me − and there is hardly any distinction between the self and the outer world.

Apparently, without reality testing which stems from frustration (i.e., from saying that "this is *not me,* and I cannot control it") and without acceptance of one's limitations, no one can ever become well adjusted. Reality testing implies accepting one's limitations for reality also includes one's self. The patient must learn to distinguish between wish and reality, to become aware of his limitations, and to use his abilities to their utmost. When the patient says, "I wish to make a million dollars," he is expressing a wish that he could act on and try to make come true. However, when he says, "I *have* a million dollars" and he doesn't have it, his reality testing is disturbed. Seeing things realistically, with no illusions about yourself or others, is one of the main elements of mental health. Reality testing is a very important function of the ego, and one strengthens the ego by testing reality.

Working through implies the resolution of conflicts which frees some amount of libido. I think of libido in quantitative terms, although I don't know how to measure it. I assume that every individual possesses some amount of mental energy, and I assume that this energy is derived from biochemical energy. At certain times and in certain moods, there is a distinct amount of mental energy in our systems. In neurotics, this energy is probably entangled in inner strife, in their inner conflicts and anxieties. When these are resolved, the person is more capable of using this energy in productive ways. Sometimes toward the end of therapy, patients become boisterous and overconfident. They don't know how to use their newly released energy and might get themselves involved in foolish adventures: they may marry the first person they meet or rush into divorce. At this point, one must invoke the *reality principle* which is a higher level of satisfying one's needs. According to Freud's structural system, the id operates on the lust principle, erroneously translated as pleasure principle. *Lust* is not pleasure; *lust* is urgency, grave need, urge. The id operates on the *lust principle,* which means that as soon as tension arises in the system, the tension leads to immediate action and immediate gratification of the need. The *reality principle* means pleasure without displeasure. The id operates on the principle of "do what you please, come what may." The ego says, "I'd better figure out the consequences. I will not take silly chances." The ego postpones gratification through reconsideration and thought processes. The reality principle is the opposite of the pleasure principle, because both agree with Freud's hedonistic philosophy of seeking pleasure and avoiding displeasure. However, while the id operates on the principle of immediate discharge of energy, with no attention to the consequences, the ego calculates. The ego may postpone gratification in order to get better gratification later. The ego may denounce gratification if it creates too much conflict or too many problems.

Strengthening the ego implies persistent application of the reality principle. A patient with an additional amount of emotional energy which has been released by the psychotherapeutic process is prone to do things that may cause him harm. Patients tend to act out their impulses because they have more energy. To use an analogy, it is like increasing the power of a car's engine without increasing the power of its brakes. People who have completed successful treatment have more powerful engines, but they need a proportionate increase in the power of their brakes. This is the process of working through. Patients must be ready to accept the consequences of their behavior. I usually ask them: "Do you really want this? Do you *really* want it? Is *this* what you wanted?" With these questions, one enters the second phase of interactional psychotherapy which will be described in Chapter 8.

The reality principle is the bedrock of a strong ego. A weak ego bypasses things. The egos of dysmutuals are sloppy, and they allow themselves to make mistakes that nobody else can do. They are careless. Mature people know what they are doing and are always in charge of their emotions. Their egos exercise full control, and they know that you don't start a war unless you have enough bullets in your gun and you don't get into a fight unless you know what you can gain or lose. Everybody can make errors, but if someone jumps blindly into a river without knowing how to swim, then his ego isn't strong enough.

There are more aspects to working through, such as neutralization and/or control of antisocial or disturbing impulses. For instance, what should be done with unwholesome sexual impulses, antisocial tendencies, and exaggerated demands or aspirations? Consider sex. According to earlier ideas, any sex unless it involved the union of the two sexual organs in the right way, penis going straight into vagina, was abnormal. Clitoral orgasm was believed to be infantile, and vaginal orgasm was considered the only normal thing. Many women were taught by their psychoanalysts − men − to believe that there was something wrong with their sexuality if they didn't reach orgasm upon insertion of the penis into the vagina. Oral sex was also believed to be perverse. There are many matters on which there is no uniformity of opinion, and people can lead their lives more than one way.

To offer direct guidance in these matters would be tantamount to imposing the therapist's private opinions. The task of psychotherapy is not to transform apples into oranges, but to enable patients to live in accordance with *what they are* and to play their cards best. All this leads to the second phase of psychotherapy − the *search for identity*. However, before we deal with this issue, a few remarks should be made about the treatment of female patients.

WOMEN AS PATIENTS

Freud was a keen observer and could not fail to notice that most of the problems that perplexed *his patients* were rooted in family life, related to the role of women in society, and most often experienced as difficulties in the psychological and physical aspects of sexual behavior. Undoubtedly, these were the most disturbing problems of Freud's time.

However, many so-called feminine traits are culturally induced behavioral patterns. In prehistoric times, when children were the main labor force, having numerous children was an economic device. A woman's task was to produce babies and take care of them; a man's task was to hunt, fish, fight, work, and provide food and protection. Motherly love and care were praised as feminine traits; courage and cunning, as male traits. While staying home, women were expected to mind the hearth, cook meals, and keep the house clean. Men were supposed to fertilize several women; thus, they were expected to be sexually aggressive. Women were supposed to attract the male sperm; thus, they were expected to be sweet, charming, and subservient. Women kept by men, whether in or outside of marriage, received every benefit as long as the men cared about them.

Apparently, women had no choice but to accept the passive role of charming girls, subservient wives, and caring mothers. They were brainwashed and conditioned to accept these social roles from their earliest days. Young men could go wherever they pleased and lead a life they liked, but a girl was her father's slave until he agreed to transfer her to her future husband. Though marriage was, in a way, the only means of escaping father's tyranny, the marital oath committed women to love, honor, and obey their new masters. Most women preferred new masters to old ones, and some of them managed somehow to outsmart their marital partners.

In the Victorian era, marriage was the only socially acceptable avenue for women. Unmarried women were ridiculed and blamed for remaining single. When a girl was unhappy being with the feminine role and preferred an active and independent life pattern, she was called tomboy, amazon, and masculine. When a woman refused to accept the three K's — *Küche, Kirche, Kinder* (kitchen, church, and children) — she was treated as an outcast. In Freud's time, masculinity and femininity were described as follows:

When you say "masculine" you mean as a rule "active," and when you say "feminine" you mean passive . . . . The male sexual cell is active and mobile; it seeks out the female one, while the latter is stationary and waits passively. This behavior of the elementary organism of sex is more or less a model of the behavior of the individuals of each sex in sexual intercourse. The male pursues the female for the purpose of sexual unity, seizes her and pushes his way into her. (Freud, 1931)

Freud did not invent *penis envy,* but he did recognize this phenomenon. Understandably, the more girls were restricted, the more they wished to escape the yoke by a magic switching to the opposite sex. Some of my female patients dream about switching railroad tracks.

One must, therefore, interpret penis envy in girls not as an envy of their little brothers or playmates, but as a wish for the possession of the large, fatherly penis and — with it — fatherly power. Penis envy is not a general and universal element of female psychology, but it should be perceived as a feminine protest against male domination. The penis, as the cherished symbol of power, was envied by women not because it was a sexual tool but because it symbolized freedom and power.

Today, some women wish to be men and some men wish to be women. Some of my male patients have dreams in which their wish to be a woman is clearly expressed. Female breasts appear in the dreams as a cherished possession, and penises and breasts are often confused.

My clinical experience suggests that neither men nor women can completely resolve their oedipal involvements, whether they be positive ones (with the parent of the opposite sex) or negative ones (with the parent of the same sex). Some residuum of the "first love" for the parent or the parental substitute seems to remain forever in almost all people.

While there is a good deal of evidence concerning the universality of oedipal involvement (though it is necessarily different in different cultures), one may doubt the universality of penis envy. Going through case reports gathered over 30 years of clinical practice in this country, I have arrived at the conclusion that penis envy occurred more frequently in the older generation of women who were brought up in traditional, father-controlled families with a clear male supremacy than in the younger generation who were brought up in families with tenuous or nonexistent supremacy of the father.

The male wish to be a woman was noted by some psychoanalysts a long time ago. Fenichel (1945) noticed that many men who are not homosexual at all identify with their mothers and later with their girlfriends. In some cases, feminine men deny that becoming a girl would mean the loss of the penis and try to stress the fact that they actually have a penis while acting as though they were girls; thus they are, as it were, girls with penises.

The gradually increasing incidence of *breast envy* requires further study, and anything said here would be sociocultural speculation. For instance, Terman and Miles found in the nineteen thirties that men are self-assertive and aggressive, while women are compassionate and sympathetic. However, these were the ideas of the thirties. Contemporary studies indicate that aggressiveness is not limited to one sex only.

In summary, the terms "masculine" and "feminine" are meaningless as long as they are indiscriminately applied. There are no "masculine" or "feminine" occupations. In France, Germany, and several other countries, teachers are predominantly male. In the Soviet Union, the majority of physicians are women. Men and women can be lawyers, mathematicians, elevator operators, mountain climbers, farmers, dentists, mailroom clerks, gynecologists, salespersons, psychiatrists, or even construction workers. Primary and secondary sexual traits have little to do with one's occupation, intelligence, tenacity, moods, and so on. Some individuals are more assertive or more subservient, more sick or more healthy, or more mature or more neurotic than other people, irrespective of sex. The whole idea of male or female personality traits is a heritage of bygone times when men owned, controlled, programmed, and brainwashed women.

Masculine and feminine identities are related to one particular aspect of life. It is absurd to call a quiet, well-adjusted man unmasculine because he does not act like an aggressive, boisterous adolescent or does not idolize cowboys and gangsters. It is no less absurd to accuse a woman of lack of femininity because she is a brilliant scientist, a shrewd businesswoman, or a gifted political leader. *Masculinity and femininity are limited* to the *exual and emotional aspects* of male-female interaction.

It is unwise to overgeneralize and assume that all human problems are related to sexual and procreative activities. On the other hand, it is also risky to overlook these highly important aspects of human life. Man and woman need each other, sexually and otherwise. They need to feel accepted and loved by someone of the opposite sex. They feel lonely if deprived of such companionship, and happy when they love and are loved.

The psychological differences between male and female behavior in courtship, marriage, sex, and parenthood are rooted in *biological differences* between the sexes. Reproductive organs, sexual cravings, menstruation, pregnancy and childbirth, breast-feeding, and menopause are not culturally induced. There are clearly observable differences in the mating and maternal behavior of male and female mammals, which are determined by gonadal hormones. In one experimental study with rhesus monkeys, androgen was administered to pregnant females and produced hermaphroditism. When faced with other females, they attempted mounting and insertion.

Research has failed to prove that human beings are born sexually dimorphic. There is no evidence that girls are born to be kind, considerate, and caring, and that boys are born competitive and belligerent. In human beings, the prenatal gonadal hormones do not determine future behavioral differences between boys and girls. Apparently, nature has ordained a major part of human gender-identity differentiation to be accomplished in the postnatal period. Gender identity is usually imprinted on boys and girls in their second and third years of life, and a considerable part of one's behavior is acquired in childhood. However, no man can learn the biological rhythms and functions of female organisms. Therapists should not overlook sexual problems or issues of psychosexual identity, but they must not assume that all emotional disorders are sex related (Wolman and Money, 1980).

8
The Search for Identity

The three phases in interactional psychotherapy are not separate entities. They overlap each other, for as soon as a patient has made significant progress in one phase, the issues related to the next phase come up. When the patient's ego gains strength and his grasp of reality improves, he begins to think realistically of himself and to look for the meaning of his life.

The analytic phase clears up emotional difficulties and enables individuals to embark upon a logical analysis of their wishes, thoughts, and deeds. Toward the end of the analytic phase, patients feel that they can do much more with their newly acquired energy which has been liberated from inner conflicts. They begin to crave self-realization and fulfillment, and they search for direction. What one is, what one should do with oneself, and what the meaning of one's life is — these are the problems to be dealt with in the second phase of psychotherapy.

Some therapists are satisfied with a mere removal of symptoms. Analytically oriented therapists go further and dig into the roots of the symptoms, hoping to prevent their recurrence. Interactional psychotherapy aims at *personality integration* which should enable individuals to withstand future hardships, adequately cope with any future stress, and conduct their lives in accordance with what they are about.

The removal of anxiety and depression is a prerequisite for, and the first step toward, personality integration, but the therapeutic work must go beyond this first step. On several occasions, I have worked with people, young and old, who were entangled in emotional conflicts that prevented them from perceiving themselves for what they really were and caused them to act in total disregard of their aptitudes, inclinations, and opportunities. Apparently, there is a good deal of truth in the saying that neurotics are their own worst enemies, and the first phase of psychotherapy should liberate them from their self-defeating way of life. Quite often, however, people don't know where to go and what to do with their new found freedom; they need help. They must be given the chance to take a fresh look at themselves and to develop a new outlook on their lives.

It is not unusual for a patient to make the following statement toward the end of the analytic phase: "I have wasted most of my life, but I have decided I don't want to waste it any longer. I want to live and to live the way I want!" Yet, as mentioned before, liberated people may not know what to do with their freshly acquired freedom from emotional entanglements and may follow momentary whims. Psychological maturity means the removal of infantile inhibitions and the establishment of a rational self-control. However, at the end of the analytic phase, there is a danger of patients' making rash decisions and acting impulsively. To return to our earlier analogy, the increased power of an engine requires a proportional increase in the power of the brakes. The realistic ego must take over, and the second phase of interactional psychotherapy is essentially a higher level of ego therapy.

A strong ego must have a *sense of direction* for even the best controlled apparatus may become futile, unless its efforts are directed toward positive goals. Human life as such is a biological phenomenon devoid of any particular meaning or purpose. The only built-in goal of all living organisms, including the human race, is survival, but there are no prescriptions for the way one's life should be conducted. As explained in earlier chapters, every human being should take stock of his abilities and interests, keep an eye on his options and opportunities, and make the best of them. In other words, every human being has a set of cards — some inherited, some acquired — and should play them.

There are no universal goals in life; therefore, every human being must develop his or her own purposes. A life without a goal is total frustration; a life with goals set by the individual represents a challenge. Victories bring joy, failures and defeats bring sorrow, but as long as one does not give up striving, one's self-esteem remains intact. Depression is a feeling of helpless anger directed toward oneself. People who did not try blame themselves for not trying and feel depressed, but a person who tries hard respects himself for doing his best even when there are disappointments and defeat. The second phase of interactional psychotherapy helps patients find out who they are and what can they do in their lives.

WHO AM I?

Mr. O. R., a 46-year-old man, came to my office. His complaints were numerous; he indicated feelings of worthlessness and depression, sleep difficulties, psychosomatic aches and pains, and a general sense of futility. He was a gifted man and quite successful in business, but he did not like his work, did not enjoy his material wealth, and felt thoroughly bored with life.

"I am an old man," he said, "and I have nothing to look for in life. There is nothing in my life that attracts me, that keeps my interest and makes me happy. When I look back, it is all the same: petty affairs with girls I didn't care for and jobs I did not like. I have done all kinds of things, and I got involved with a great many silly issues. Now I am doing things I do not care about. What a waste!"

I went with Mr. O. R. through the analytic phase of interactional psychotherapy, struggling with his infantile conflicts and hang-ups. Psychological treatment cannot create abilities one does not possess, but it can and does free emotional energies which are tied up in a neurotic knot. Then the point came at which the rejuvenated Mr. O. R. began to ask the questions, Who am I? How can I find out who I am? How can I become myself?

Who are you? Your origins are rather humble. A man and a woman, in a moment of great love or simple boredom, driven by intimate love or motivated by sexual arousal, laid the foundations for your life. That's how it all started. Since then, many things have happened. The little zygote, a tiny piece of living matter, grew and developed, and went through prenatal stages similar to other mammals. Then a baby was born — a helpless piece of flesh and a confused mass of neuromechanisms exposed to millions of stimuli. Years passed; some people took care of you, some neglected you; some loved you, some did not care. You learned creeping and crawling, talking and screaming, crying and laughing, and here you are — a grown woman or a grown man. Who are you? A link in the chain of events. A minute on the clock of life. A social security number. A taxpayer. Who are you?

Only one thing is sure. Whatever is around you — whatever you relate to, see, hear, touch, and sense — all this will disappear the minute you disappear, as far as you are concerned. You are not the center of the entire universe, but the universe will cease to exist for you the minute you cease to exist.

Your parents, friends, relatives, husband or wife, children, and loved ones — they come and go. Only one person will stay with you as long as you live and never leave you — and that person is you. How humble and how magnificent this relationship is! You, a speck of dust, a piece of flesh, a bubbling organism. You, the splendid center of whatever is going on. If you close your eyes forever, nothing else will count, nothing else will matter.

Think about it. You cannot give bread unless you have bread to give. You cannot save drowning people unless you know how to swim. You cannot be anything unless you are yourself. You are the origin, the zero point, and the everything of your life.

Before you decide to be good or bad, you must decide to be yourself. Before you decide how to live, you must accept the fact that you have nothing else but your own life. You are your life, and your life is you. Because you are yourself and because you cannot be anything else but yourself, the time has come — at this point in your life — to find who you are, what you are, and what you want. Are you yourself or are you not you? The prerequisite for any decision, for any judgment, for any planning, is to accept the fact that you have just one life. Today you are here, and tomorrow you are not. What is your life about and what would you like to be?

Me and Not-Me

A newborn infant cannot separate himself from the environment and especially from the one who takes care of him — his mother or a maternal substitute. A newborn infant, though he is physically separate from his mother and the umbilical cord has been cut, is not aware that something is "me" and something is "not-me."

One of the early psychoanalysts, Sandor Ferenczi, maintained that the newborn infant hallucinates omnipotence. He wishes to receive milk, and the milk comes through. He wishes to be taken care of or to be picked up, and the wish comes true. As long as an individual hallucinates omnipotence, the hallucination bears witness to his weakness because only very weak people hallucinate power.

As the infant learns to creep and crawl, to grasp and loose things, to hold and give up, he comes to grips with reality and realizes that there are things which do not yield to his will and are not wish fulfillment. The door that doesn't open, the chair that cannot be pushed away, the doorknob that doesn't move when the child grabs it — all are "not-me." "Me" is what you can do with yourself: the finger that you can put in your mouth, the hair that you can pull from your own head. "Me" is yourself, but whatever else is around you is "not-me." The "not-me" stands in contradistinction to whatever is "me," and "me" is in contradistinction to whatever is "not-me."

In the process of separating oneself from the environment, the recognition of the environment antecedes the recognition of oneself. "Not-me" comes first; "me" comes later. Infants are not too clear where they are, who they are, and what the boundaries of their bodies are. They merge with the toys they play with and the cushions they hug. All things and all people belong to them and are perceived as a part of themselves.

Some immature adults also treat money and other possessions as if these things were a part of their own personality. Once, one of my patients told me that he contemplated suicide because he lost a huge amount of money on the stock market and perceived the loss of this money as if it were a part of himself. More serious is the loss of a beloved person. Ever so often, my patients think of committing suicide when they lose someone dear. Mrs. E. told me that her husband had left her and that she felt she had nothing to live for because her entire life had been invested in this man. Here are excerpts from this session:

"Doc, I promised to tell you my feelings and tell you the entire truth about myself, but I think this will be our last session."

"Why?" I asked.

"Because since Steve left me, I have nothing to live for," Mrs. E. replied." It's like a part of me broke away and I have nothing to live for. We lived together for so many years. I walk around the house and I find it empty. There is a hole, a hole in my life, can you see it? I can see the hole — I sit at the table with the children and one chair is empty. It's empty, it's hollow, there's a hole. I put the dishes on the table and one place is empty. I go to bed and half of the bed is empty. There is a hole, hole, hole."

We sat for a minute in silence. "Where am I going to turn?" she asked. "Part of me is missing. How can I live? How can one live when he has lost a limb, or an eye, or an ear? I don't know, I was never an invalid. But I lost everything − all my life, all my feelings, all my emotions were devoted to this man. I lost everything."

"Everything?" I asked. "Is that true?"

"I know what you have in mind," she said. "We had our fights. Sometimes I hated him. Sometimes I wished he would leave. And yet, I cannot give him up."

"Do you want him back?" I asked.

Mrs. E. cried. "Yes and no," she said. "Should he come back, I would hate him because he broke away. I don't know if I want him back. He was not good to me. He was not nice. He was unfriendly. He was unfaithful. You know it."

"Yes," I replied, "I know it. You told me."

"I don't want him back and I don't want to lose him," she said. "Because losing him is just like losing part of myself. I don't know what I am. Am I a part of him? He is disgusting! Doc, what do I want? Who am I? Why do I cry? What is this all about?"

Identity and Separation

In the case of this woman, marriage was not an alliance of two free people: it was a kind of possessiveness. Was it colonialism or imperialism? She felt that the man belonged to her and that she belonged to him. Part of her life was invested in him, cathected in him. He was her possession. She couldn't give him up because he was part of her life, of her daily routine − having breakfast together, going to work separately, meeting at dinner for angry exchanges, fighting about children and household, and leaving home with the excuse of having meetings. Most probably, he was going out with other women. Meanwhile, she was home crying, calling him up, running after him. She had had one extramarital affair; her husband had one affair after another. Was this what they missed? They certainly were unhappy and he finally broke away, but she couldn't take the separation, couldn't be herself. She was unable to perceive marriage as a union of two individuals, each with his own life, relating to one another in love and friendship. Would she ever be prepared to face this reality?

Every human being is alone, always alone. People come and go. Friendships start and come to an end. The only true, faithful, never-giving-up friend is oneself. Can people rise to this understanding and accept the fact that what they do and whom they relate to are up to them? It is their own decision to choose friends and alliances, husbands and wives, occupations and business associates. It is up to them to make their choices and to become aware that the outer world is an outer world and not a part of them. They can and should relate to other people, but they do not belong to anyone and no one belongs to them.

How does a child develop the feeling of a clear distinction between "me" and "not-me"? There is one, simple answer: by frustration. Frustration is both the curse and the blessing of life. Frustration is a curse because no one wants to be frustrated. It hurts and is discouraging, but without frustration, no one could ever be aware of what life is about. Perhaps we need darkness to appreciate light, and we need light to find soothing relief in darkness. If everything were as we wanted it to be, if we could have everything we wished in childhood, we would never develop a feeling of reality. The thumb that the child puts in his mouth is part of him, but the doorknob that cannot be taken off the door is not a part of him. The foot that can be raised above the floor belongs to him, but the floor does not. The doorknob that doesn't move, that resists pushing and pulling is "not-me"; it frustrates the child's wishes and is clearly "not-me." The floor, too, is a "not-me": one can move one's fingers, but one cannot move the floor. The rain that comes and doesn't go away – even when Johnny wants to play – is "not-me": it's rain. "Me" is me, part of what I wish and can manage to do with myself. Everything else is "not-me."

Other people are also "not-me." Parents are "not-me" unless they are too indulgent and too permissive, and give the child the erroneous impression that he can manipulate the world. The door that doesn't yield to pressure, the floor that doesn't move away, the mother that doesn't obey the child – these give the child a realistic perception of the outer world. Whatever resists our wishes, whatever frustrates, is "not-me." "Me" is pitted against the outer world and must negotiate

with all the innumerable "not-me's." Through interaction one becomes aware of oneself, and one can relate to others when one becomes
aware that they are "not-me."

Identity and the Clinical Types

The issues of identity and purpose take on different behavioral patterns in the three clinical types described. Hypervectorials tend to
get overinvolved with people and overcommitted to purposes alien to
their own needs, interests, or abilities. They often become self-
righteous fanatics, self-styled martyrs, prophets, idealists, and/or big
or small dictators who impose their beliefs on others. They do care
for people, but they seem to believe that their overprotective and
sometimes domineering love is what the other person needs. Quite
often, they offer unsolicited and unwelcome help, and impose themselves on people they care for.

Hypervectorials are usually devoted parents, but they tend to be
overprotective and to make their children feel guilty for being unable
to reciprocate the way their parents expect them to. The more the
parents are disturbed, the heavier is the yoke of guilt that they
impose on their children. In many instances, latent and manifest
schizophrenic parents do not treat their children as separate individuals but as appendages or extensions of themselves. Some hypervectorial parents live vicariously through their children, overidentify
with them, and hold on to them. They often resent the inevitable
fact that the child must grow up and try to prolong the child's dependent attitude.

One of my patients Mrs. K., a 46-year-old schizoid character neurotic, was indignant when her 24-year-old son told her that he was in
love and planned to marry. Mrs. K. was critical of her son's choice
and tried to prevent the marriage. The analytic phase of psychotherapy enabled her to break away from her own parents and to develop
a more rational attitude toward her children, but she still faced the
identity crisis. After cutting her own umbilical cord and accepting
the rights of her 24-year-old son to cease being a child and to make
his own decisions, she feared that the "child" would leave her and
she would have to face "an empty house." She pleaded: "Where am
I? I understand that I was unnecessarily involved first with my

parents and then with my son. But what now? How can I adjust to the new situation?"

Obviously, she needed some help in order to accept herself, develop her own interests, and plan her own activities. She did well in the second phase of therapy. She went back to college and renewed her studies in anthropology which had been interrupted when she married 25 years before. She was a meticulous, precise, and logical person, and she soon obtained a research assistantship — the first step toward a productive and rewarding research career which she decided to pursue in addition to continuing her reasonably good relationship with her very busy surgeon-husband.

The treatment of hyperinstrumental, narcissistic, selfish sociopaths is quite difficult and not always rewarding. In the analytic phase, the therapist endeavors to allay their fear of being taken advantage of by everyone and their resulting need to take advantage of everyone they come across. Their inferiority feelings make them seek self-aggrandizement at the expense of other people. They tend to boast about non-existent achievements, and tell lies about their association with powerful and famous individuals. They are never themselves, and in their exploitative and parasitic lives, they assume various roles in pleasing those they look up to and stepping on those they believe to be defenseless.

Toward the end of the analytic phase, they are ready to give up their selfish, narcissistic behavior, their role playing, and their pretense. They become more humble and willing to accept themselves for what they really are, but they hardly know who they are and where to turn. The second phase of therapy must enable them to accept other people as equals and develop group identification (this will be explained later in this chapter).

Dysmutual neurotics, hysterics, depressives, and so on, swing from one extreme to another: from unselfish love for everyone, to extreme resentment and hatred for those who dare not to love them. The analytic phase, as described in Chapter 7, must help them to establish the balance of intraindividual cathexes that would make them less sensitive to being loved or rejected by others. They are overdependent on what other people think of them or, rather, what they believe others think of them. Their behavior is usually directed toward pleasing those who "love them" and fighting their "enemies."

The acceptance of themselves is the first step in the dysmutuals' search for identity. They must realize that "being loved by everyone" means preciously little in their lives. One patient of mine boasted about finally being liked by the elevator operator in my office building; another complained that people in his office did not show much affection; another thought of quitting a good job because the boss did not praise his work; still another felt bad because the neighbors in his apartment house did not show him much respect.

Self-confidence and self-respect are initially acquired in childhood in child-parent interaction. Parental approval gives the child the feeling of security, and the child's own efforts respectfully acknowledged by the parents contribute to the child's self-confidence. As the child grows older, peer approval becomes more important. Finally, mature men and women learn to depend mainly on themselves, and approval by others plays a less significant role.

At the second phase of psychotherapy, dysmutual patients don't need the therapist's approval. Having resolved their transference, they become more capable of depending on themselves. They set realistic goals for themselves and begin to objectively evaluate their wishes, thoughts, and deeds. They come to terms with themselves and develop a realistic appraisal of themselves.

Self-centeredness

One must draw a clear distinction between being self-centered and being selfish. Selfish people are people who love themselves and don't care for others. They are narcissistic sociopathic individuals who have invested their entire libido or emotional energy in themselves and have very little, if any, left for other people. They tend to exploit the world, use others, and take advantage of whomever they can. They are takers who want to take without giving. They treat others as instruments to be used, which is why I call them "hyperinstrumentals."

Self-centered people are not necessarily selfish. They believe themselves to be of utmost importance to themselves. They can be loving, congenial, and considerate people who direct their energies toward helping themselves as well as others. All great thinkers, and all creative men and women, have been self-centered: they concentrated on themselves. They used their energies to build themselves up and to enrich their mental, emotional, and intellectual lives. They respected themselves and treated their lives as a most important chain of events. They believed themselves to be the center of whatever was going on around them, and being self-centered, they respected the rights of others. One could compare self-centeredness to the solar system: the sun is the center, and all other things are planets or satellites. Yet the sun doesn't borrow light; it gives light. The sun does not take away anything from anybody; being rich, it distributes its enormous energy and to all the celestial bodies that revolve around it.

Self-centered individuals can radiate warmth, affection, love, and creativity, and can give all the wealth of their hearts and minds to other people. Being self-centered, they do not waste their energies — they distribute them. Being self-centered, they do not mismanage their resources but manage them toward the well-being of themselves and others.

Being self-centered is a prerequisite for creative art. A creative artist must concentrate on himself and pay attention to his intellectual, artistic, and other capabilities in order to develop them fully. Then, the artist can enrich other people's lives by his creations, the works he has made. Imagine a man who has a million dollars. He can distribute this million dollars to a million different people, giving everybody one dollar. Doing this, he does not help anyone, but he impoverishes himself and becomes a pauper and a beggar. He can, however, act in another way. He can put the million dollars in an investment that yields tax-free income and use this money in a productive manner. Let's say he might have $100,000 of tax-free income every year. He can use one-half of this income for himself, and the other half can be continuously distributed in a productive way to other people. He can be a giving person without destroying himself as in the first case.

Self-centered individuals take care of themselves: they learn to swim before they try to save drowning people; they taste bread before trying to distribute it to hungry people; they develop strong muscles before using them for plowing the earth and giving its fruits to those who need it. Self-centered people are people who care for themselves, who realize that as far as they are concerned nothing exists if they perish. They know that they will be useless if they neglect themselves. Self-sacrificing, helpless martyrs are of no help to their fellowmen.

Self-mismanagement

"Who am I?" asked a 59-year-old patient. His life was a chain of inconsistencies and haphazard decisions. He was changing occupations, switching businesses, doing things he never liked, getting involved in issues he didn't care about, and making money he didn't need. He was married to a woman he didn't love, lived in a place he didn't enjoy, and associated with people he despised. "Who am I?" he asked. "I am 59 years old; soon I'll be 60. Is my life over? Am I coming to the end of my road hating myself and feeling that this is the life I wasted?"

I told him, "Life begins the day you begin it."

He smiled. "Where should we begin? When should we begin?"

"Where?" I asked. "In you. When? Today."

He smiled again, but after a minute, the smile disappeared and a deep cloud covered his face. "Doctor," he said, "I don't know what I want. I don't know who I am. I am going to continue to be a wheeler-dealer, making money and losing money, speculating, coniving, hating myself, hating what I do, hating my wife and my partners, and everyone else. I don't know who I am."

I responded, "That's what you are here for. We are the same age. I am not smarter than you are. I don't know more than you do. In many areas of life, you have more knowledge than I have. You are certainly wiser in economic life, and you know much more about finances than I do. You probably have had more experiences in your life than I have had and will ever have. Why should you come to me and not I to you?"

He raised his eyes. "That's the question, Doctor. Why should I pay you and not you me?"

"If I were in need of your help, I would come to you. Why did you come to me?" I asked.

"Just because I don't want to waste the rest of my life," he said. "Maybe I'll die tomorrow. Maybe I'll live another 30 years. I am still in excellent physical health. I think clearly. I have a good mind. Why should I waste the rest of my life? What should I do?"

What should he do? First, he should get a realistic estimate of his intellectual potentialities and emotional resources. He should be helped in developing the ability to take hardship, to make decisions, and to stand by them, as well as to be capable of changing them whenever necessary. He must realistically evaluate his wishes, likes, and dislikes. What does he really want? How can he make his wishes come true? What are his potentialities, and which way should he go in life to optimally fulfill himself? What is his fulfillment? Every human being is a bud, and every human can become a flower. Every life can bear fruit, and every human life will come to an end and wither away. Before it withers away, it should blossom and bear fruit. This is the immanent goal of all life.

What does blossoming and bearing fruit mean? This is highly individual and means different things for different people. It is transient, and every human being must find his or her particular way. Evaluating one's potentialities is a step in the right direction. Evaluating one's inclinations, needs, likes, interests, and aspirations must follow. The next step is a realistic appraisal of one's situation, potentialities, and possibilities, and of the responsibilities one carries in life. One must find out how to apply one's abilities and interests in both present and future situations.

Whenever people ask me what they should do in the future, I usually advise them to imagine their last day of life and look backward. When one looks forward, one faces unknown options. It is far more important to project oneself into the last day of life, look backward, and ask, "Is this the life I wanted to live? If I were given the opportunity to live a second life, would I choose to live it the way I lived my first? I had no choice in terms of genetics and childhood, but am I proud of my adult years? If not, I have wasted the greatest gift one can ever get — the gift of life! But if I feel proud of my efforts and with some exceptions am willing to live again the way I have lived, then life was worth living."

The tasks of the second therapeutic phase are far from simple. The therapist must not try to remake the patients' personalities but rather must help them realize what cards they have and enable them to play those cards in the best possible way, according to the nature of the cards and the nature of things around them.

Whatever people do, they do on purpose, but often they are unaware of the purposes that are submerged in the depths of the unconscious. The task of the therapist is to help patients discover themselves and realize that it is up to them to lead their lives accordingly. As mentioned previously, the task of the therapist is not to willfully and arbitrarily attempt to change an apple tree into an orange tree, but to help the apple and the orange trees grow well and bring out the best possible fruit.

One must not be too optimistic in regard to psychotherapy. The therapist must accept his or her own limitations as well as the limitations of the patient. Not all gardeners can produce miracles, and not all fruit trees can bear perfect fruit, but it is the gardner's task to offer the best possible help to every plant.

HIERARCHY OF GOALS

She was shouting, "Never! Never again! I don't want to be married again! I don't want a husband, a kitchen, babies, and diapers! I want to live the way I want to live without all that status and glory of marriage! I don't need the security and boredom of suburbia! Am I abnormal or maladjusted or neurotic?"

She was 35, a college professor, and quite a successful researcher in biology. She was furious, and cursed Sigmund Freud, Carl Jung, and Herman Wouk. "I am not going to be a sweet Eve or a hausfrau or a Marjorie Morningstar!" she screamed. "I am not going to sacrifice my scientific work, my moral convictions, my integrity, my intellectual curiosity, for the dubious pleasures of marriage! I am a modern woman. Security? I have it. I have tenure in college. No one can fire me. I was just promoted to associate professor. I got a fabulous research grant. My time is divided between teaching and research. In my leisure time, I listen to music, go to concerts and opera. Men? I can have as many as I please!"

Many contemporary women face the conflict between career and family life. Some choose a career, some prefer family life, and may find a way of combining both. Modern marriage and family require the equal participation of men and women, which can enable both to pursue their distinct careers.

Many people face difficulties in making decisions and planning their lives. No human being can have everything he or she wishes to have, and no one could be omniscient nor omnipotent. The second phase of psychotherapy helps people to scrutinize their wishes and options, and to establish a hierarchy of goals. There are no universal rules; every individual must set his or her own goals in life and pursue them in a rational manner.

Survival is the built-in, immanent goal of human life. Ultimately, there is an end to every human life. There is no need to pursue death; it comes to everyone anyway. However, the pursuit of a meaningful life requires mobilization of all the resources a human being possesses. One must *perspire* in order to survive and to provide food, shelter, rest, health care, and so on for oneself; one must *aspire* to live one's life the way one would like to.

There are no intrinsic goals in human life except to stay alive. People may spend all their days on earth practicing respiration, circulation, and digestion, and leading a meaningless life of sheer biological existence. They may, however, if they want, create a meaningful life for themselves — a life of dignity and fulfillment.

A life without goals is a life of boredom and futility. Setting goals presents a challenge and an opportunity to fully utilize one's energies and realize one's potentialities. Whatever abilities one does possess deserve to be put to full use, but in most instances, people must be helped to choose between various inclinations and aptitudes.

Consider, for instance, the choice of career. Working with young people, I have often tried to help them arrive at rational conclusions by pointing out four relevant criteria, namely, aptitudes, interests, practical considerations, and overall personality.

Most people have more than one aptitude, but they should follow the one that offers the best chances for success. Some people have a spectacular ability in music, mathematics, or business, and their choice is self-evident. Most people, however, are forced to make hard choices because they have limited talents or are gifted in more than one direction. On several occasions, I have advised patients to take a battery of aptitude tests which would enable them to obtain a realistic picture of their abilities and compare themselves to the national averages. These aptitude tests helped them decide which field offered optimal chances of success.

The choice of a career is a lifelong commitment. People spend most of their waking hours in fields, factories, and offices, and their interests must be taken into consideration in their occupational choice. Some individuals are fortunate since their interests and aptitudes coincide. In the case of equal aptitudes in different fields, the person's main interest should serve as the decisive criterion, and in the case of equal interest in various fields, one's highest aptitude should determine the vocational choice.

One must also take into consideration practical issues such as job availability, job security, potential income, and chances of progress and promotion. I once had in treatment a law school student who was determined to pursue maritime law. Apparently he was both gifted and interested in this field. I advised him to check the job opportunities in this highly specialized profession. After several interviews with his professors and, on their recommendation, with leading experts in maritime law, he decided to change his plans. He was told that maritime law is a small field with very few openings which are usually available to the relatives and friends of owners of maritime businesses who need legal help related to insurance and casualties.

I also had as a patient a 40-year-old businessman, married and the father of two children, who was quite displeased with himself and his business activities. Eighteen years before, for reasons beyond his control, he had dropped out of medical school. Now, eighteen years later, he was still subscribing to medical journals. His special interest was medical equipment: he loved medical gadgets, and whenever he visited a physician's office, he was anxious to examine them and discuss them with the doctor.

Unfortunately, it was too late for this man to go back to medical school and he did not intend to become a student. "Even if I had the chance to be admitted," he explained, "who would support my wife and our little children?" A partial solution to his problem was within his reach. He continued his interest in practical considerations and became involved in selling medical equipment to hospitals and to private practitioners.

The overall personality outlook is the last, though certainly not the least, criterion of vocational choice. People identify themselves with their occupation and should be able to take pride in their success and competence. Moreover, people identify themselves with their peer group, join their professional or trade organizations, and are recognized and identified by others as teachers, physicians, plumbers, writers, brokers, and so on. I frequently ask my patients to project their self-image into the future. "Imagine you are 20 years older," I suggest, "and take a look at yourself. Let us assume that you are successful in the field that you intend to enter. How do you feel about yourself 20 years later?"

This question is directed to one of the most relevant issues of mental health, namely, *self-respect*. Success and failure come and go, but whatever one does and whatever happens must not undermine one's self-respect. Every human being wants to be successful in his or her endeavors, but no one is promised an unbroken chain of success, and it is highly important to retain self-respect even in defeat.

Those who don't try can never be happy. They can't have the excitement of challenge and the victory of attainment. Failure brings pain, but it need not affect one's self-esteem. One can say, "At least I did what I could. I did not give up, and I am not a quitter. I can be proud of myself despite what happened."

No human being can have all his or her wishes come true, nor can anyone always be happy. Happiness is a winged creature; it comes and goes. Striving toward a goal is a challenge, and attaining a difficult goal brings feelings of victory and happiness. Triumphs make one happy, and those who have no goals know no happiness.

During the second phase of psychotherapy comes a moment of serenity and awareness when the patient realizes *who he is and what he could and should do*. "This is what I am," a patient may say. "No use to pretend, to play silly games, and to try to be what I am not. These are the cards given to me by heredity and experience. I must play them the best I can. I don't know how long I will live, but I shall live the way that offers fulfillment and self-realization." During the second therapeutic phase, patients acquire *courage and wisdom*. They have the courage to be aware of their potentialities; the courage to face life and determine how to live; the courage to decide what they *should do*. Then comes a careful checking against reality and a determination of what one realistically *could do*. Courage is not enough; mature people also need the *wisdom* to make rational decisions. Rational decisions imply coping with hardships and taking advantage of opportunities.

ALONE BUT NOT LONELY

Toward the end of the first phase of psychotherapy, many patients feel lonely. The umbilical cord is cut. Adult patients realize that they have no daddies and mommies to depend on. They no longer expect to be taken care of by, or to rebel against, their parents. Past attachments and grievances have been resolved; infantile emotions are neutralized; and patients accept adult responsibilities for their actions.

Patients also outgrow the infantile transference relationship and no longer worship the therapist. They treat him as an equal; they know they are more competent than the therapist in several areas of life, but they continue psychotherapy expecting to receive help in their search for identity and meaning. Furthermore, in the course of the second therapeutic phase, patients realize that every human being is a separate entity: "My toothache or my conjunctivitis or my bronchitis is mine only. Other people may be friendly and compassionate, but their teeth, eyes, or bronchi are not affected. It is me, and only me, who is in pain. I am alone, always alone. My parents will die on me. My boyfriend or husband, my girlfriend or wife, may or may not stay with me forever. My children must leave me. The only person who will never leave me as long as I live — is myself." Every human being is alone, but he need not be lonely. No human being can be self-sufficient, and every human being needs allies.

Children need to be loved, for parental love carries the promise of food and protection. It is a one-way street: the weak child needs strong and friendly allies. The child's attitude toward his parents is *instrumental;* the child needs to be accepted, and his feelings of security depend on being loved by strong and friendly adults.

Adult men and women are not omnipotent either. They too need strong and friendly allies. Yet unless they themselves are strong and friendly, who needs their friendship? Children have parents or parental substitutes. Adults do not have loving daddies and mommies. Aged parents may need help from their adult sons and daughters.

Childhood is dependence, but adulthood does not imply independence. No human being can be totally independent. Maturity means *interdependence.* It is a balance of instrumental, mutual, and vectorial attitudes. Mature adults are instrumental in breadwinning activities, mutual in friendships and marriage, and vectorial in parenthood and in charitable and idealistic tasks.

Mature adults are mainly self-reliant and only partially dependent on others. In their instrumental pursuit of economic success, they do not expect anyone to bring them income on a silver platter. In friendship and marriage, they are ready to give and expect the same from their partners. In parenthood, they are willing to give without expecting anything in return.

Most social interactions occur on a give-and-take basis. One must be strong in order to give, and must be aware of one's power to do things for oneself and for others. Self-respect is another name for the awareness of one's power to satisfy one's own needs as well as being able to help others.

Children's self-respect depends on parental approval. A child does not know whether he or she is strong or weak, big or little, pretty or ugly, smart or silly. Wise parents praise their child and contribute to the child's self-esteem: the child accepts the parents' opinions.

Gradually, as children grow and become capable of mastering tasks they could not master earlier, they develop an awareness of their own power. They can, for instance, ride a bike, skate, play ball, and do well on a test in school. Gradually, their self-esteem depends more on their evaluation of their own resources and less on approval by others.

The need to be accepted, liked, and respected by others never disappears; all people need to be liked (acceptance) and respected (power) by others. In late childhood and adolescence, the need for peers' approval leads to identification with one's group and a willing acceptance of group rules, norms, and expectancies. The superego develops as the child's identifies himself with his parents and accepts their dos and don'ts as guiding principles. Teenagers tend to identify with their peers and, in the process of socialization, develop the we-ego, which represents their acceptance and sharing of the norms and ideas of their peers. Adulthood does not imply a shedding of these earlier developmental phases but, rather, their synthesis into a harmonious personality structure.

PERSONALITY INTEGRATION

Split personality is a misnomer, for no personality is a monolithic structure. Every human being is a conglomeration of tissues, muscles, and organs, and every human functioning is comprised of the functions of several systems, among them the glandular, nervous, digestive, cardiovascular, and so on. Human behavior also (I am using this term in its broadest meaning is motivated, activated, and controlled by scores of diverse and often opposite impulses, drives, emotions, thoughts, memories, and so on. Mental systems have been conceptualized in diverse manners by psychological theorists.

Apparently, every human being is a "split personality," but some personalities are more split than others. Some are badly disorganized, and their feelings, thoughts, and actions contradict each other, and bring defeat and misery. The task of the analytic phase of psychotherapy is to resolve infantile conflicts and remove the stumbling blocks that prevent personality growth and integration. The task of the second phase is to help the patient in his search for identity and personality integration.

Setting goals and establishing their order of priority are of vital importance in personality integration. One cannot follow all one's whims, wishes, and desires; a person must choose what is important for him and pursue his selected objectives. The integration of personality and inner harmony are attained through a reconciliation of one's *shoulds* and *coulds*. The goals reflect what an individual believes should be done, but some goals might be unattainable and their pursuit might produce unnecessary frustration. It is, therefore, advisable to carefully check the roads leading to the desired land and, if necessary, to modify or even abandon one's goals. In some of the cases described earlier in this book, people pursued unattainable goals and needed corrective guidance. Sometimes, in the second phase of therapy, the patient's energies, freed from inner conflict, give the patient the feeling of unlimited possibilities and inspire clarity, but not always rational actions. In such instances, testing reality becomes imperative, and patients must be helped to take stock of their own resources and objective possibilities.

As explained in Chapter 1, perceiving things as they are is one of the main criteria of mental health, and the second phase of interactional psychotherapy reaffirms the need for avoiding too easy as well as too difficult tasks. The level of aspiration should correspond to the person's psychological resources and to what could be done at a given time in a given environment. The courage to be oneself (the shoulds) must be combined with the wisdom of acting in a rational manner (the coulds).

The French existentialist writer Albert Camus described the human tragedy in an essay entitled "The Myth of Sisyphus." The Greek mythological figure of Sisyphus was supposed to lift a rock to the top of a hill, but as soon as he was close to the top, the rock slid back. Camus's Sisyphus was supposed to symbolize the futility of human endeavors.

I maintain that Sisyphus is, indeed, a symbol of futility, but it is the futility of human beings who refuse to be themselves and get involved in tasks alien to their psychological makeup. It is indeed a waste to spend one's life rolling a barren boulder uphill on the steep road of life. One can do more in life than carry a heavy and useless load, and find out that nothing has been accomplished in a task that serves no purpose.

Many people are going nowhere and leading a life that offers no challenges and no victories. Many people indulge in weakness, follow momentary impulses, and yield to self-destructive temptations. One must choose between self-discipline and self-defeat, and the mastery over one's whims and impulses must be attained in the second therapeutic phase.

Human life has a built-in, inevitable final point, and ultimately all of us will fall off a cliff and that will be the end of our journey on earth. However, as long as we live, we must set our eyes on the next hill, which is a bit higher and a bit closer to the stars. No one can reach the stars, but why not reach toward them?

The task of human life is not an achievement, for no achievement can be final and no achievement should justify resting on one's laurels. Life is a process of achieving and following the bumpy road toward new achievements and new peaks. One must look backward and forward. Looking backward gives the sense of what one has achieved so far, how many hardships were coped with, and what opportunities were used or missed. Looking forward inspires fresh efforts toward new achievements. The three main phases of psychotherapy – the analytic phase, the search for identity, and self-realization – should serve as guidelines for the psychotherapist who wants to help human beings understand the limitations of human life and the potentialities of living a full life.

9
Becoming: Self-Realization

The third phase of interactional psychotherapy should enable patients to develop meaningful goals. They will decide in which direction they are going, and how they intend to utilize their intellectual and emotional resources.

Human beings do not live in a vacuum. They are surrounded by people and must relate to them. Earlier in this book, the theory of three types of interindividual relationships was introduced, namely, the instrumental, mutual, and vectorial. The infant versus mother relationship is a prototype of instrumentalism: infants are takers, and they need to *receive* care, food, shelter, and so on. Genuine friendship, mature sexual behavior, and marriage are prototypes of mutual, *give-and-take relationships*. Responsible parenthood is *giving without expecting anything in return*, and it is the prototype of vectorial relationships.

Earning a living is based on an instrumental attitude. Both employers and employees think of themselves and interact with each other in order to satisfy their own needs. There are, however, numerous interactions on a give-and-take basis, in which people seek to satisfy their own needs as well as the needs of others. The need to give and take originates in the desire to have one's own needs satisfied, but as the child grows older, the need to share and to give leads to a separate, independent behavioral pattern. Even when one does not need people, one needs to be with them. The need to be accepted is a derived need, but it is nevertheless a powerful need which determines the nature of friendship relations and, often, also of sexual relations and marriage.

Mature adults are capable of caring for those who need help. In many instances, mature adults do not relate to other people for personal gain, nor are they interested in having their actions reciprocated, for they enjoy helping others. People join charitable organizations for the purpose of helping others and take part in idealistic organizations to work for the good of mankind. Their attitude is vectorial.

My theory of social development stresses the ability to relate to other people within the framework of the four possible interactional patterns: hostility (H), instrumentalism (I), mutualism (M), and vectorialism (V). Well-adjusted, mature individuals act *rationally* in all four directions. They can display hostile behavior in self-defense; they are instrumental (takers) in the pursuit of a livelihood; they are mutual (givers and takers) with friends, sex partners, and spouses; and they are vectorial (givers) toward children, as well as in charitable and idealistic activities. A mature individual interacts in all four types of relationships.

It might be advisable at this point to briefly summarize my theory of moral development described in Chapter 2. According to this theory (Wolman, 1982), people are born *anomous.* They know no restraint and no consideration for anyone. Intrauterine life is clearly parasitic: the zygote-embryo-fetus is all out for itself, whereas mother's body is vectorial and self-sacrificing.

Birth changes little in this parasitic attitude. Infants follow their impulses and operate on the principle of immediate gratification. Infants are anomous, that is, amoral and selfish.

Fear of retaliation and punishment is the first, though preciously small, step toward moral behavior. The earliest restraints are based on fear; thus, the earliest phase of primitive morality should be called *phobonomous.* With the development of a rudimentary awareness of potential consequences, which Freud called the "archaic ego," the child's selfishness faces restraints. The child learns to obey because he fears. Fear is not morality, but this restraint from without breaks the ground for more advanced phases of morality.

As children become aware of parental love and care, they appreciate what they get and begin to reciprocate. The child needs parental love and fears he may lose it; thus, his attitude toward his parents is a combination of love and fear. The child willingly and fearfully accepts parental rules and prohibitions, and gradually absorbs these rules and perceives them as if they were his own. He may blame himself for occasional disobedience and develop *guilt feelings* whenever he violates parental rules. His behavior is *heteronomous,* for he willingly obeys norms instituted by others whom he perceives as loving and powerful authority figures. In Freud's personality model, this self-regulatory agency was called the *superego*.

Preadolescents and adolescents develop close interpersonal relations with their peers, and form cliques and gangs. Identification with the peer group to which one chooses to belong becomes the guiding principle for years to come, and often this loyalty goes on until the end of life. The willing acceptance of social norms — be they of a certain religious denomination, racial or ethnic group, or political party — leads to the formation of a new part of one's personality, which I call the *we-ego*. I have referred to this group identification period as *socionomous*.

The ultimate moral development goes beyond socionomy. Imagine an Omnipotent Being: an Omnipotent Being does not fear or need anything; thus he cannot hate or hurt anyone. The only thing he can do is to give what he has. He *must* build and create, love and protect. Those who have reached this divine point, such as Christ, Prometheus, Antigone, have developed a *vector-ego* that goes out of themselves and reaches toward others. They have the *courage to give*. They are *autonomous*.

THE DRIVE FOR POWER

The drive for power is the chief corollary of the universal struggle for survival. All human beings strive to possess maximum power, which is defined as the ability to satisfy needs. All human beings share the basic biological needs for oxygen, food, water, and sleep, and also have acquired needs related to the highly diversified personality make-up of individuals. Some of these needs might be rooted in genetic and organic factors, and some are a product of learning and socio-cultural influences. The common denominator of all these highly diversified needs is the *need to feel powerful*.

The need to feel powerful appears under many names and in many forms, shapes, disguises, and degrees. It is often called self-esteem, self-respect, self-confidence, and so on. It may lead to extensive efforts to accumulate wealth, to acquire property, to win a contest, to conduct a war, to gain fame, and so forth. In many instances, the need to feel powerful is gratified when a man seduces a woman or vice-versa, when a student receives a high mark in school, when a tennis player wins a tournament, when a swimmer crosses the English channel, when a mountain climber reaches the top of Mount Everest, when a woman gives birth, when a writer finishes a book, and also when a crook outsmarts honest people, a criminal kills a cop, or a soldier kills many enemies.

The need to feel powerful is always *goal directed*. One feels strong when one sets a goal and attains it. The more difficult the task, the more power accrues to the winner. Pleasure and displeasure are daily occurrences, but happiness is a winged creature that comes at moments of great victory and triumph.

Life without goals is meaningless drudgery. Having nothing to live for deepens the existential crisis of lack of identity and purpose. The intrinsic, built-in goal of human life is to stay alive, but every human being has the right to choose how he or she wants to live.

The second phase of interactional psychotherapy helps patients become aware of themselves and their potentialities, and enables them to realistically perceive their environment and take stock of what can they do. In the third phase, the time arrives when all these factors are put together, and satisfactory and obtainable goals are set.

The realistic striving toward a goal enhances one's self-esteem, that is, the awareness of one's power. People who have no goal often feel at the mercy of outside forces. They perceive themselves as victims of fate or helpless onlookers. People who set goals for themselves may win or lose. Obviously, they feel "great" (i.e., powerful) when they win, but even when they lose, they respect themselves for trying, for being brave and tenacious, and for being able to live the way they want. The mastery over one's own personality, which enables one to feel that he can live the way he wants, creates a priceless sense of achievement that brings with it a feeling of self-respect. Some of my patients may have to face grave adversities, but when they reach the point of living in accordance with their convictions, they will never fall apart — come hell or high water.

Everyone's life brings ups and downs, successes and failures, victories and defeats. No human being is immune to illness and accident, material gains and losses, approval and rejection, love and hate. The second phase of psychotherapy enables individuals to enjoy success and to cope with hardship and defeat. The third phase enables them to gain mastery over themselves and develop constructive plans.

As mentioned in Chapter 8, every personality is "split," that is, a conglomeration of diverse impulses, feelings, experiences, habits, thoughts, and so on. The second phase of interactional psychotherapy should contribute personality integration; the third phase should help one choose direction and purpose, thereby giving meaning and dignity to one's life.

Competing with other people is often a necessity, but one must be aware of the fact that other people might deliver better products and better services. No one can be the best, and certainly no one can retain first place forever. Even Miss America reigns for only a year, and no scientist can win Nobel prizes year after year. No one should be expected or, even worse, pressured to always be better than others. One need not live up to what other people expect, but one should *live up to oneself and make the best use of whatever potentialities one has.*

Therefore, one kind of competition should go on as long as possible, namely, the *competition with oneself.* No human being can be an overachiever, but many are underachievers. It is irrational to try the impossible and to aspire to reach the unreachable, but it is no less irrational not to try to do the best one can.

Some people play cards they don't have, and some don't play the cards they have. The second phase of interactional psychotherapy helps patients to become aware of who they are and what can they do. The third phase should help them toward fulfilling their potentialities and making their dreams come true.

Those who don't have any dreams, ambitions, and aspirations lead a dull life void of challenge and achievement. Those who do have ambitions and dreams, but live in their dreams doing nothing about them, are neurotics. The third phase of psychotherapy should help individuals to develop their own particular aspirations and to forge ahead in a realistic manner.

People who know what they want and are aware of their own potentialities endeavor to accomplish whatever is really possible. They do not build castles in the air, nor do they shy away from hardships. When they reach a peak, they give themselves credit, but they do not rest on their laurels — they set themselves another target higher than the one they have already reached.

BECOMING

The main principles of interactional psychotherapy can be summarized as follows: the fight for survival is the universal driving force common to all living organisms, but only human beings are sadly aware of the ultimate futility of this struggle and the inevitability of death. Perplexed human beings usually seek consolation in two different directions, namely, religion or hedonism. Religion preaches *lasting;* hedonism preaches *being.* Interactional psychotherapy proposes *becoming.*

Religion promises immortality, that is, *lasting forever.* Some primitive and ancient people believed in the survival of the mummified body, and provided food and shelter for the deceased. Sophisticated religions postulate immortality of the soul, and promise resurrection. The fear of death is somewhat assuaged by the hope that the deceased will "rest in peace" and that the soul will be well received in the hereafter. Life is presented as a short and not too pleasant corridor that leads into death and eternal peace. The phrase *sub specie aeternitatis* carries with it the bittersweet pill of the tragedy of death and the glorious promise of immortality.

Not everyone believes in God, and many people do not believe in souls or their immortality. Some people choose to accumulate as much physical prowess, material wealth, political power, and so on, as possible — as if all these real or symbolic acquisitions could make them omnipotent and capable of defying death. Especially during periods of economic insecurity, political tension, social disorder, and international conflict, the search for sensual pleasure offers a tempting escape from the fear of death. There has never been greater use of liquor and sex than during the period of decline of the Roman Empire, and there was never more fun than in Pompeii on the eve of its destruction. Fear of the future may drive people to seek escape into infantile regression and blissful forgetting. The widespread abuse of drugs and alcohol, as well as the growing wave of violent behavior, is indicative of escape into an instant and illusory feeling of power. Some people seem to believe that they can outsmart death by living a loud, sensuous, hedonistic life. In contradistinction to the mystical *lasting* and *sub specie aeternitatis,* hedonists practice *being* and *carpe diem.*

Human beings have three choices: being, lasting, or becoming. One can *be* by satisfying his immediate needs for food, sex, fun, prestige, and violence. One may try to *last* by believing in a hereafter or by building pyramids and monuments in the hope that he will exist forever as a mummy. To *become* human implies accepting the inevitability of death without sinking into animalistic hedonism and violence, or escaping into mystical superhuman beliefs.

Man is suspended in midair between God and animal. He may descend into animalistic *being* or hallucinate godlike *lasting.* Nature has provided neurotic ropes with which men can hang themselves on their animalistic or mystical beliefs. There is, however, a third road — the road of *becoming* human. Becoming human means continuously changing in order to become more human than one was yesterday.

There are two fundamental differences between men and animals: intelligence and morality. All animals, including man, fight for survival, breathe, take in food and water, and are governed by biochemical laws. Mankind, however, can satisfy its needs without using claws, teeth, guns, or nuclear weapons. Violence is the prerogative of the animal world, and the survival of the fittest is the law of the jungle.

One can fight *against* others, but one cannot become human alone. To be human means to be human to other human beings. Animals fight *against* one another; humans work *with* one another. Whatever has been created by human beings — houses, castles, bridges, ships, factories, schools, art galleries, symphonic orchestras, or space travel — was created by people *working together.* Whatever has been destroyed, was destroyed by animalistic regression to selfishness and violence.

To become human implies the use of human *intelligence* and *compassion* to help other human beings. To *become human* means to be understanding and considerate of the needs and rights of other human beings. Human intelligence has created enormous scientific and technological power. This power need not be dissipated in being or lasting: it can be harnessed for or against humanity, and employed in a universal effort to become human or in mass murder.

To advocate racial, religious, ethnic, socioeconomic, or international hatred is not human; animal species invented racism long before Hitler. Mobbing an animal that belongs to another species is common practice in the animal world. Violence is animalistic; consideration and cooperation are human. A pecking order is the law of animal society; equal rights for all is a law of human societies.

People cannot "love" one another and become angels. However, people can strive to become more human, and *becoming* is a continuous striving toward the humanization of humanity.

The human idea of God is an idea of Being that creates: God has created something out of nothing. All religions describe their gods as beings who *created* the world. Creation is the symbol of power; creation is also the main road toward fulfillment of oneself and real happiness.

No human being can always achieve, always create, always do something pleasing to himself and to others. No human being can continuously be successful in his endeavors. No human being can reach the sun and the stars, but a human being can go in the right direction. Not to have achieved, but achieving; not arriving at the inn, but walking toward the inn; not resting on one's laurels, but moving toward those laurels, realizing more of one's abilities, and putting one's talents to their most constructive, productive, and creative use — these constitute the main sense of life and the only possible answer to the existential crisis that cripples human efforts and maims human minds.

Not all human beings can attain the same level of achievement, the same level of progress, the same level of fulfillment. That is why every psychotherapist must correctly assess the resources of his patients and not to try to accomplish the impossible. However, the three main phases of therapy — the analytic phase, the search for identity, and self-realization to — should serve as guidelines for the psychotherapist who wants to help human beings understand the limitations of human life and the potentialities of living a full life.

The second psychotherapeutic phase helps patients develop the courage to be themselves, that is, the *courage to live* the way they think they should. The third phase helps them develop the *courage to give*. Children and weak, immature, infantile adults need help; they are on the receiving end. Mature adults are capable of giving, and the more one gives, the richer one becomes.

The more one has, the more one tends to give. The more power one has, the more one tends to do, to create, to help — one's spouse, children, relatives, community, religion, nation, or all of humanity.

Gifted people are culturally rich, and they create art, music, and science for everyone. Even cowards and weaklings can kill, but it takes power, wisdom, and skill to heal and to save human lives.

In order to give, one must have. In order to save a drowning person, one must be a forceful swimmer. In order to help, one must be strong. Then, the more love one gives, the richer his personality becomes.

Parental love and devotion constitute the prototype of vectorialism. A vectorial attitude can be directed toward one's children, one's family, and the members of one's group. However, it can also be objectified and directed toward humanity and the universal values of religion, science, art, and morality. The third phase of psychotherapy should help people to function on this vectorial level and pursue values that serve humanity and help people to become more humane.

References

Abraham, K. (1911). *Selected papers.* New York: Basic Books, 1953. (a)

Abraham, K. A short study of the development of the libido viewed in the light of mental disorders (1924). *Selected papers.* New York: Basic Books; 1953, pp. 418-479. (b)

Ackerman, N. W. Preventive implications of family research. In G. Caplan (Ed.), *Prevention of mental disorders in children.* New York: Basic Books, 1961, pp. 142-167.

Adler, K. A. Adler's individual psychology. In B. B. Wolman (Ed.), *Psychoanalytic techniques.* New York: Basic Books, 1967.

Albee, G. W. Emerging concepts of mental illness and models of treatment. *American Journal of Psychiatry,* 1969, *125,* 870-876.

Alexander, F. *Fundamentals of psychoanalysis.* New York: Norton, 1948.

Alexander, F. and French, T. *Psychoanalytic therapy.* New York: Ronald, 1946.

Alexander, F. G. and Selesnick, S. T. *The history of psychiatry.* New York: Harper & Row, 1966.

Barber, T. X. Experimental hypnosis. In B. B. Wolman (Ed.), *Handbook of general psychology.* Englewood Cliffs, N.J.: Prentice Hall, 1973.

Bellak, L. and Loeb, L. (Eds.). *The schizophrenic syndrome.* New York: Grune & Stratton, 1969.

Berkowitz, L. (Ed.). *Advances in experimental social psychology,* Vol. 6. New York: Academic Press, 1972.

Bernstein, A. The psychoanalytic technique. In B. B. Wolman (Ed.), *Handbook of clinical psychology.* New York: McGraw-Hill, 1965, pp. 1168-1199.

Blanck, R. and Blanck, G. *Ego psychology.* New York: Columbia University Press, 1974.

Bour, P. Proposition concrète en matière de nosologie psychiatrique. *Annales Medico-Psychologiques,* 166, 2, 508-511.

Bower, E. M. Primary prevention of mental and emotional disorders. In N. M. Lambert (Ed.), *The protection and promotion of mental health in schools.* New York: Basic Books, 1970.

Claghorn, J. L. (Ed.). *Successful therapy.* New York: Brunner-Mazel, 1976.

Colby, A., Gibbs, J., and Kohlberg, L. *Standard form scoring manual.* Cambridge, Mass.: Center for Moral Education, 1980.

Devereux, G. Some criteria for the timing of confrontations and interpretations. *International Journal of Psychoanalysis,* 1951, *32,* 19-24.

DSM II. *Diagnostic and statistical manual of mental disorders* (2nd ed.). Washington, D.C.: American Psychiatric Association, 1968.

DSM III. *Diagnostic and statistical manual of mental disorders* (3rd ed.). Washington, D.C.: American Psychiatric Association, 1980.

Downey, T. W. Psychoanalysis: Recent developments. In B. B. Wolman (Ed.) *International Encyclopedia of Psychiatry, Psychology, Psychoanalysis and Neurology: Progress Volume 1.* New York: Aesculapius Publishers, 1983, pp. 336-343.

Edwards, G. Diagnosis of schizophrenia: an Anglo-American comparison. *British Journal of Psychiatry,* 1972, *120,* 385-390.

Ehrenwald, J. Parapsychology and the healing arts. In B. B. Wolman (Ed.), *Handbook of parapsychology.* New York: Van Nostrand Reinhold, 1977, pp. 541-555.

Eisenbud, J. Paranormal photography. In B. B. Wolman (Ed.), *Handbook of parapsychology.* New York: Van Nostrand Reinhold, 1977, pp. 414-430.

Eissler, K. R. The effect of the structure of the ego on psychoanalytic technique. *Journal of the American Psychoanalytic Association,* 1953, *1, 104-143.*

Eysenck, H. J. The effects of psychotherapy. In H. J. Eysenck (Ed.), *Handbook of abnormal psychology.* New York: Basic Books, 1961.

Federn, P. *Ego-psychology and the psychoses.* New York: Basic Books, 1952.

Fenichel, O. *The psychoanalytic theory of neurosis.* New York: Norton, 1945.

Feynman, R. P. *Quantum electrodynamics.* New York: Benjamin, 1961.

Freud, S. (1932) *New introductory lectures on psychoanalysis.* New York: Norton, 1933.

Freud, S. *A general introduction to psychoanalysis* (1915-1917). New York: Garden City, 1943.

Freud, S. *An outline of psychoanalysis* (1938). New York: Norton, 1949.

Freud, S. *Beyond the pleasure principle* (1920). New York: Liveright, 1950. (a)

Freud, S. Analysis terminable and interminable (1937). In *Collected Papers,* Vol. 5. London: Hogarth Press, 1950. (b)

Freud, S. The interpretation of dreams (1900). *The standard edition of the complete psychological works of Sigmund Freud,* Vol. 4. London: Hogarth Press and the Institute of Psychoanalysis, 1962, pp. 339-627. (a)

Freud, S. Three essays on the theory of sexuality (1905). *The standard edition of the complete psychological works of Sigmund Freud.* London: Hogarth Press, 1962. (b)

Freud, S. The future prospects of psychoanalytic therapy (1910a). *The standard edition of the complete psychological works of Sigmund Freud,* Vol. 11. London: Hogarth Press, 1962, pp. 139-152. (c)

Freud, S. "Wild" psychoanalysis (1910b). *The standard edition of the complete psychological works of Sigmund Freud,* Vol. 11. London: Hogarth Press, 1962, pp. 219-230. (d)

Freud, S. The handling of dream-interpretation in psychoanalysis (1911). *The standard edition of the complete psychological works of Sigmund Freud,* Vol. 12. London: Hogarth Press, 1962, pp. 89-96. (e)

Freud, S. Observations of transference-love (1915). *The standard edition of the complete psychological works of Sigmund Freud*, Vol. 12. London: Hogarth, 1962, pp. 157-171. (f)

Freud, S. Turnings in the ways of psychoanalytic therapy (1919). *The standard edition of the complete psychological works of Sigmund Freud*, Vol. 17. London: Hogarth, 1962, pp. 157-168. (g)

Freud, S. Female sexuality (1931). *The standard edition of the complete psychological works of Sigmund Freud*, Vol. 21. London: Hogarth Press, 1962, pp. 225-243. (h)

Fromm-Reichman, F. *Principles of intensive psychotherapy*. Chicago: University of Chicago Press, 1950.

Glover, E. *The technique of psychoanalysis*. New York: International Universities Press, 1955.

Glover, E. *Birth of the ego*. New York: International Universities Press, 1968.

Glover, E. Remarks on success and failure in psychoanalysis and psychotherapy. In B. B. Wolman (Ed.), *Success and failure in psychotherapy*. New York: Macmillan, 1972, pp. 131-152.

Grinker, R. W. Emerging concepts of mental illness and models of treatment: the medical point of view. *American Journal of Psychiatry*, 1969, *125*, 865-879.

Hill, L. B. *Psychotherapeutic intervention in schizophrenia*. Chicago: University of Chicago Press, 1955.

Horwitz, L. *Clinical prediction in psychotherapy*. New York: Aronson, 1974.

Jackson, D. D. (Ed.). *The etiology of schizophrenia*. New York: Basic Books, 1960.

Jacobs, T. Psychoanalytic technique: Changing views. In B. B. Wolman (Ed.), *International Encyclopedia of Psychiatry, Psychology, Psychoanalysis and Neurology: Progress Volume 1*. New York: Aesculapius, 1983, pp. 349-353.

Jeans, J. *Physics and philosophy*. Ann Arbor, Mich.: University of Michigan Press, 1958.

Jones, E. *The life and work of Sigmund Freud*. New York: Basic Books, 1953-1957, 3 vols.

Kernberg, O. *Object relations theory and clinical psychoanalysis*. New York: Aronson, 1976.

Koestler, A. *The heel of Achilles*. New York: Random, 1974.

Kohlberg, L. *The meaning and measurement of moral development*. Clark University Press, 1979.

Kohut, H. *The analysis of the self*. New York: International Universities Press, 1971.

Kraepelin, E. *Psychiatric*. Leipzig: Barth, 1904.

Krauss, H. H. and Krauss, B. J. Manic-depressive disorder: Wolman's view. In B. B. Wolman (Ed.), *International Encyclopedia of psychiatry, psychology, psychoanalysis, and neurology*, Vol. 6. New York: Van Nostrand/Aesculapius, 1977, pp. 487-488. (a)

Krauss, H. H., and Krauss, B. J. Nosology: Wolman's system. In B. B. Wolman (Ed.), *International encyclopedia of psychiatry, psychology, psychoanalysis, and neurology,* Vol. 8. New York: Van Nostrand/Aesculapius, 1977, pp. 86-88. (b)

Laing, R. D. *The politics of experience.* New York: Ballantine, 1967.

Langs, R. *The therapeutic interaction.* New York: Aronson, 1976.

Latane, B. and Darley, J. *The unresponsive bystander. Why doesn't he help?* New York: Appleton, 1970.

Lidz, T. *The origin and treatment of schizophrenic disorders.* New York: Basic Books, 1973.

Margenau, H. *Science and ethics.* Princeton, N.J.: Van Nostrand, 1964.

Marmor, J. (Ed.) *Modern psychoanalysis.* New York: Basic Books, 1962.

Philips, I. *Human adaptation and its failures.* New York: Academic, 1968.

Philips, I. and Draguns, J. G. Classification of behavior disorders. *Annual Review of Psychology,* 1971, *22,* 447-482.

Pinsker, H. and Spitzer, R. Classification of mental disorders (DSM-III). In B. B. Wolman (Ed.), *International encyclopedia of psychiatry, psychology, psychoanalysis, and neurology,* Vol. 3. New York: Van Nostrand/Aesculapius, 1977, pp. 160-164.

Prichard, J. C. *Treatise on insanity.* London: Gilbert and Piper, 1835.

Rangell, L. Psychoanalysis and the dynamic psychotherapies. Panel report. *Journal of the American Psychoanalytic Association,* 1961, *9,* 585-609.

Reich, W. *Character analysis* (2nd ed.). New York: Orgone Institute, 1945.

Rest, J. R. *Development in judging moral issues.* Minneapolis: Minnesota University Press, 1979.

Rosenbaum, M. (Ed.). *Ethics and values is psychotherapy.* New York: Free Press, 1982.

Scheff, T. J. and Scheff, T. I. *Being mentally ill: A sociological theory.* Chicago: Aldine, 1966.

Selesnick, S. T. *The techniques of psychoanalysis developed by Franz Alexander and Thomas French. In B. B. Wolman (Ed.), Psychoanalytic techniques: A handbook for the practicing psychoanalyst.* New York: Basic Books, 1967.

Servadio, E. Psychoanalysis and telepathy. *Imago,* 1935, *21,* 489-497.

Simon, G. C. Ethical and social issues in professional psychology. In B. B. Wolman (Ed.), *International encyclopedia of psychiatry, psychology, psychoanalysis, and neurology,* Vol. 4. New York: Van Nostrand/Aesculapius, 1977, pp. 380-383.

Spotnitz, H. Techniques for the resolution of the narcissistic defense. In B. B. Wolman (Ed.), *Psychoanalytic techniques: A handbook for the practicing psychoanalyst.* New York: Basic Books, 1967.

Stein, A. *Causes of failure in psychoanalysis and psychotherapy.* New York: Macmillan, 1972, pp. 37-52.

Stone, L. The widening scope of indications for psychoanalysis. *Journal of the American Psychoanalytic Association,* 1954, *2,* 567-594.

Stone, L. *The psychoanalytic situation.* New York: International Universities Press, 1961.

Strupp, H. H. Ferment in psychoanalysis and psychotherapy. In B. B. Wolman (Ed.), *Success and failure in psychoanalysis and psychotherapy.* New York: Macmillan, 1972, pp. 71-103.

Strupp, H. H., Hadley, S. W., and Gomes-Schwartz, B. *Psychotherapy for better or worse: An analysis of the problem of negative effects.* New York: Aronson, 1977.

Sullivan, H. S. *Conceptions of modern psychiatry.* Washington, D.C.: White Foundation, 1947.

Sullivan, H. S. *Interpersonal theory of psychiatry.* New York: Norton, 1953.

Szasz, T. *The myth of mental illness.* New York: Harper, 1961.

Tarachow, S. *An introduction to psychotherapy.* New York: International Universities Press, 1963.

Thompson, C. *Psychoanalysis, evolution and development.* New York: Norton, 1950.

Tolman, E. C. The intervening variable. In M. H. Marx (Ed.), *Psychological theory.* New York: Macmillan, 1951.

Witenberg, E. G. How not to succeed in psychotherapy. In B. B. Wolman (Ed.), *Success and failure in psychoanalysis and psychotherapy.* New York: Macmillan, 1972, pp. 177-192.

Witenberg, E. G. and Caligor, L. The interpersonal approach to treatment with particular emphasis on the obsessional. In B. B. Wolman (Ed.), *Psychoanalytic techniques: A handbook for the practicing psychoanalyst.* New York: Basic Books, 1967.

Wolman, B. B. *Vectoriasis praecox or the group of schizophrenias.* Springfield, Ill.: Charles C. Thomas, 1966.

Wolman, B. B. *Children without childhood.* New York: Grune & Stratton, 1970.

Wolman, B. B. (Ed.). *Success and failure in psychoanalysis and psychotherapy.* New York: Macmillan, 1972.

Wolman, B. B. *Dictionary of behavioral science.* New York: Van Nostrand Reinhold, 1973. (a)

Wolman, B. B. *Call no man normal.* New York: International Universities Press, 1973. (b)

Wolman, B. B. (Ed.). *Handbook of parapsychology.* New York: Van Nostrand Reinhold, 1977. (a)

Wolman, B. B. (Ed.). *International encyclopedia of psychiatry, psychology, psychoanalysis, and neurology.* New York, Van Nostrand/Aesculapius, 1977. (b)

Wolman, B. B. (Ed.). *Clinical diagnosis of mental disorders.* New York: Plenum, 1978. (a)

Wolman, B. B. Classification and diagnosis of mental disorders. In B. B. Wolman (Ed.), *Clinical diagnosis of mental disorders: A handbook.* New York: Plenum Press, 1978. (b)

Wolman, B. B. The crisis of identity and purpose. *Clinical Psychologist,* 1978, *32,* 3-7. (c)

Wolman, B. B. (Ed.). *Handbook of dreams.* New York: Van Nostrand Reinhold, 1979.

Wolman, B. B. and Money, J. (Eds.). *Handbook of human sexuality.* Englewood Cliffs, N.J.: Prentice-Hall, 1980.

Wolman, B. B. *Contemporary theories and systems in psychology* (2nd ed.). New York: Plenum, 1981.

Wolman, B. B. Interactional theory. In B. B. Wolman (Ed.), *Handbook of developmental psychology*. Englewood Cliffs, N.J.: Prentice Hall, 1982. (a)

Wolman, B. B. Treatment of schizophrenia. In B. B. Wolman (Ed.), *Therapist's handbook* (2nd ed.). New York: Van Nostrand Reinhold, 1982. (b)

Wolman, B. B. (Ed.). *International encyclopedia of psychiatry, psychology, psychoanalysis and neurology: Progress Volume 1*. New York: Aesculapius Publishers, 1983.

Zetzel, E. R. The theory of therapy. *International Journal of Psychoanalysis,* 1965, *46,* 39-52.

Zilboorg, G. and Henry, G. W. *A history of medical psychology*. New York: Norton, 1941.

Zubin, J. Classification of behavior disorders. *Annual Review of Psychology,* 1967, *18,* 373-406.

Author Index

Subject Index